FRANCIS BACON

on

Communication & Rhetoric

Francis Bacon

on

Communication & Rhetoric

OR: *The Art of Applying*

Reason to Imagination for the Better Moving

of the Will

By

KARL R. WALLACE

CHAPEL HILL

The University of North Carolina Press

1943

To

HERBERT AUGUST WICHELNS

and

ALEXANDER M. DRUMMOND

PREFACE

The aim of this study is to present and to evaluate Francis Bacon's theory of communication and rhetoric as it emerges from his letters and occasional writings, and from his philosophical, scientific, and literary compositions. The method of the study may perhaps be characterized as descriptive and comparative. With some modification, it is the method of the literary historian that Edwin Greenlaw, among American scholars, has presented in *The Province of Literary History*. On the descriptive side, I have tried to explain briefly how Bacon looks at any communicative process that involves the use of symbols, and to suggest at some length how he views the essential problems of all discourse, whether the discourse be written or oral, scientific or persuasive. In greater detail the study fills in the Lord Chancellor's opinions on public address and the principles of rhetoric. The study, accordingly, is not concerned with Bacon as a writer of philosophical and literary essays, nor as a speaker in Parliament and in the law court; rather, it deals directly with Bacon as a rhetorical theorist.

The description rests on the general hints and special suggestions that Bacon made from time to time and in various works. Often the suggestions are general, without benefit of example and discussion; occasionally they are specific precepts, without benefit of their relevant, general principles. Consequently, the investigator who presents Bacon's views on oral and written communication must conjecture and interpret to a greater extent than he who expounds Bacon's philosophical opinions. I have endeavored to interpret with reasonable conservatism, possibly with the result that the scholar may find Bacon somewhat less of a revolutionary than a classicist. But revolutionary or not, James's Lord Chancellor holds much that is profoundly significant to the student of communication, whether he be a student of history and theory, or a writer and speaker.

On the comparative side, this study seeks merely to arrive at Bacon's peculiar or distinctive contribution to rhetorical theory. By setting Bacon's views beside those of ancient rhetoricians and those of his contemporaries it is possible to indicate wherein the Elizabethan is in some degree novel. I have not attempted to show wherein Bacon is directly indebted to other rhetoricians, partly because the limits of the study will not allow it, chiefly because his direct indebtedness rarely can be demonstrated conclusively. Whether Bacon's ideas on discourse are as significant to our day as his views on scientific method, one can scarcely say with finality; one can only venture the opinion that had the writer, the speaker, and the pedagogue of the last three centuries understood Bacon's position, we should have been spared much "fine" writing and "elocutionary" speaking—in fact, much that springs from the doctrine of Art for Art's sake.

Although it may not be possible to determine Bacon's indebtedness to others, I can in some measure recognize my own. To those who have contributed to the bibliographies, thanks must be given elsewhere. I wish here to acknowledge the kindness of the curators of the rare books in the following libraries: the Chapin Library at Williams College, the Congressional Library, the Duke University Library, the Folger Memorial Library, the Newberry Library, the New York Public Library, and the Harvard College Library. To Mr. Jack Dalton of the Alderman Library at the University of Virginia, I am indebted for generous help in preparing the final manuscript; and to the Committee on Research at the University of Virginia, I am very grateful for financial assistance in publication.

Perhaps my principal obligation is to the training received some years ago in studying for the doctorate. To make the acknowledgment in print may offend the esthete's taste and transgress the cynic's hard proprieties; yet I want to record it, partly because there seems to be a general disposition to belittle the value of re-

search in the humanities and social sciences as compared to research in the physical sciences, and partly because in my own case
the graduate experience appears in retrospect as a distinct turning
point in academic endeavor. For those teachers who were chiefly
instrumental in that experience, I reserve the dedicatory page.
Finally, I desire once again to pay homage to the judgment and
fortitude of my wife.

KARL R. WALLACE

University of Virginia
Charlottesville, Virginia
August 1, 1942

CONTENTS

FRANCIS BACON

on

Communication & Rhetoric

CHAPTER ONE

GENERAL VIEW

OF

RHETORIC AND PUBLIC ADDRESS

The purpose of this study is to set forth and to evaluate Francis Bacon's theory of public discourse. The attempt to reveal public address as Bacon himself understood it leads to a view of prose as the art of oral and written communication, or, in Elizabethan phraseology, as the Art of Elocution, the Art of Tradition, or the Art of Transmission. By such nomenclature Bacon meant to designate a broad, practical art of communication whose ends are to instruct men and to move them to action. The ends, in fact, give rise to his principal classification of discourse; for when man undertakes to teach he is engaged in scientific and didactic discourse; when he intends to influence conduct he employs persuasive address. The medium of such prose forms is, to Bacon, either gesture or language. But although the Baron of Verulam was thus aware of a general art of communication having its special ends and media, he was concerned principally with a species of the art, called Rhetoric. To him this is the art whose theory and principles teach man to illuminate, to illustrate, and to make effective ideas that are to awaken response in others. In the hope of preserving Bacon's emphasis, accordingly, this investigation will deal with his theory of communication in brief, and with his theory of rhetoric *in extenso*.

For the determination of his theory of rhetoric and public address, the most valuable of Bacon's writings are *The Advancement of Learning* (1605) and its expanded Latin translation, *De augmentis scientiarum* (1623). In these works Bacon deals with the art of oral and written communication more fully than in any other place. In these works, moreover, he considers the essential nature of rhetoric more analytically than elsewhere, for the two compositions taken together examine the departments of human knowledge, state their relationships, and determine their peculiar functions. Other works, if their relation to the entire Baconian *opera* be respected both temporally and philosophically, serve occasionally to correct the estimate afforded by the cyclopedic *De augmentis*, more often to smooth off rough edges and to supply illustrations. *Valerius terminus of the Interpretation of Nature*, probably an early work, and the *Novum organum* (1620) help in understanding the Idols, or those errors of perception and judgment inherent in human nature. It would appear that their recognition, by the prose artist, has profound implications for a theory of communication. *The Colours of Good and Evil*, published in part in 1597, is indispensable to the deliberative or political speaker who would appreciate the strength and weakness of the premises from which his everyday arguments stem, whether directly or by implication. The *Apophthegmes, New and Old* (1625) also belong to a Baconian system of rhetoric, for with their help the prose artist gives spice and flavor to discourse. From the *Promus of Formularies and Elegancies* comes the chief suggestion for an art of delivery. Many of the *Essays*, in their early editions as well as late, seem originally to have been intended as aphorisms on human nature from which a speaker or writer could derive aid in sizing up his audience. Even Bacon's letters and speeches, beyond being examples of his own rhetorical practice, afford references and allusions to the principles and methods of composition. Accordingly, this study regards the view of communication outlined in the *Advancement* and the *De augmentis* as the *sine qua non*; it takes the allusions to public address that appear in Bacon's other writings, harmonizes them with the outline of the cyclopedia, and forms the picture of the whole.

One who endeavors to sketch an accurate, intelligible picture of Bacon's views on public discourse must deal with sources that resemble patchwork. There are a multitude of suggestions and they are scattered throughout Bacon's writings. In the *Advancement* and its expanded translation, moreover, the remarks on discourse do not form a nicely-developed system of rhetoric; rather, they pick out and throw into relief those elements which Bacon thought had been neglected. For the most part, the *Advancement* tells us, "that science which we call Rhetoric, or Art of Eloquence" has in the past been "excellently well laboured." [1] Men have always pursued it avidly, largely because "the emulation of Aristotle with the rhetoricians of his time, and the eager and vehement zeal of Cicero doing his utmost to ennoble it, coupled with his long experience, has made them in their works on rhetoric exceed themselves. Again those most brilliant examples of the art which we have in the orations of Demosthenes and Cicero, added to the perfection and skill of the precepts, have doubled the progression in it." [2] Hence, Bacon declares, he will write rather of the deficiencies which "as handmaids attend the art, than in the rules and use of the art itself." [3] It is manifest, then, that Bacon's works do not present a systematic exposition of rhetorical theory; and in trying to present an ordered picture one must select what appears to be the proper point of emphasis, and must arrange relevantly about it a background that shows some balance, harmony, and perspective. Doubtless the result will exhibit closer kinship to a line-drawing than to an oil canvas resplendent with color and detail.

With considerable reluctance this study will forego the tempta-

---

[1] *The Advancement of Learning, Works,* III, 409. In this study, the symbol *Works* designates *The Works of Francis Bacon,* ed. by J. Spedding, R. L. Ellis, and D. D. Heath (London, 1876-1883).

[2] *De augmentis scientiarum,* VI, 3; *Works,* IV, 455.

[3] *Ibid.* Bacon explains that *The Advancement of Learning* consists of two parts: "the former concerning the excellency of learning and knowledge, and the excellency of the merit and true glory in the augmentation and propagation thereof; the later, what the particular acts and works are which have been embraced and undertaken for the advancement of learning, and again what defects and undervalues I find in such particular acts. . . ." (*Adv. of L., Works,* III, 263-264.) When he wished to translate the *Advancement* into Latin, he characterized it to Dr. Playfer thus: ". . . my purpose was rather to excite other men's wits than to magnify my own; I was desirous to prevent the incertainness of my own life and times, by uttering rather seeds than plants; nay and furder . . . by sowing with basket, than with the hand . . . I have only taken upon me to ring a bell to call other wits together. . . ." [*The Letters and the Life of Francis Bacon including All His Occasional Works . . . ,* collected and edited by James Spedding (London, 1861-1874), III, 301.]

tion to delineate Bacon as a speaker and writer, though his contemporaries suggest that a portrait of him as a prose artist would well reward the energy. Discerning Ben Jonson once applied a passage of Seneca's to the Lord Chancellor:

. . . there happened in my time one noble speaker who was full of gravity in his speaking; his language, where he could spare or pass by a jest, was nobly censorious. No man ever spake more neatly, more presly, more weightily, or suffered less emptiness, less idleness, in what he uttered. No number of his speech but consisted of his own graces. His hearers could not cough or look aside from him without loss. He commanded where he spoke, and had his judges angry and pleased at his devotion. No man had their affections more in his power. The fear of every man that heard him was lest he should make an end.[4]

More vulgarly, Jonson is supposed to have declared to Drummond that "My Lord Chancellor of England wringeth his speeches from the strings of his band, and other Councellours from the pyking of their teeth." [5] When Bacon was Elizabeth's Attorney General, Essex wrote him that the Queen "did acknowledge you had a great wit and an excellent gift of speech. . . ." [6] But though Bacon proved an effective speaker at the bar and in Parliament, we shall in this study use his speeches sparingly, partly because their texts are incomplete and in error, partly because his principles and precepts of rhetoric have so much more meaning to the modern student of oral and written communication. So far as we draw upon them, the speeches serve mainly to help resolve ambiguities and inconsistencies of theory, and to suggest, where stylistic inaccuracies of text could not greatly hurt the general sense of what was said, how Bacon's own practice conformed to his principles.

Once Bacon's theory of rhetoric and public address is limned and framed, the last step in this study will be a short appraisal and judgment of it. Can it be said that Bacon has made a significant contribution to our knowledge of the principles of discourse? By setting the Baconian system beside the theories of Tudor and early Stuart rhetoricians, the observer can see contrasts in subject mat-

---

[4] *Timber,* ed. by F. E. Schelling (Boston, 1892), 30.
[5] *Notes of Jonson's Conversations with William Drummond of Hawthornden,* ed. by David Laing (London, 1842), 25.
[6] *Letters and Life,* I, 297.

ter and emphasis that mark Bacon along with Thomas Wilson as one who viewed rhetoric in its full classical hues, rather than with those who, like Sherry and Peacham, reduced prose to flashy exercises in tint. To Bacon, rhetoric appears as a full-bodied, independent art of composition in which the discovery, selection, and arrangement of ideas are at least as important as their manner of phrasing and delivery. To Sherry and Peacham and the rest of the Ciceronian stylists, the choice of content and the management of the structure and form of a composition seem unimportant, for they restricted the scope of rhetoric mainly to the delicate art of turning tropes and figures. Furthermore, one must look to Bacon's uniqueness of contribution, not merely by setting him over against his contemporaries, but by comparing him with his classical forbears to whom, like any educated Elizabethan, he is inevitably indebted. In many respects his rhetorical theory reveals striking comparisons with that of Plato, Aristotle, Cicero, Quintilian, and the unknown author of the *Rhetoric to Herrennius*. Occasionally there are direct borrowings acknowledged by Bacon himself, but in most cases the influence of the classical rhetoricians on him cannot be demonstrated explicitly, and the scholar must therefore be content with the revelation of interesting correspondencies. Finally, one must try to measure the significance of Bacon's contribution by looking briefly to the greater English rhetorics that have appeared since the mid-seventeenth century and indicate wherein they betray the Lord Chancellor's touch. Are there other theorists, like Bishop Whateley in the nineteenth century, who definitely acknowledge their inspiration and indebtedness to Jonson's "noble speaker?"

Bacon's classification of knowledge is based on the presumption that the mind is capable of division into a number of "faculties" or powers, each with its own function. In the *Advancement* and the *De augmentis*, his theory of communication stems from Philosophy, a branch of learning that utilizes the rational powers of the mind. It is a striking fact that for Bacon, communication is at bottom an intellectual activity, no matter whether its purpose is instruction or persuasion, whether its symbols are visual or oral. By the position given to communication in his hierarchy of knowledge, he makes it a part of logic, if it is not in a large measure coextensive with it.

Bacon's early classification of knowledge divides all knowledge into History, Poetry, and Philosophy, according to the three rational faculties of the mind, Memory, Imagination, and Reason. Of these mental activities, the memory is chiefly engaged in the production of History, the imagination is the principal faculty at work in composing Poetry, and the reason is the preponderant power in formulating Philosophy.[7] Bacon holds history in esteem and accordingly carefully examines its parts at some length. But poesy, because it is a part of learning that is "extremely licensed"[8] and obeys no rational law, is later eliminated from serious investigation. Bacon's chief concern is, of course, Philosophy, which he partitions into First or Primary Philosophy, and Particular Philosophy. Under the last occur two principal divisions: Divine and Human. The philosophy of man is, in turn, treated in two parts, one dealing with a general science that concerns "the Nature and State of Man,"[9] and the other comprising a particular science that treats of man first as an individual and second as a social creature.[10] The division by dichotomy, however, does not stop here, even though Bacon professes to disparage Plato's method.[11] The doctrine of man segregate properly treats of his body and of his soul or mind. The study of the body gives rise, among other things, to Medicine and Athletic, but it is the soul or mind which claims most of Bacon's attention, for it is through the intellect that man will eventually learn to interpret and control nature, the great end toward which all learning advances.

The mind, in Bacon's system, has two principal parts: the rational and the sensible. The first is peculiar to human beings, but the second is discovered also in animals. Now this duality of mind

[7] *Adv. of L., Works,* III, 329.
[8] *Ibid.,* 343.   [9] *De aug.,* IV, I, *Works,* IV, 373.
[10] The doctrine of man as a social creature Bacon calls Civil Knowledge. It is divided according "to the three summary actions of Society; *the knowledge of conversation, the knowledge of negotiation, and the knowledge of empire or government.* For there are three kinds of good which men seek in society, comfort against solitude, assistance in business, and protection against injuries; and there are three wisdoms of divers natures, which are often separate; wisdom of behavior, wisdom of business, and wisdom of state." (*De Aug.,* VIII, I, *Works,* V, 32.)
[11] *De aug.,* VI, 2, *Works,* IV, 448. Ellis suggests that Bacon here is disparaging the method of Peter Ramus. (*De aug.,* VI, 2, *Works,* I, 663.)

must be regarded in three ways, according to its substance, its faculties, and the uses and objects of the faculties. The substance of the mind, we note, may perhaps be called spirit,[12] but of this little can be known. With the faculties or operations of the soul, however, we are well acquainted: They comprise the "understanding, reason, imagination, memory, appetite, will; in short, all with which the logical and ethical sciences deal." [13] We may in the future have real knowledge of the faculties by an examination of their origins, "and that physically, as they are innate and inherent in the soul," [14] but at present we best understand them by their uses and objects. In referring the faculties to their uses and objects, Bacon finally reaches two important parts of philosophy: ethics, and the four Intellectual Arts or logic. "Logic discourses of the Understanding and Reason; Ethic of the Will, Appetite, and Affections; the one produces determinations, the other actions." [15] In Bacon's view, then, the mind employs its faculties either as instruments of knowing or as means of action. The mind perceives and understands facts and objects; it infers and determines; it pictures; it remembers; it desires; it wills——all with the purpose of allowing man either to know or to act.

In arriving at the four Intellectual Arts one at last comes to the precise position of communication in the Baconian cyclopedia. The four arts, Bacon declares, are "divided according to the ends whereunto they are referred; for man's labour is to *invent* [16] that which is *sought* or *propounded;* or to *judge* that which is *invented;* or to retain that which is *judged;* or to *deliver over* that which is *retained.* So as the arts must be four: Art of Inquiry or Invention; Art of Examination or Judgement; Art of Custody or Memory; and Art of Elocution or Tradition." [17]

The Arts of Invention and Memory, as shall later be observed are necessary in any act of communication. So also is the Art of Judgement that deals with proofs and demonstrations. It is the Art of Elocution—called in the *De augmentis* the Art of Transmission—which is the art of communication:

---

[12] *De aug.,* IV, 3, *Works,* IV, 398.   [13] *Ibid.*   [14] *Ibid.,* 399.

[15] *De aug.,* V, 1, *Works,* IV, 405.

[16] Spedding declares that Bacon uses the word "invent" simply as equivalent to *invenire*—to find out. (*Works,* III, 384n.)

[17] *De aug.,* V, 1, *Works,* III, 384-385.

Let us now proceed to the Art of Transmitting, or of producing and expressing to others those things which have been invented, judged, and laid up in the memory; which I will call by a general name the Art of Transmission. This art includes all the arts which relate to words and discourse. For although reason be as it were the soul of discourse, yet in the handling of them reason and discourse should be kept separate, no less than soul and body. The art of transmission I will divide into three parts; the doctrine concerning the Organ of Discourse, the doctrine concerning the Method of Discourse, and the doctrine concerning the Illustration or adornment of Discourse.[18]

The Illustration of Discourse, Bacon continues, is rhetoric; the Organ of Discourse, although it has been popularly called Grammar, is language symbols, both oral and written; and the Method of Discourse refers to ways of forming, arranging, and managing a composition as a whole. In other words, Bacon is here thinking of the elements of communication—the sounds and visual components of words, *i. e.*, the smallest independent and meaningful language-units; the combination of these units, not merely to make up "sentences" but to form the entire composition; and the "adornment" or *vivid* presentation of the composition so that the reader or hearer may be properly instructed and moved. Although he deals but sketchily with the "Organ" and the "Method," his remarks show how profoundly he understood the fundamental problems of language communication.

In treating of the organ or medium of discourse, Bacon refers to any system of symbolic formulation, except the conventional alphabets of the world and their oral counterparts, that has sufficient diversity, variety, and stability to render possible all effective distinctions among ideas. As a kind of intellectual currency, a system of communicative symbols need meet only one rule: "that whatever can be divided into differences sufficiently numerous to explain the variety of notions (provided those differences be perceptible to the sense) may be made a vehicle to convey the thoughts of one man to another." [19] The symbols that measure up to this rule, so Bacon continues, are the conventional letters or alphabet of any language, together with the sounds of speech and certain schemes of gesture and of hieroglyphics.

---

[18] *De aug.*, VI, 1, *Works*, IV, 438–439.   [19] *Ibid.*, 439.

After thus pointing out the essence of a language, Bacon sets forth two main divisions of the organ of discourse. One division is reserved for Grammar, or the art that deals with "Speech and Words;" the other division is labelled, in the *De augmentis*, the "Notations of Things," and in the *Advancement*, the "Notes of Cogitations," or *signs* of thought. In this class Bacon includes *all* language symbols that fall outside speech sounds and letters, and subdivides the class into two parts: "The Notes of Things ... which carry a signification without the help or intervention of words, are of two kinds: one *ex congruo*, where the note has some congruity with the notion, the other *ad placitum*, where it is adopted and agreed upon at pleasure." [20] The first kind of "notation" is a language of representive symbols whose meanings are carried by a visual picture or *emblem* that either directly or by analogy points to the things referred to. Of this kind of symbol are Hieroglyphics and Gesture, the former consisting of written symbols whose pictures may be permanent, the latter consisting of movements whose images are evanescent. But despite this difference, Bacon recognizes that both Hieroglyphics and Gesture are truly representative, for both "have always some similitude to the thing signified, and are a kind of emblems." [21] In thus recognizing a language of representative gesture, he apparently restricts it to what we speak of today as descriptive and locative gesture. Excluded are the gesture of emphasis and the gesture that reveals mood or attitude, for these would seem to have no congruity with the notion expressed.

The second kind of notation is termed "real characters." These have "nothing emblematic in them, but are merely surds, no less than the elements of letters themselves, and are only framed *ad placitum*, and silently agreed upon by custom." [22] As surds, real characters are abstract symbols that exhibit no direct analogical connection with the thing or the idea they stand for. Apparently Bacon feels that their meaning is due to repetition and association, rather than to representation; hence they have the seemingly "irrational" aspect that a surd, in one sense, possesses. Furthermore, as surds they derive their sanction through silent and tacit agreement. It is true, of course, that many of the symbols of speech and

---

[20] *Adv. of L., Works*, III, 400; *De aug.*, VI, 1, *Works*, IV, 439-440.
[21] *De aug.*, VI, 1, *Works*, IV, 440.   [22] *Ibid.*

ordinary writing are likewise surd-like in aspect, but Bacon evidently has in mind here a scheme of symbolic language to which he gives no name. Unfortunately he offers the reader no illustration of a real character, and is content to round out his sketchy hints by suggesting that "there ought to be as many of them as there are radical words," [23] and by asserting that in China and the far East they are in extensive use. It should be possible, he concludes, that "a number of nations whose languages are altogether different, but who agree in the use of such characters . . . [could] communicate with each other in writing; to such an extent indeed that any book written in characters of this kind can be read off by each nation in their own language." [24]

Bacon speaks of Grammar as "the harbinger of other sciences," [25] a department of learning not very noble, but deserving of dignity because "it serves for an antidote against the curse of the confusion of tongues." [26] As a division of the Organ of Discourse, it has two species, "the one being Literary, the other Philosophical. The one is used simply for languages, that they may be learned more quickly or spoken more correctly and purely; the other ministers in a certain degree to philosophy." [27]

About Literary Grammar, Bacon has nothing directly to say. Perhaps he thought the art of learning languages had been so well worked over by others that it showed no glaring deficiencies which he would undertake to remedy. But upon Philosophical Grammar, "the noblest species of Grammar," he spends some time, and specifically alludes to the content of studies that we now speak of broadly as philology and phonetics. Acknowledging that he has taken the hint from Caesar's books on *Analogy*, he recognizes "a kind of grammar which should diligently inquire, not the analogy of words with one another, but the analogy between words and things, or reason; not going so far however as that interpretation which belongs to Logic." [28] This branch of grammar does not deal with the invention and discovery of ideas and arguments, whether by way of the traditional deductive methods or by means of the new induction as exemplified by the *Novum organum;* nor does this kind of grammar have traffic with the arrangement and ordering

---

[23] *Ibid.,* 440.   [24] *Ibid.,* 439.   [25] *Ibid.,* 440.
[26] *Ibid.,* 440-441.   [27] *Ibid.,* 441.   [28] *Ibid.*

of the larger units of discourse, a study that Elizabethan logicians customarily included in their treaties under the head of "Disposition." This aspect of grammar, moreover, does not deal profitably with "the imposition and original etymology of names," [29] because only too often such study is undertaken on the erroneous supposition that words were originally "derived and deduced by reason and according to significance." [30] Here Bacon fleetingly implies that there is no one correct, final word for an object or a concept; to study etymologies on such an assumption may be a subject that claims both elegance and reverence, but nevertheless is "sparingly true and bearing no fruit." [31] Rather than pursuing such fruitless inquiry, Philosophical Grammar studies etymologies, if at all, as they have been "arbitrarily fixed," [32] according to custom and usage. Furthermore—and of far greater importance—it will call upon linguists who know "a great number of tongues, learned as well as vulgar," to handle the various "properties of *languages;* showing in what points each excelled, in what it failed." [33] Bacon thus seems to have in mind that grammar embraces the study of *all* words and speech, whether literary or colloquial. To him the results of such study are profound. First, all languages would not only be "enriched by mutual exchanges, but the several beauties of each may be combined (as in the Venus of Appelles) into a most beautiful image and excellent model of speech itself, for the right expressing of the meanings of the mind." [34] Second, such inquiry will produce "signs of no slight value, but well worthy of observation . . . concerning the dispositions and manners of peoples and nations, drawn from their languages." [35] Bacon's illustrations of the results of a comparative study of languages are sufficiently significant and interesting to warrant quotation at length:

I like well that remark of Cicero's that the Greeks had no word to express the Latin *ineptus;* 'because,' says he, 'that vice was so familiar among the Greeks that they did not perceive it in themselves;' . . .And how came it that the Greeks used such liberty in composition of words, the Romans on the contrary were so strict and sparing in it? One may plainly collect from this fact that the Greeks were fitter for arts, the

---

[29] *Ibid.,* 441.
[30] *Ibid.*   [31] *Ibid.*   [32] *Ibid.*
[33] *Ibid.*   [34] *Ibid.,* 442.   [35] *Ibid.*

Romans for business; for the distinctions of arts are hardly expressed without composition of words; whereas for the transaction of business simpler words are wanted. Then again the Hebrews have such a dislike to these compositions that they had rather abuse a metaphor than introduce a compound word: and the words they use are so few and so little mixed, that one may plainly perceive from their very language that they were a Nazarite nation, separated from the rest of the nations.[36]

It is evident, then, that out of a study of the medium of communication, Bacon sees man gathering information not merely about language as a tool, but about the customs, habits, and operations of the mind that employs the tool. "Certainly words are the footsteps of reason, and the footsteps tell something about the body." [37] It is partly for this reason that the art of communication appears in the Baconian cyclopedia as an expression of the rational faculties of the mind.

Besides the Literary and Philosophical branches of grammar, Bacon recognizes yet another division that concerns the "accidents of words . . . such as Sound, Measure, and Accent." [38] Under this

---

[36] *Ibid.*, 442.

[37] *Ibid.*, 441. In the *Novum organum*, I, aphorisms 59, 60 (*Works*, IV, 59-62), Bacon also alludes to the relationship between the word-symbol and "reason." There he points out to the scientist how uncertainly and inexactly a word may refer to the thing signified. He suggests, first, that although reason may at times govern word-formation, the symbols of language are "commonly framed and applied according to the capacity of the vulgar. . . ." He indicates, second, that when the learned man unguardedly uses everyday terms he is not only fostering and passing on hazy meanings but also is thinking with inexact counters. It is this disposition to think with inexact words that Bacon calls the Idol of the Marketplace. The Idol can be circumvented in questions that are in the realm of the probable and the contingent when men in dispute will start out with definitions and agree upon their terms. But in the realm of the exact and demonstrable, the scientist cannot mitigate error by using the definition solely; he must either frame his definitions and axioms by basing them originally on the observation of individual instances, or test current definitions by referring them to the particular instance. In brief, Bacon in the *Novum organum* (1620) adds nothing essential to his sketch for a theory of language in the *De augmentis* (1623). I might suggest, in passing, that if this account of aphorisms 59 and 60 is correct, Professor Jones may be writing somewhat strongly in asserting, on the basis of the same passages, that Bacon "condemned" language. See his "Science and Language in England of the Mid-Seventeenth Century," *Journal of English and Germanic Philology*, XXXI (July, 1932), 316.

[38] *De aug.*, VI, 1, *Works*, IV, 442.

part of grammar, he alludes first to the behavior of sounds, not as isolated phonemes, but as they combine in connected speech to produce "sweetnesses and harshnesses." Having in mind the judgment of the ear as to the pleasing and agreeable qualities of pronunciation, he suggests, on the one hand, that all nations have agreed that certain sound combinations are harsh and offending; "for there is no language that does not in some degree shun the hiatus caused by vowels coming together, and the harshnesses caused by consonants coming together." [39] On the other hand, he declares that preference for one sound combination over another differs from nation to nation, and from language to language. The Greek language, for instance, "abounds in diphthongs; the Latin is much more sparing of them. The Spanish dislikes thin letters, and changes them immediately into those of a middle tone." [40]

It is regrettable that in offering his hints on the sweetness and harshness of speech sounds, Bacon has not seen fit to be more explicit. To the phonetician especially, his account raises fundamental questions. Does he mean to imply that a description of linguistic phenomena will admit an absolute yardstick of sweetness and harshness, consonance and dissonance, to which all men agree? Does he want us to infer, from the phrases "shun the hiatus" and "consonants coming together," that pronunciation is to a large degree determined by what our speech agents find it *easiest* to do? Or does he mean merely to suggest that sweetness and harshness of sounds are determined by custom and convention? Probably Bacon does not intend to imply that there is an absolute criterion of the pleasing and agreeable qualities of speech sounds. To hold this view and at the same time to maintain that many of our language symbols are silently agreed upon by custom and that many words and names have been fixed arbitrarily would lead him into contradictory principles of language behavior, for he would be holding on the one hand that symbols are determined by custom and experience, and on the other that sound phenomena are governed by some abstract, a priori principle. Furthermore, Bacon is probably not aware that pronunciation, in the past as well as at present, is governed to a considerable degree by the tendency of the articulatory agents to form sounds in the easy way—with a

---

[39] *Ibid.,* 443.   [40] *Ibid.*

minimum expenditure of energy. He appreciates, of course, that a
study like phonetics would examine the manner by which speech
sounds are formed—"by what percussion of the tongue, by what
opening of the mouth, by what meeting of the lips, by what effort
of the throat, the sound of each letter is produced." [41] But although
he realizes that systematic observation of pronunciation may involve separate study, and despite his interest in experimentation,
he himself never observed pronunciation scientifically. Had he done
so, he might have seen, and have stated for us, that articulatory
habits tend to follow the easy path. It would appear more probable,
accordingly, that Bacon's measuring rod for sweetness and harshness of speech is custom and tradition. He means merely that the
users of one dialect will find certain sound combinations pleasing
and acceptable in quality, the users of another dialect will not;
and that their acceptance of one sound as sweet and the rejection
of another as harsh is due to usage, habit, and association, rather
than to the existence and application of an abstract, aesthetic
principle. In dealing with the sound of words, therefore, grammar
will seek to discover what each language and what each dialect will
admit as pleasing and agreeable qualities of speech sounds. A Baconian grammar, it is manifest, would be descriptive, not prescrip-
tive.

The second accident of speech with which grammar must deal is
measure. By the "Measure of words," Bacon has reference "to the
style and form of words: That is to say, metre or verse. . . ." [42]
In its development poetry has given us many examples of measured
cadence, but systematic study and observation of metrical patterns has been "a very small thing." Hence, Bacon believes that
this part of grammar should handle three matters. First, it shall
deal with prosody, and address itself "to the teaching of kinds and
measures of verse." [43] Second, it must include precepts as "to the
kinds of verse which best suit each matter or subject. The ancients
used hexameter for histories and eulogies; elegiac for complaints;
iambic for invectives; lyric for odes and hymns. Nor have modern
poets been wanting in this wisdom, so far as their own languages
are concerned." [44] Third, grammar must observe what metrical

---

[41] *Ibid.*, 442–443.
[42] *Ibid.*, 443.   [43] *Ibid.*   [44] *Ibid.*

schemes are peculiarly appropriate to a language. The modern writers, so Bacon asserts, "out of too much zeal for antiquity, have tried to train the modern languages into the ancient measures (hexameter, elegiac, sapphic, etc.) ; measures incompatible with the structure of the languages themselves, and no less offensive to the ear." [45] In determining what rhythms a language will stand, Bacon cautions, "the judgment of the sense is to be preferred to the precepts of art;—as the poet says, 'The dinner is for eating, and my wish is that guests and not that cooks should like the dishes.' " [46] By thus making the sensible and sensuous the basis of judging what cadences are tolerated by a language, Bacon is once more appealing to custom and usage as arbiter; the ear, as guest, selects and accepts what it is accustomed to.

The third accident of speech that falls to the business of grammar is accent. Since "it is too small a matter to speak of," Bacon passes it by swiftly. Enough is said, however, to reveal that he thinks of accent, first, as stress on the syllable and the word, and second, as the intonation pattern of a sentence. ". . . the accentuation of *sentences* has not been observed at all. And yet it is common to all mankind almost to drop the voice at the end of a period, to raise it in asking a question, and other things of the kind not a few." [47] Is Bacon in this passage alluding not merely to changes of pitch or inflection, but to the *pattern* of pitch variations in the sentence?

Bacon's final division of grammar is reserved for Writing. This, in turn, he sub-partitions into orthography that makes use of the common alphabet, and writing that employs *ciphers*. The former characters are open and evident; the latter, secret and private. We need not, in this study, be concerned with Bacon's description of cipher writing, for in everyday communicative efforts, ciphers are clearly unimportant. But his remarks on ordinary writing, though brief, yield at least one word of advice: Spell and pronounce a language according to its conventions of spelling and of utterance. The attempt of his contemporaries to reform spelling and thus make English a more phonetic language "in which the spelling should agree with the pronunciation" merely belongs "to the class of unprofitable subtleties. [48] . . . For the pronunciation itself is con-

---

[45] *Ibid.*, 443. [46] *Ibid.* [47] *Ibid.*, 444. [48] *Ibid.*

tinually changing; it does not remain fixed; and the derivations of words, especially from foreign tongues, are thereby completely obscured. And as the spelling of words according to the fashion is no check at all upon the fashion of pronunciation, but leaves it free, to what purpose is this innovation?" [49] It is manifest, then, that so far as writing goes, a Baconian grammar will favor spelling and pronunciation habits that conform to custom and convention. If it is possible to make spelling and speech agree with one another, the harmony is only temporary. Tomorrow pronunciation will change, and if it is to keep abreast orthography must also. Furthermore, the effort to modernize spelling will not serve as a guide to pronunciation, because the written symbol does not stabilize its manner of utterance. Thus, with respect to the symbols that carry meaning to others Bacon fully appreciates that the written sign exhibits a behavior all its own, and similarly that the oral sign obeys laws peculiar to it. To him, the oral symbol and the written symbol are independent.

The significance and importance that Bacon attaches to the Method of Discourse, or disposition, are strikingly indicated by its place in the cyclopedia. As has been observed already, that part of natural philosophy which relates to man's intellect gives rise to four intellectual arts: the art of invention, the art of judgment, the art of memory, and the art of transmission. The art of transmitting knowledge—the art of producing and expressing to others what has been invented, judged, and laid up in the memory—had, before Bacon's time, included principally the studies of grammar, rhetoric, and logic. But Bacon thought that the *method* and the form of communication was of such importance to the dissemination of knowledge that he removed it from its traditional place under rhetoric and logic, and elevated it to the status of a study or doctrine in its own right:

The Method of Discourse . . . has been commonly handled as a part of Logic; and it also finds a place in Rhetoric, under the name of *Disposition*. But the placing of it in the train of other arts has led to the passing over of many things relating to it which it is useful to know. I have therefore thought fit to make the doctrine concerning Method a substan-

---

[49] *Ibid.*, 444.

tive and principal doctrine, under the general name of Wisdom of Transmission.[50]

Bacon, then, sees disposition as a part of the Art of Transmission, co-ordinate with grammar and rhetoric. That it may be a part of rhetoric he admits, but for the advancement of science and learning he would have it a separate art.

By disposition or method Bacon means the plan or system of marshalling the content of a written or oral composition; it is the scheme of arrangement that gives composition its order and form. Within the scope of disposition, Bacon includes also the *selection* of ideas. In other words, an author has not only the problem of discovering or inventing all the possible ideas he might say—a process that Bacon holds to be distinct from disposition—but in planning his discourse he must decide what to include, what to reject. That order and selection are interdependent is manifest when Bacon divides the doctrine of method into two parts: ". . . the one relating to the disposition of the whole work or argument of a book; the other to the limitation of propositions. For there belongs to architecture not only the frame of the whole building, but also the formation and shape of the several beams and columns thereof; and Method is as it were the architecture of the sciences." [51] The first part, accordingly, classifies patterns for organizing discourse as a whole. The second, relating to the limitation of propositions, leads an author to consider how inclusive his product is to be. What Bacon has in mind is the restriction of a work or book to its own professed subject; it must not "intermeddle within the province of another," [52] in order that "repetition, excursion, and all confusion" may be avoided.[53] Beyond keeping an eye upon the latitude of his subject, an author must watch its longitude, for he must determine "unto what degree of particularity a knowledge should descend." [54] By thus looking to the scope of his composition, a writer or speaker may avoid being a splitter of the cummin seed and falling into fine distinctions without a difference. He may avoid, too, discoursing on generalities that are too remote to be useful to men.[55] Under "limi-

---

[50] *De aug.*, VI, 2, *Works*, IV, 448.   [51] *Ibid.*, 453.
[52] *Adv. of L.*, *Works*, III, 408.   [53] *De aug.*, VI, 2, *Works*, IV, 453.
[54] *Adv. of L.*, *Works*, III, 408.   [55] *De aug.*, VI, 2, *Works*, IV, 453-454.

tation of propositions," then, Bacon is considering questions of unity, of scale and proportion, of degree of comprehensiveness and detail in treatment, and he thinks of them as involving not the plan of the discourse as a whole, but selecting the propositions that make up the discourse.

The classification of the kinds of method that pertain to discourse as a whole comprehends the rest of what Bacon says formally on Method of Discourse. He believes that the kinds of arrangement, when classified and made a separate study, would be to the art of communication what the forms of reasoning are to the art of judgment: ". . . as the doctrine of Syllogisms comprehendeth the rules of judgment upon that which is invented, so the doctrine of Method containeth the rules of judgment upon that which is to be delivered. . . ." [56]

The first kind of method is division by dichotomy, the "one and only method" of Platonic and Ramean analysis. Of this Bacon unhesitatingly disapproves. The form leads to error, whether in everyday affairs or in science. To try to press all one's information and arguments into two members results either in missing some parts or in forcing knowledge out of its natural shape: "this kind of method produces empty abridgments." [57]

The next two methods Bacon seeks to distinguish from all other schemes of arrangement by the ends at which they aim. He calls these methods the *Magistral* and the *Initiative*. The former aims to instruct in the application and use of knowledge already at hand; the latter communicates knowledge in much the same order as it was discovered and thereby encourages the progression and continuation of learning. The former method assumes a popular audience willing to believe; the latter postulates an audience of critical examiners: "The magistral method teaches; the initiative intimates. The magistral requires that what is told should be believed; the initiative that it should be examined. The one transmits knowledge to the crowd of learners; the other to the sons, as it were, of science. The end of the one is the use of knowledges, as they now are; of the other the continuation and further progression of them." [58] In Bacon's time, the transmission of knowledge for the

---

[56] *Adv. of L., Works*, III, 403.
[57] *De aug.*, VI, 2, *Works*, IV, 449.   [58] *Ibid.*

sake of further investigation—the *Handing on of the Lamp*— seemed like "a road abandoned and stopped up":

. . . there is a kind of contract of error between the deliverer and the receiver; for he who delivers knowledge desires to deliver it in such form as may be best believed, and not as may be most conveniently examined; and he who receives knowledge desires present satisfaction, without waiting for due inquiry; and so rather not to doubt, than not to err; glory making the deliverer careful not to lay open his weakness, and sloth making the receiver unwilling to try his strength.[59]

The mechanical arts are fortunate in that their material is lasting; any improvement made by one man is preserved and may be taken up and further improved generations later by another investigator who, in turn, may again be improved upon. But in the realm of thought and of communication of ideas, successive generations spend most of their energy in interpreting and defending the ideas of former thinkers, much as medieval and Renaissance scholars have championed Aristotle uncritically. Bacon feels, therefore, that "since the labour and life of one man cannot attain to perfection of knowledge, the wisdom of the Tradition is that which inspireth the felicity of continuance and proceeding. And therefore the most real diversity of method is of method referred to Use, and method referred to Progression. . . ."[60] Knowledge that is to grow in the hands of others should be delivered *in the same method wherein it was invented:*

. . . a man may revisit and descend unto the foundations of his knowledge and consent; and so transplant it into another as it grew in his own mind. For it is in knowledges as it is in plants: if you mean to use the plant, it is no matter for the roots; but if you mean to remove it to grow, then it is more assured to rest upon roots than slips. . . . if you will have sciences grow, it is less matter for the shaft or body of the tree, so you look well to the taking up of the roots.[61]

Bacon places the Acroamatic and the Exoteric methods next in

---

[59] *Ibid.*   [60] *Adv. of L., Works,* III, 403.

[61] *Ibid.,* 404. In *Of the Interpretation of Nature,* an early draft of the *Advancement* and the *Novum organum,* Bacon seemed to doubt that the transmission of ideas could follow exactly the order in which they came into being; no knowledge ever was delivered "in the same order it was invented." *Works,* III, 248.

order. The latter is the form of arrangement that comes about when a writer makes a special effort to be clear. The Acroamatic or Enigmatical arrangement is a method of ordering and handling ideas that is manifest in obscurity of exposition and development. It is, in brief, esoteric.[62] Like the Initiative method, it separates the vulgar auditors from the select, but unlike the progressive method, it employs a way of delivery more secret than most: "The intention of it . . . seems to be by obscurity of delivery to exclude the vulgar (that is the profane vulgar) from the secrets of knowledges, and to admit those only who have either received the interpretation of the enigmas through the hands of the teachers, or have wits of such sharpness and discernment as can pierce the veil." [63] Bacon thinks that the ancients employed an obscure delivery with judgment and discretion, but in later times it has been disgraced by many "who have made it as a false and deceitful light to put forward their counterfeit merchandise." [64] Perhaps the Enigmatical method is used by some who would appear wise: ". . . some are so close and reserved, as they will not shew their wares but by a dark light; and seem always to keep back somewhat; and when they know within themselves they speak of that they do not well know, would nevertheless seem to others to know of that which they may not well speak." [65]

As the fifth and sixth forms of communication, the aphoristic plan and the "methods" of conventional discourse are opposed to each other. The aphoristic kind of method is that form of writing which learned men of science employ to convey the heart of their learning to other specialists. Usually the form is that of a small, pithy tractate such as Bacon himself uses in the second book of the *Novum organum*, and seems to be conditioned entirely by subject matter:

Aphorisms, except they should be ridiculous, cannot be made but of the pith and heart of sciences; for discourse of illustration is cut off; recitals of examples are cut off; descriptions of practice are cut off; so

---

[62] Bacon appears to be employing "acroamatic" in the sense that medievalists applied it to Aristotle's extant works. Addressed to hearers who as disciples were capable of following the abstruse lectures of the master, they were regarded as examples of deep learning delivered to a select audience.

[63] *De aug.*, VI, 2, *Works*, IV, 450.

[64] *Ibid.*   [65] *Of Seeming Wise, Works*, VI, 436.

there remaineth nothing to fill the Aphorisms but some good quantity of observations; and therefore no man can suffice, nor in reason will attempt, to write Aphorisms, but he that is sound and grounded.[66]

Such a method contrasts with other methods, particularly the Magistral, in that it exhibits less coherence, less connection and joining of the parts. Most methods, indeed, are more fit to win consent or belief than to invite men to inquire further, for "they carry a kind of demonstration in orb or circle, one part illuminating another, and therefore satisfy." [67]

Opposed to the aphoristic form of writing is the usual method of connected and continuous discourse, in which unity and coherence are scrupulously maintained for the purpose of teaching or persuading a more or less popular audience. In both the *Advancement* and the *De augmentis*, Bacon cryptically describes this form as "methods." As one method of continuous discourse, it is probable that Bacon here is thinking of what the sixteenth-century logicians referred to as the great "Methode" of arranging systematic treatises.[68] The arrangement consisted of an order that moved from the general to the particular, and that at the same time progressed from the familiar to the unfamiliar and from the most important to the less important.

Other "methods" appear to consist of those that Bacon merely alludes to as traditional, or "vulgar and received." They are listed as the Analytic, Systatic, Diaeretic, Cryptic, and Homeric.[69] As to the essence of the Homeric and Cryptic methods, Bacon gives no hint. As to the determining characteristic of the other kinds, he offers a clue. The Analytic scheme is that of "Resolution," [70] in which particular judgments and instances are presented with no special effort at revealing their logical relationships. The Systatic method is opposed to the Analytic, for in it the writer logically and systematically demonstrates the results of analysis; he pulls together his particular judgments, he classifies and shows the rela-

---

[66] *Adv. of L., Works*, III, 405.   [67] *Ibid.*

[68] Consult *The Logike of the Moste Excellent Philosopher P. Ramus Martyr,* newly translated. . . . (London, 1574), Book II, 14-16. Cf. the edition of 1626, pp. 181 ff., and Dudley Fenner's *The Artes of Logike and Rhetoricke.* . . . (London, 1584), Book I, 7. See also F. P. Graves, *Peter Ramus and the Educational Reformation of the Sixteenth Century* (New York, 1912), 151-154.

[69] *De aug.,* VI, 2, *Works,* IV, 452.   [70] *Adv. of L., Works,* III, 407.

tionship of the particular to the general, and in Bacon's phrase produces a work that is a "Constitution." [71] In addition, the method of systatis implies that the writer is addressing an audience of learners and pupils who are being *introduced* to a subject. The method appears to differ from the Initiative, in that it is used for learners in subjects other than the sciences, whereas the Initiative plan is reserved for students of the sciences only. The Diaeretic method is a conventional arrangement in which the proposition or theme of a composition is divided, sub-divided, and broken down into its logical parts and relevant qualifications. It is well exemplified in the non-conformist sermon of the sixteenth century where it became a stereotyped pattern in which a proposition unfolded in this sequence: definition, division or partition, treatment of causes, treatment of effects, application of the theme, and exposition of contrary meanings of the theme.[72]

The seventh method that Bacon distinguishes is one determined by the subject matter that is handled. There can be no "uniformity of method in multiformity of matter." [73] and hence there exists "a great difference in delivery of the Mathematics, which are the most abstracted of knowledges, and Policy, which is the most immersed." [74] Just as techniques of invention and discovery vary from subject to subject, so will forms and patterns of arranging and presenting material.[75]

Two other kinds of method are called *"assertions and proofs,"* and *"questions with determinations,"* both schemes which Bacon fails to explain. Perhaps the assertion-and-proof aspect of the first plan indicates an arrangement in which the speaker first states a theme and then supports it with arguments, much in the manner of the modern speaker. The question-and-determination scheme may be one in which the problem or thesis is first stated, and is then discussed, pro and con, by question-and-answer, according to the mode of the scholastical disputation. The arrangement may also refer to the plan of some contemporaneous school books that

---

[71] *Ibid.*, 407.

[72] See Neils Hemmingsen, *The Preacher, or Methode of Preaching*, trans. by John Horsfall (London, 1574), facing 26-33.

[73] *Adv. of L.*, *Works*, III, 406.

[74] *Ibid.*

[75] *De aug.*, VI, 2, *Works*, IV, 452.

present the elements of a subject by a sequence of alternate questions and rejoinders.[76]

An important method is that which depends upon "the informations and anticipations already infused and impressed on the minds of the learners concerning the knowledge which is to be delivered." [77] If the scientist tries to popularize his knowledge, he must adopt an order and form that will render his meaning clear; "those whose conceits are beyond popular opinions have a double labour; the one to make themselves conceived, and the other to prove and demonstrate." [78] Frequently the endeavor to be clear will drive the man of specialized knowledge to rely on parables and similitudes. This is perhaps the most natural and most elemental method to aid understanding: ". . . in the infancy of learning, and in rude times, when those conceits which are now trivial were then new, the world was full of Parables and Similitudes; for else would men either have passed over without mark or else rejected for paradoxes that which was offered, before they had understood or judged." [79]

The last method that Bacon discusses is named the method of Imposture, and is distinguished by a writer's desire to appear deeply learned when actually his knowledge is superficial. Like the Art of Lullius, Bacon says, "the object of it is to sprinkle little drops of a science about, in such a manner that any sciolist may make some show and ostentation of learning." [80]

With Bacon's account of disposition before us, we may well look to the principles that emerge from it. First, there is the clear dictum that all communication in language ultimately is derived from and is oriented by the audience. In fact, Bacon is definitely aware of at least two classes of audience—those who possess special knowledge and those without it; indeed, it is this classification of hearers that leads him to distinguish the Initiative Method from the Magistral, the Exoteric from the esoteric. At the focal point of such a distinction is the man who, having specialized knowledge, either speaks or writes to pupils—his intellectual inferiors—that

---

[76] For an example of such presentation, see Charles Butler's *Rhetoricae libri duo* (London, 1598).

[77] *De aug.*, VI, 2, *Works*, IV, 452.

[78] *Adv. of L., Works*, III, 406.

[79] *Ibid.*, 407.

[80] *De aug.*, VI, 2, *Works*, IV, 454.

they may understand merely; or addresses himself to his equals—
critics or scientists—that they may evaluate or criticize. On the
other hand are those who learn and those who judge and act, *i. e.*,
those who unquestioningly appreciate and those who weigh and
consider, acquiesce or reject, the while undergoing modification of
attitude and conduct. Second, the classification of hearers gives
rise, in Bacon's view, to two principal kinds of discourse: exposition and persuasion. Where a writer is confronted with pupils,
whether they be learned, like the scientist, or ignorant, like the lay-
man and beginning student, his task is to explain; where he treats
of controversial matters of everyday discussion before a popular
audience, his purpose is to influence belief and conduct. In his
treatment of disposition as a separate art, Bacon is of course
basically interested in scientific exposition, and he evaluates most
of the methods with the peculiar purpose of the scientist in mind.
For the moment he merely alludes to the conventional methods that
are fit "to win consent or belief," reserving them for persuasive or
rhetorical discourse. Nevertheless he suggests, although he does
not develop, a classification of prose according to the audience addressed and the end intended. Third, the subject matter of a composition influences its form of expression, and special subjects
accordingly make use of unique forms of presentation. Finally,
Bacon's belief that the audience ultimately governs communication
and that the kinds of discourse have their own ends gives rise to
the conviction that the form and structure of all utterance must
be *functional*. His methods manifestly indicate that order and arrangement in a composition must be adapted to the audience's
knowledge and belief, to the subject matter, and to the purpose
the speaker or writer intends to achieve. No one method for the
orderly, systematic communication of ideas can be squeezed to fit
a variety of purposes and occasions, least of all the logician's
stock method of dichotomatic division and the Ramean formula
of progressing from the most evident, general statement, to the
least evident, particular item.

We have now arrived at the third and last division of the Art
of Transmission. Bacon names it the Illustration of Discourse, or
rhetoric, and his views on it as the great art of public address will
comprise the remainder of our study. Upon none of the four in-

tellectual arts except invention do the Baconian *opera* devote more time in critical analysis and in illustration than upon rhetoric. The technique of scientific discovery or "new induction" claims most of Bacon's attention, especially as described and illustrated in the longish *Novum organum*. Yet rhetoric gets hardly less devotion, for when one puts together the long sections given over to Antitheta, the early Essays, the Colours of Good and Evil, the Apothegmes, the *Promus of Formularies and Elegancies*, and the sophisms of everyday argument in the *De augmentis*, they constitute a very sizable proportion of Bacon's writings.

As the exposition of Bacon's views on rhetorical address is undertaken, it is well to emphasize its position and place in the cyclopedia. Rhetoric, in the first place, is located in the logical arts and is thus rational in character. Rhetoric, moreover, as one of the three divisions of the Art of Transmission, shares the function of conveying ideas with the other offspring of the parent art. Finally, although Bacon is at some pains to distinguish rhetoric from the Organ of Discourse and from the Method of Discourse, he does not intend the three divisions of the Art of Elocution to be mutually exclusive or to be strictly parallel with one another. The Organ of Discourse leads to a theory of language, and must therefore be employed by anyone engaging in rhetorical endeavor. As has been noted, the medium of discourse, whether scientific or rhetorical, is language. The Method of Discourse, although mentioning several modes of communication, is chiefly concerned to distinguish didactic, expository writing from rhetorical address. Furthermore, Bacon might not only have explicitly included rhetorical address under Method of Discourse, but were he not interested in emphasizing scientific writing, he might also have put disposition under rhetoric, where, so he asserts, it has a legitimate place.[81] Or had he not desired his special emphasis, Method itself might have been an offshoot of the Art of Judgment, "and that not amiss." [82] Indeed, Bacon deserves tribute for permitting his classifications to overlap, not only in the intellectual arts, but in the method of arranging the entire *Advancement*. He saw that Ramus, in making grammar, rhetoric, and dialectic mutually exclusive, had fallen upon the

[81] *De aug.*, VI, 2, *Works*, IV, 448.
[82] *Adv. of L.*, *Works*, III, 403.

shallows of knowledge. Accordingly, in the attempt to present Bacon's theory of rhetorical discourse, we too shall try to follow Bacon's practice, rather than Ramus's.

CHAPTER TWO

THE SPECIAL PROVINCE

OF RHETORIC

The faculty psychology which dominates Bacon's classification of knowledge in the *Advancement of Learning* and the *De augmentis* appears also in his definition of rhetoric. Not only is all knowledge divided into three parts, History, Poesy, and Philosophy, that are referred to the corresponding mental faculties, memory, imagination, and reason, but the function of rhetoric is also described in terms of a faculty psychology. "The duty and office of Rhetoric," Bacon writes, "is to apply Reason to Imagination for the better moving of the will.[1] . . . Rhetoric is subservient to the imagination, as Logic is to the understanding; and the duty and office of Rhetoric, if it be deeply looked into, is no other than to apply and recommend the dictates of reason to imagination, in order to excite the appetite and will."[2] It is worth observing that Bacon intends here to offer, not a complete descriptive definition, but a strict logical definition in which the *essence* or characteristic mark of rhetorical activity is set off from other activities.

Such a conception of rhetoric is maintained consistently throughout Bacon's works. Rhetoric is the only art, serious in intent, which utilizes the imagination in obedience to the dictates of reason. In poetry, the artistic or creative imagination obeys no law and responds to every caprice; and this fact leads Bacon in his later years to banish verse from the rank of arts and sciences.[3] Rhetoric,

---

[1] *Adv. of L., Works,* III, 409.
[2] *De aug.,* VI, 3, *Works,* IV, 455.   [3] *De aug.,* V, I, *Works,* IV, 406.

on the other hand, employs the reproductive imagination that, ever having rationally related ideas as an ultimate base, endeavors to render vivid didactic and argumentative discourse. Thus rhetoric by the manner in which the imaginative faculty is subservient to reason as well as by its place in the Baconian cyclopedia is rational in character.

When Bacon looks at the individual as a composite of "faculties," he is regarding the mental life, the psychological activities, within the human organism. As a consequence, the mind is held to be in a constant state of flux; the human being is at all times *active*. Bacon goes beyond this, however. He postulates, not an isolated individual, but a social being whose life and actions are inextricably bound up with his fellow beings. The social being, moreover, is no static creature; rather he is constantly in action, capable by his activities of influencing the movements of others and in turn of being influenced by their actions. Bacon's world, in other words, is dynamic; in social intercourse the end, either immediate or ultimate, is action.

Such a conception of the individual and of society is important, because it explains why Bacon does not set up, as the end of rhetoric, belief. Whereas modern theorists of rhetoric sometimes deem it expedient to distinguish belief and action as separate purposes that may be achieved by the speaker, Bacon does not recognize that so far as the immediate end of a given speech is concerned, the speaker may aim either to establish belief or to influence action. For Bacon, all rhetorical address seeks to influence action. In Bacon's psychology, the appetite and the will are those agents which impel action; to influence the will is therefore to secure action. Hence, to declare that rhetoric recommends reason to imagination "in order to excite the appetite and the will" is to assign, as the end of public address, the persuasion of men to action.

That Bacon thinks of the speaker as moving men to action is suggested by his attempt to mark off didactic discourse from scientific or critical discourse, and to distinguish both of these in turn from rhetorical address. His early work, *Of the Interpretation of Nature*, represents Bacon as a teacher and scientist who sees as the ends of communication, knowledge to be accepted and used or knowledge to be appraised and criticized:

. . . there are forms and methods of tradition wholly distinct and differing, according to their ends whereto they are directed. That there are two ends of tradition of knowledge, the one to teach and instruct for use and practice, the other to impart or intimate for re-examination and progression. That the former of these ends requireth a method not the same whereby it was invented and induced, but such as is most compendious and ready whereby it may be used and applied. That the latter of the ends, which is where a knowledge is delivered to be continued and spun on by a succession of labours, requireth a method whereby it may be transposed to another in the same manner as it was collected, to the end it may be discerned both where the work is weak, and where it breaketh off.[4]

In the Preface of the *Great Instauration*, Bacon again thinks of himself as teacher of all mankind, and hence, in setting forth his ideas to others, he will aim above all else to employ a clear style. He will avoid majesty of writing, and will refrain from confutations and pleadings:

. . . the same humility which I use in inventing I employ likewise in teaching. For I do not endeavor either by triumphs of confutation, or pleadings of antiquity, or assumption of authority, or even by the veil of obscurity, to invest these inventions of mine with any majesty; which might easily be done. . . . I have not sought . . . nor do I seek either to force or ensnare men's judgments, but I lead them to things themselves and the concordances of things, that they may see for themselves what they have, what they can dispute, what they can add and contribute to the common stock.[5]

In brief, the end of communication for the teacher is belief or acceptance, for the scientist, evaluation and criticism.

On the other hand Bacon customarily describes as persuasive those situations in which words are adapted to influence action. Such, for example, is the advice to the government that "consciences are not to be forced, but to be won and reduced by the force of truth, with the aid of time and the use of all good means of instruction and persuasion." [6] In advising James on the union of Scotland with England, he carefully distinguishes speech designed for persuasion and that planned merely for information. ". . . the length and ornament of speech are to be used for persuasion of

---

[4] *Works*, III, 248.   [5] *Works*, IV, 19.   [6] *Letters and Life*, I, 98.

multitudes, and not for information of kings. . . ." [7] Bacon closes
the advice to James with the words: "Thus have I made your Majesty a brief and naked memorial of the articles and points of this
great cause, which may serve only to excite and stir up your
Majesty's royal judgment, and the judgment of wiser men whom
you will be pleased to call to it. Wherein I will not presume to persuade or dissuade any thing, nor to interpose mine own opinion." [8]
At another time he recommends to Cecil that the English religion
is the most effective means of restoring the affection of the Irish
toward England, the method of "advancing religion" to be principally "the sending over of some good preachers, especially of the
sort which are vehement and zealous persuaders, and not scholastical, to be resident in principal towns. . . ." [9] This is entirely consonant with the doctrine laid down in the little treatise entitled
Helps for the Intellectual Powers, when Bacon speaks of the sensi-
tiveness and mobility of man's will and of the means by which it can
be influenced:

> And as to the will of man, it is that which is most maniable and obe-
> dient; as that which admitteth most medicines to cure and alter it. The
> most sovereign of all is Religion, which is able to change and transform
> it in the deepest and most inward inclinations and motions. And next to
> that is Opinion and Apprehension; whether it be infused by tradition
> and institution, or wrought in by disputation and persuasion.[10]

Here we perceive once more that Bacon has his eye on a social
creature whose point of control is the will. Religion is the great
force which can move the will and thereby influence conduct. But
next to that is popular belief and opinion which may determine
action by being part of every man's intellectual heritage or by
operating as subject matter for the persuasive speaker. Bacon,
then, seems to describe as persuasive and rhetorical those circumstances in which one man seeks to influence the actions of others.

But although rhetorical address seeks directly to influence
action, the type of conduct urged ought to be in the realm of the
virtuous and the good. To give to rhetoric the office of rousing the

---

[7] *Letters and Life*, III, 219.

[8] *Articles Touching Union of Scotland with England, Letters and Life*, III,
234.

[9] *Letters and Life*, III, 49.   [10] *Works*, VII, 100.

emotions by means of imaginative appeal without any qualification of purpose whatsoever would be repugnant to one whose cardinal article of faith was belief in reason. If the passions are to be aroused, they must work toward a *good* end as dictated by the understanding and reason. The office of rhetoric is to apply reason to imagination for the *better* moving of the will. "The end of Logic is to teach a form of argument to secure reason, and not to entrap it; the end of Morality is to procure the affections to obey reason, and not to invade it; the end of Rhetoric is to fill the imagination to second reason, and not oppress it. . . ." [11] Bacon cannot sympathize with Plato for condemning rhetoric merely because it can make the worse appear the better reason. The true function of rhetoric is to picture the good:

. . . it was a great injustice in Plato (though springing out of a just hatred of the rhetoricians of his time) to place rhetoric among arts voluptuary; resembling it to cookery, which did as much to spoil wholesome meats, as by variety and delicacy of sauces to make unwholesome meats more palatable. But God forbid that speech should not be much more conversant in adorning that which is good, than in colouring that which is evil; for this is a thing in use everywhere; there being no man but speaks more honestly than he thinks or acts. And it was excellently noted by Thucydides as a censure passed upon Cleon, that because he used always to hold on the bad side, therefore he was ever inveighing against eloquence and grace of speech; as well knowing that no man can speak fair of courses sordid and base; while it is easy to do it of courses just and honourable. For Plato said elegantly . . . 'that virtue, if she could be seen, would move great love and affection;' and it is the business of rhetoric to make pictures of virtue and goodness, so that they may be seen.[12]

Bacon thus insists that imaginative appeal must be subordinate to reason, because he distrusts the power of the imagination when uncontrolled. In his psychology the imagination properly fulfills one of its roles by acting as a messenger between the reason and the affections. Normally the imagination is under the restraint of reason, but occasionally it slips off its shackles and springs up, free and powerful:

---

[11] *Adv. of L., Works*, III, 410-411; *De aug.*, VI, 3, *Works*, IV, 455-456.

[12] *De aug.*, VI, 3, *Works*, IV, 456.

Neither is the imagination simply and only a messenger; but it is either invested with or usurps no small authority in itself, besides the simple duty of the message. For it was well said by Aristotle, 'That mind has over the body that commandment which the lord has over a bondman; but that reason has over the imagination that commandment which a magistrate has over a free citizen,' who may come also to rule in his turn . . . it is no small dominion which imagination holds in persuasions that are wrought by eloquence; for when by arts of speech men's minds are soothed, inflamed, and carried hither and thither, it is all done by stimulating the imagination till it becomes ungovernable, and not only sets reason at naught, but offers violence to it, partly by blinding, partly by incensing it. . . .[13]

Man's conduct, Bacon reasons, ought to be governed by reason, but as society is constituted, the proper functioning of the reason is disturbed by three agencies:

. . . we see that the government of reason is assailed and disordered in three ways: either by the illaqueation of sophisms, which pertain to Logic; or by juggleries of words, which pertain to Rhetoric; or by the violence of the Passions, which pertains to Ethics. For as in negotiations with others, men are usually wrought either by cunning, or by importunity, or by vehemency; so likewise in this negotiation within ourselves, we are either undermined by fallacies of arguments, or solicited and importuned by assiduity of impressions and observations, or agitated and transported by violence of passions. And yet the nature of man is not so unfortunately built, as that those arts and faculties should have power to disturb reason, and no power to strengthen or establish it; on the contrary they are of much more use that way. For the end of logic is to teach a form of argument to secure reason, and not to entrap it; the end likewise of moral philosophy is to procure the affections to fight on the side of reason, and not to invade it; the end of rhetoric is to fill the imagination with observations and images, to second reason, and not to oppress it.[14]

---

[13] *De aug.*, V, 1, *Works*, IV, 406; cf. *Adv. of L.*, *Works*, III, 382.

[14] *De aug.*, VI, 3, *Works*, IV, 455-456. Of the uncivilized and turbulent actions of man and of their modification by social agencies into an harmonious society, Bacon writes in his interpretation of the fable of Orpheus. That part of the fable in which Orpheus soothes the warring beasts by music, so Bacon suggests, aptly describes "the nature and condition of men; who are full of savage and unreclaimed desires, of profit, of lust, of revenge, which as long as they

Here Bacon regards logic and ethics and rhetoric as three means of counteracting evil tendencies inherent in human nature, and rhetoric, like its psychological counterparts, becomes an instrument of reason to induce right action. When virtue "cannot be shewed to the Sense by corporal shape, the next degree is to shew her to the Imagination in lively representation." [15] If we cannot persuade by example and imitation, we must rely upon word-images.

That rhetoric should function to second reason and not to oppress it, becomes clear upon perceiving how Bacon regarded the passions and the reason in their capacity of controlling individual action. Both the affections and the reason in their normal activity naturally impel the individual to do good. The passions, however, are inferior guides to conduct, for they regard only immediate or *present* action. Reason, on the other hand, looks to *future* action, and hence is the superior guide. The imagination, standing between the affections on the one side and reason on the other, may ally itself with either. If to the passions, then the individual is impelled to unreasonable, shortsighted acts that take no thought of the future. If to the reason, then the individual acts with better direction; deliberate, rational action becomes possible because the imagination exhibits the future as though it were actually present. Rhetoric therefore provides a body of rules whereby the imagination may be won from the affections and applied to the dictates of reason for the better moving of the will. Reason would become captive and servile without eloquence, ". . . if Eloquence of Persuasions did not practice and win the Imagination from the Affection's part, and contract a confederacy between the Reason and Imagination against the Affections. For the affections themselves carry ever an appetite to good, as reason doth; the difference is, that *the affection beholdeth merely the present; reason beholdeth the future and sum of time;* and therefore, the present filling the imagination more, reason is commonly vanquished; but after that force of elo-

---

give ear to precepts, to laws, to religion, sweetly touched with eloquence and persuasion of books, of sermons, of harangues, so long are society and peace maintained; but if these instruments be silent, or that sedition and tumult make them not audible, all things dissolve into anarchy and confusion." (*Adv. of L.*, *Works*, III, 302; and *The Wisdom of the Ancients*, *Works*, VI, 720-722.)

[15] *De aug.*, VI, 3, *Works*, IV, 456.

quence and persuasion hath made things future and remote appear as present, then upon the revolt of the imagination reason prevaileth." [16]

The enlistment of rhetoric in the cause of truth and goodness is of course an integral part of Bacon's scheme to advance learning. If true knowledge is unearthed, according to his great scheme of scientific inquiry, eloquent men must aid in its communication. Scientists and learned men may discover profound knowledge, but their true estimation and price lies with men at large. And in order that they may accept new knowledge, their imaginations must be roused to action:

. . . the property and breeding of knowledges is in great and excellent wits, yet the estimation and price of them is in the multitude, or in the inclinations of princes and great persons meanly learned. So as those knowledges are like to be received and honoured, which have their foundation in the subtility or finest trial of common sense, or such as to fill the imagination; and not such knowledge as is digged out of the hard mine of history and experience, and falleth out to be in some points as adverse to common sense or popular reason, as religion, or more. Which kind of knowledge, except it be delivered with strange advantages of eloquence and power, may be likely to appear and disclose a little to the world and straight to vanish and shut again.[17]

Such a statement, of course, rests on the assumption that man can be improved through education, an assumption to which Bacon heartily subscribed: ". . . as the most excellent of metals, gold, is of all other the most pliant and most enduring to wrought; so of all living and breathing substances, the perfectest (Man) is the most susceptible of help, improvement, impression, and alteration. And not only in his body, but in his mind and spirit. And there again not only in his appetite and affection, but in his power of wit and reason." [18]

The end of rhetoric, then, is the influencing of right action. We turn now to a consideration of the legitimate means by which rhetoric, in Bacon's eyes, is permitted to attain its end. Bacon realized that to define the function of rhetoric as the application

---

[16] *Adv. of L., Works*, III, 410-411; cf. *De aug.*, VI, 3, *Works*, IV, 456-457.
[17] *Filum labyrinthi, Works*, III, 503.
[18] *Helps for the Intellectual Powers, Works*, VII, 99.

of reason to imagination for the better moving of the will, was to imply also the principal methods of proof or support by which a speaker accomplishes his purpose. The definition implies, in the first place, that reasons and arguments must be discovered and selected, for Bacon, like Plato and Aristotle, feels that reason is "the soul of discourse." [19] In deliberative speaking in particular, where the "persuader's labour is to make things appear good or evil," it may be performed most soundly by "true and solid reasons." [20] The kinds of argument most useful to the speaker are those types of proof spoken of as induction, syllogism, and example, most of these belonging by right to logic, but made use of by rhetoric. Another type of proof may be called the imaginative. The speaker's peculiar problem is to move his audience by rendering his argument vivid, and hence any material or any manner of expression which will engage the imaginative faculty of his hearers will at once make acceptable the logic of his speech. By "imaginative proof," then, is meant in part ideas whose *content* incites the emotions, and in part is meant a style of expression which translates passionless reason into vivid terms. Bacon recognizes, finally, a third type of proof which depends upon the orator's disclosing and revealing himself, upon the speaker's setting himself forth to advantage.

Bacon views the processes of oral and written composition virtually as did the ancients. This should not be taken to mean, however, that he was content with the classical rhetorical categories of Aristotle, Cicero, and Quintilian, by which prose composition was divided into five operations: invention, disposition, elocution, memory, and pronunciation. He regarded these operations as comprising the body's *intellectual* or logical activities, and they could only be improved, in his view, when each one for the sake of study and analysis was subjected to separate scrutiny. To serve this purpose, accordingly, he removes them from the train of any one art, and calls them the "logical arts": Invention, Judgment, Memory, and Elocution. Although this grouping may have been suggested by the famous Peter Ramus,[21] Bacon did not follow the

---

[19] *De aug.*, VI, 1, *Works*, IV, 439.
[20] Preface to the *Colours of Good and Evil*, *Works*, VII, 77.
[21] So Ellis indicates, *Works*, I, 616n.

Rameans who made the compartments mutually and irrevocably exclusive of one another. He sees that some of the methods of invention are "common to both, logic as well as rhetoric" and are useful "where we are disputing with one another." [22] The art of judging deals with proofs, arguments, and disputations; and disposition, "commonly handled as a part of Logic . . . also finds a place in Rhetoric." [23] Furthermore, Bacon's art of memory derives some of its material from the rhetorician's precepts concerning recall; indeed, in showing how the recall of concepts can be facilitated by associating them with images, Bacon's illustration is for the sake of the rhetorician: ". . . you will more easily remember the image of a hunter pursuing a hare, of an apothecary arranging his boxes, of a pedant making a speech, of a boy repeating verses from memory, of a player acting on a stage, than the mere notions of invention, disposition, elocution, memory, and action." [24] It seems evident that although Bacon, for the sake of analyzing intellectual activity, removes invention, disposition, and memory from the skirts of rhetoric, he still perceives that they are operations that any creative speaker or writer must undertake.

In discussing the logical arts Bacon makes no direct reference to elocution and delivery as parts or as processes of rhetoric as such. Quite unlike both the Rameans and the classicists he does not treat of *pronuntiatio* systematically, nor does he think of elocution as style. In fact, Bacon's broad use of "elocution" as signifying the whole process of communication or transmission is his own. Nevertheless, he refers often, albeit unsystematically, to both style and pronunciation in their traditional senses. Accordingly, it seems clear that Bacon's view of the operations and divisions of public discourse is essentially classical, for when his view is set in the historical perspective of rhetorical theory its emphasis is ancient rather than Ramean; its color is that of Greek and Roman rhetoric rather than that of the Ciceronian stylists of the late Renaissance. Again, this is not to say that when Bacon uses some of the terminology of classical rhetoric he means the same things as Aristotle or Quintilian;[25] as shall eventually be shown, his own understanding

---

[22] *De aug.*, V, 3, *Works*, IV, 423.   [23] *De aug.*, VI, 2, *Works*, IV, 448.
[24] *De aug.*, V, 5, *Works*, IV, 437.
[25] This is well illustrated when the student tries to decide how Bacon might

of rhetoric and the processes of discourse may at times be quite different, even unique.

In order fully to understand rhetoric as Bacon conceives it, one must do more than merely set forth its end, its principal means of proof and the operations involved in pursuing the art. One must inquire somewhat further into what Bacon means by the dictum that rhetoric applies reason to imagination for the better moving of the will. This requires, first, an examination of what Bacon says concerning the imagination and its function, and second, a consideration of the relations of rhetoric to knowledge in general, and to logic and to ethics in particular.

Bacon regards the imagination as a rational faculty, and holds that its preponderant function over the other faculties gives rise to poetry. This at least is his stated view at the opening of *The Advancement of Learning*. But with the gradual development of the *Advancement*, he shows a marked distrust of the power of the imagination, even to the extent of denying poetry a place in his scheme of knowledge. "The knowledge which respecteth the Faculties of the Mind of man is of two kinds; the one respecting his Understanding and Reason, and the other his Will, Appetite, and Affection; whereof the former produceth Position or Decree, the latter Action or Execution." [26] The imagination, as a faculty in its own right, disappears, and along with it, poetry.

What, then, becomes of the imagination? Though now denied the distinction of a faculty proper, it is the great instrument or agent of both the Reason and the Will. It is a go-between, or messenger.

---

classify the species of discourse, for his vocabulary is at times markedly classical, at times original. When referring to occasions for public address, Bacon employs such terms as "law court" pleadings, "forensics," "deliberatives," speeches of "policy," and "ceremonials," thus suggesting that his principal kinds of rhetorical address are the three classical species: forensic, deliberative, and demonstrative. Apparently he intends both preaching and letter-writing to fall within these three divisions. Had he undertaken a formal classification of rhetorical address, the arrangement might have been both specific and practical: "Orations are pleadings, speeches of counsel; laudatives, invectives, apologies, reprehensions; orations of formality, or ceremony, and the like." (*Adv. of L., Works*, III, 342.) "Letters are according to all the variety of occasions; advertisements, advices, directions, propositions, petitions, commendatory, expostulatory, satisfactory, of compliment, of pleasure, of discourse, and all other passages of action." (*Ibid.*)

[26] *Adv. of L., Works*, III, 382.

Perhaps Bacon at this stage in the composition of the *Advancement* is, as Professor Bundy suggests, "conscious of inconsistency in having assigned poetry to the realm of imagination and in having at the same time denied to imagination any primary function," [27] for Bacon continues:

> It is true that the Imagination is an agent or *nuncius* in both provinces, both the judicial and the ministerial. For Sense sendeth over to Imagination before Reason hath judged: and Reason sendeth over to Imagination before the Decree can be acted; for Imagination ever precedeth Voluntary Motion: saving that this Janus of Imagination hath differing faces; for the face towards Reason hath the print of Truth, but the face towards Action hath the print of Good. . . .[28]

Bacon means that an individual in the process of inventing and of judging what he has found out either sees in his mind's eye the objects or things which he is to judge, or at least has an image of the words and propositions which make up a chain of reasoning and which form the basis for judgments. The significance of images *incites* the understanding. Similarly, an individual who wills to act morally cannot do so without first "seeing" to some extent the end for which he strives. What Bacon seems to be driving at is the notion that the use of language is always accompanied in some degree either by an imaginative picture of the objective world or by a picture of the words themselves. If one is engaged in scientific inquiry, the imaginative accompaniment of language has the face of Truth, for the end of science is the discovery of truth; if one is concerned with human conduct and behaviour, with the influencing of men in society, the imaginative picture evoked by language has the face of Good, for the goal of ethics is right action. In short, without the aid of the imagination, human reason cannot operate and the human will cannot determine upon a line of action. The imagination, then, is an agent both in logic and in ethics.

It seems probable that the imagination, as Bacon conceives it in the passage under consideration, has but one operation—the production of images, the calling up of images of past experience,

---

[27] "Bacon's True Opinion of Poetry," *Studies in Philology* XXVII (1930), 260.

[28] *Adv. of L., Works*, III, 382.

whenever one reads or writes or talks.[29] But earlier in the *Advancement*, when the imagination is considered as a faculty, it has another function. It calls up images and in addition moulds ideas and objects of experience into *new combinations*. Here, then, Bacon marks an image-producing faculty which is not *re-productive*, but *creative*. In its creative operation, moreover, it obeys no law:

Poesy is a part of learning in measure of words for the most part restrained, but in all other points extremely licensed, and doth truly refer to the Imagination; which, not being tied to the laws of matter, may at pleasure join that which nature hath severed, and sever that which nature hath joined. . . .[30]

The lawless action of the creative imagination is again apparent when Bacon contrasts the two imitative arts, poetry and history:

Poesy . . . is . . . concerned with individuals; that is, with individuals invented in imitation of those which are the subject of true history; yet with this difference, that it commonly exceeds the measure of nature, joining at pleasure things which in nature would never have come together, and introducing things which in nature would never have come to pass; just as Painting likewise does. This is the work of the Imagination.[31]

It is obvious, therefore, that the creative imagination can have no proper place in prose composition if rhetoric is to fulfill its end. Rhetoric legitimately seeks to secure the reign of reason. It employs the imagination only to make "things future and remote appear as present." [32] Consequently, the image-making faculty that serves rhetoric cannot conjure up ideas willy-nilly, nor join ideas at pleasure. The creative imagination, highly emotional and uncontrollable, has no place in rhetorical endeavor. The reproductive imagination, on the other hand, serving merely to call up simple memory images or pictures in the mind of the audience, is useful to the speaker. After the invention and selection of arguments, he can translate his case into vivid terms, thereby better moving his audience than he would by reason alone. But in this

---

[29] ". . . of things that have been in no part objects of the sense, there can be no imagination, not even a dream." (*A Description of the Intellectual Globe, Works*, V, 504.)

[30] *Adv. of L., Works*, III, 343.   [31] *De aug.*, II, 1, *Works*, IV, 292.

[32] *De aug.*, VI, 3, *Works*, IV, 457.

translation it is essential that the imagination remain subservient
to reason. To state this, however, is not to minimize the importance
of the imagination to rhetoric. In Bacon's eyes rhetorical address
would be impossible without imagery. Reason and imagination
work hand in hand; each depends on the other. So essential is this
relationship that Bacon at one time cites as the subject of rhetoric,
"Imaginative or Insinuative Reason." [33]

If we follow Bacon's lead and look deeply into the office of
rhetoric, we shall discover how precisely he has set forth the
scope of rhetoric as distinct from the scope of other arts.

Bacon believes that the proper province of ethics is a rational
study of the good, in order that the affections may follow the
dictates of reason rather than their own unbridled fancy; "the
end . . . of moral philosophy is to procure the affections to fight
on the side of reason, and not to invade it." [34] Accordingly, in his
encyclopedia of knowledge he briefly discusses what he calls the
"culture of the mind" or, in other words, the nature of the good,
and the ways and means whereby the mind may be trained toward
right action. One of the ways in which rhetorical address contributes to ethical conduct consists, as we have already observed,
in reenforcing the dictates of reason by wooing the imagination
from the passions and vividly presenting the claims of rational conduct. Rhetoric, in addition, shares the purpose of ethics because,
in deliberative speaking especially, the orator must consider what

---

[33] *Adv. of L., Works,* III, 383. Spedding has an interesting footnote relative
to Bacon's notion of the imagination: "Poesy, which belongs properly to the
Imagination, is not to be considered as a part of knowledge; and the two other
offices of the Imagination belong, one to the doctrine *de anima,* the other to
Rhetoric. There is no occasion therefore to make a place for Imagination among
the parts of knowledge which concern the faculties of the human mind."
(*Ibid.*) In the text, we noted the kinds of imagination relating to poesy and
to rhetoric. Of that relating to *de anima,* Bacon says in the *Sylva sylvarum,*
Century X: "Now we will speak of the force of Imagination upon other bodies,
and of the means to exalt and strengthen it. Imagination in this place I
understand to be, the representation of an individual thought. Imagination,
is of three kinds: the first joined with belief of that which is to come; the
second joined with memory of that which is past: and the third is of things
present; for I comprehend in this, imaginations feigned and at pleasure;
as if one should imagine such a man to be in the vestments of a Pope, or to have
wings." (*Works,* II, 653-654.)

[34] *De aug.,* VI, 3, *Works,* IV, 456.

is good or evil with respect to the action he is urging; "the persauder's labour is to make things appear good or evil, and that in higher or lower degree." [35] Rhetoric, furthermore, will make use of ethical studies, not only as they furnish material concerning the good and evil, but also as they supply knowledge concerning men's natures, particularly the evil tendencies of the affections. Bacon commends Aristotle for discussing the abstract nature of good and evil in the *Nicomachean Ethics*, but he finds it strange "that Aristotle should have written divers volumes of ethics, and never handled the affections, as a principal portion thereof; yet in his Rhetoric, where they are considered but collaterally and in a second degree (as they may be moved and excited by speech), he finds a place for them, and handles them acutely and well, for the quantity thereof." [36] Ethics, then, is the province which takes for its peculiar study the nature of the good, its kinds, the "sound and true distributions and descriptions of the several characters and tempers of men's natures and dispositions," [37] and the knowledge of man's affections. Rhetoric may deal with these "but collaterally."

Rhetoric and ethics are related, then, in that both consider the nature and kinds of the good, the latter quite properly, the former secondarily and in so far as the good is linked up with what the writer and speaker propose. Rhetoric, in other words, merely utilizes the knowledge of right conduct that ethics makes available. Both studies also meet at the point where each has the special problem of adapting its appeals to the person or persons addressed. One of the great deficiencies which Bacon found in traditional ethics was in character analysis. If ethics can train the mind to mould the affections and to regulate character—and Bacon deemed these very important functions of ethics—then it must know the tempers and dispositions of character so thoroughly that, in the case of any given individual, it can apply the appropriate remedy. Rhetoric, similarly, if it is to influence action, should know character so well that the speaker before any given audience may select his proof according to the character of those addressed. This, I think, is the point of Bacon's statement that "Aristotle doth wisely place Rhetoric as between Logic on the one side and

---

[35] *Colours of Good and Evil, Works,* VII, 77.
[36] *De aug.,* VII, 3, *Works,* V, 23.   [37] *Adv. of L., Works,* III, 434.

moral or civil knowledge on the other, as participating of both: for the proofs and demonstrations of Logic are toward all men indifferent and the same; but the proofs and persuasions of Rhetoric ought to differ according to the auditors . . . which application, in perfection of idea, ought to extend so far, that if a man should speak of the same thing to several persons, he should speak to them all respectively and several ways. . . ." [38]

The relationship of rhetoric to logic may be understood upon perceiving the various senses in which Bacon employs the term "logic." In the first place, logic is used to describe the four Intellectual Arts; the Arts of Invention, of Judgment, of Memory, and of Transmission are, as was previously observed, logical arts as opposed to poetry, history, and ethics. According to this conception of logical activity, then, rhetoric is a part of logic; Bacon has extended logic over the field commonly assigned to rhetorical address.

Bacon, in the second place, designates as logic, the special method of scientific inquiry which in the *Novum organum* he often refers to as the "new logic." By this is meant an inductive scheme of invention which, when applied to the interpretation of Nature, yields universally valid knowledge previously unknown to mankind. The method that produces this new knowledge having universal validity is a scheme of tabulating scientific observations in order that one may draw off general conclusions from the tabulated particulars. The aim is to *discover new facts*, to search for causes; and to facilitate the understanding in this task tables are formed.[39] If, for example, we are examining the cause of heat in order to understand its nature, Table I will cite all the phenomena where heat is present. Table II will consist of a collection of phenomena similar to those appearing in Table I, but where heat is *absent*. By deliberately looking for analogous phenomena where the quality is absent, Bacon hopes to prevent error. Table III will contain comparisons with reference to the *quantity* of heat, (1) within the various parts of the body exhibiting it, and (2) between different,

---

[38] *Ibid.*, 411.

[39] This account of the principal feature of Bacon's method is that of Basil Montagu, *The Life of Francis Bacon* (London, 1833), 285-290. His is the clearest of all interpretations that I have consulted.

distinct bodies. Table IV will comprise a collection of exclusions, by listing (1) those phenomena which are not found where heat is present, (2) those phenomena which are found where heat is absent, (3) those phenomena which became more numerous or more marked when heat decreases, and (4) those phenomena which disappear or become less marked as heat increases. Table V will consist of a collection of the phenomena which always accompany heat, increase with its increase, and decrease with its decrease. Then by inspecting this final Table it is at once apparent, says Bacon, that the nature or cause of heat is the motion of particles. What we have here, then, is a systematic procedure that applies the logical questions of presence and absence, of like and unlike, to a given problem, and that arranges the answers in a series of tables for the purpose of drawing a general, scientific axiom or principle from particular instances. A new logic like this, Bacon explains, differs from traditional logic:

For the end which this science of mine proposes is the invention not of arguments but of arts; not of things in accordance with principles, but of principles themselves; not of probable reasons, but of designations and directions for works. And as the intention is different, so accordingly is the effect; the effect of the one being to overcome an opponent in argument, of the other to command nature in action.[40]

Bacon's declaration that his science proposes "the invention not of arguments but of arts" suggests that he thought of his method as applying, not solely to science, but to all arts, humanistic as well as physical. And the *Novum organum* leaves no doubt concerning the applicability of the new induction to the social sciences:

It may also be asked . . . whether I speak of natural philosophy only, or whether I mean that the other sciences, logic, ethics, and politics, should be carried on by this method. Now I certainly mean what I have said to be understood of them all; and as the common logic, which governs by the syllogism, extends not only to natural but to all sciences; so does mine also, which proceeds by induction, embrace everything. For I form a history and tables of discovery for anger, fear, shame, and the like; for matters political; and again for the mental operations of mem-

---

[40] From "The Plan of the Work," part of the Preface to the *Great Instauration, Works*, IV, 24.

ory, composition and division, judgment and the rest, not less than for heat and cold, or light or vegetation, or the like.[41]

It is clear, then, that the rhetorician as a theorist, like the politician, the logician, and the ethical theorist in their fields, may apply to rhetoric a systematic scheme of inductive inquiry which will result in establishing a body of rules pertaining properly to the art of speaking and writing. Bacon, of course, has not specifically referred to rhetoric in this connection, because he holds that the art has been "extremely well laboured" and studied; little remains to be done. Nevertheless, new precepts that are to be added to rhetorical theory may be correctly derived by the new logic. And the results obtained, it should be observed, will be in the realm, not of contingent truth, but of universal truth.

It is probable, furthermore, that to some extent the practical-minded speaker as well as the rhetorical theorist finds the new logic useful as a tool for uncovering ideas that are new to him, although not new to all men. His new induction, Bacon holds, finds broad application; by it, he seeks to "supply the mind with such rules and guidance that it may in every case apply itself aptly." [42] Hence he delivers in the *Novum organum* many and diverse precepts in the doctrine of discovery, because it is necessary in some measure to "modify the method of invention according to the quality and condition of the subject of the inquiry." [43] The speaker, then, may use the apparatus of scientific topics or suggestive questions, and he, like a scientist, may collect and assemble his observations and answers on popular problems in the form of tables, drawing from them conclusions he might not otherwise obtain. The conclusions obtained, however, will be probable in character, not universal, nor will they be new to anyone except the speaker himself.

The term logic is applied, in the third place, to the process of "rhetorical inventions." By this is meant the recall and recovery of ideas by a speaker or writer; it is "no other but *out of the knowledge whereof our mind is already possessed, to draw forth or call before us that which may be pertinent to the purpose which we take*

---

[41] *Nov. org., Works,* IV, 112. The *Novum organum* affords an illustration of the Baconian method as applied to the determination of the principles of memory (*Works,* IV, 162-163).

[42] *Nov. org., Works,* IV, 112.   [43] *Ibid.*

into our consideration." [44] The questions and topics which facilitate the recovery of knowledge are primarily logical in character; they supply ideas, not by the new instrument but by the topics of conventional logic. Hence the speaker who takes advantage of them employs logic as an instrument.

In one other sense Bacon conceives of logic. Often he describes the Art of Judgment, the second of the four Intellectual Arts, as ordinary or "common logic." After invention comes criticism, and the Art of Judgment, accordingly, operates to test the validity of inference. Rhetoric as a practical art uses judgment, partly in testing the strength of its reasonings, but chiefly in the refutation of opponents. In short, traditional logic as distinct from the logic of scientific inquiry may be "very properly applied to civil business and to those arts which rest in discourse and opinion. . . ." [45] We observe, however, that the use of reasoning in rhetorical situations differs somewhat from its employment in formal logic. Whereas the proofs of the logician are addressed to no definite audience, the proofs of the rhetorician are always adapted to the nature of the auditors. Because of this, "Logic differeth from Rhetoric," writes Bacon in a paraphrase of Zeno, "as the fist from the palm, the one close the other at large." [46]

To summarize, then, rhetoric relates to logic, first, as a part does to the whole; second, as a science which may utilize the logical methodology of scientific discovery, thereby adding to extant rhetorical theory, and as a practical art which may adapt a scientific method of inquiry to the finding of probable facts unknown to the speaker; third, rhetoric as a practical art employs the topics of ordinary logic; and finally, as a practical activity rhetoric will utilize the precepts of everyday logic for the criticism of the inference that appears in discourse.

Although it is true, as has heretofore been pointed out, that Bacon seeks in his classification of knowledge to isolate the functions peculiar to each species, yet when he comes to consider the peculiar subject matter of each branch of learning he is fully aware that they overlap and that each fills out and renders more accurate

---

[44] *Adv. of L., Works,* III, 389.
[45] Preface to the *Great Instauration, Works,* IV, 17.
[46] *Adv. of L., Works,* III, 411.

and more significant the other. Quite significantly for our study, Bacon is nowhere more explicit in his remarks on the fundamental unity of all subject matter than in those few passages in which he refers to rhetoric as it relates to knowledge in general.

Bacon is not so much interested in the ideas which, discovered by one science and belonging properly to it, may be utilized *in toto* by another science or art, as he is interested in the notion that the discoveries and principles of one science may serve to correct and to render more accurate the axioms and principles of another part of human learning:

> . . . I that hold it for a great impediment towards the advancement and further invention of knowledge, that particular arts and sciences have been disincorporated from general knowledge, do not understand one and the same thing which Cicero's discourse and the note and conceit of the Grecians in their word *Circle Learning* do intend. For I mean not that use which one science hath of another for ornament or help in practice, as the orator hath of knowledge of affections for moving . . . ; but I mean it directly of that use by way of supply of light and information which the particulars and instances of one science do yield and present for the framing or correcting of the axioms of another science in their very truth and notion.[47]

Bacon deplores the undue specialization which he feels is rampant in the study of the sciences; for the sciences ought to "have a dependence upon universal knowledge to be augmented and rectified by the superior light thereof, as well as the parts and members of a science have upon the *Maxims* of the same science, and the mutual light and consent which one part receiveth of another." [48] The arts of speech, similarly, would be improved by a study of Grammar which underlies them all. "So likewise," Bacon continues, "in this same logic and rhetoric, or arts of argument and grace of speech, if the great masters of them would but have gone a form lower, and looked but into the observations of Grammar concerning the kinds of words, their derivations, deflexions, and syntax; specially enriching the same with the helps of several languages, with their differing proprieties of words, phrases, and tropes; they might

---

[47] *Of the Interpretation of Nature, Works,* III, 228-229.
[48] *Ibid.,* 229.

have found out more and better footsteps of common reason, help of disputation, and advantages of cavillation, than many of these which they have propounded." [49] Furthermore, a knowledge of rhetoric would be enhanced by knowing music:

> . . . a man should be thought to dally, if he did not note how the figures of rhetoric and music are many of them the same. The repetitions and traductions in speech and the reports and hauntings of sounds in music are the very same things. . . . The figure that Cicero and the rest commend as one of the best points of elegancy, which is the fine checking of expectation, is no less well known to the musicians when they have a special grace in flying the close of cadence. And these are no allusions but direct communities, the same delights of the mind being to be found not only in music, rhetoric, but in moral philosophy, policy, and other knowledges, and that obscure in the one, which is the more apparent in the other, yea and that discovered in the one which is not found at all in the other, and so one science greatly aiding to the invention and augmentation of another. [50]

Bacon suggests that the "continuance and entireness of knowledge be preserved. For the contrary hereof hath made particular sciences to become barren, shallow, and erroneous; while they have not been nourished and maintained from the common fountain. So we see Cicero the orator complained of Socrates and his school, that he was the first that separated philosophy and rhetoric; whereupon rhetoric became an empty and verbal art." [51] Bacon, it seems apparent, would condemn the prose artist who studied his rhetoric and nothing else. Excellence in any study depends upon broad, fundamental training as well as upon specialization.

In his conception of the essential unity of knowledge, Bacon emphasizes, as we have said, that the axioms and principles of one study rectify and render more sound the principles of another study. He does not seem to hold highly the idea that one study may appropriate to itself facts which may legitimately belong to another, as, for example, the speaker's rhetoric making direct use of the knowledge of human characters which it derives from ethics. This is particularly true, Bacon maintains, as regards the relationship of the First Philosophy and rhetoric. The First or

---

[49] *Ibid.*, 230.　　　　[50] *Interpretation of Nature, Works,* III, 230.
[51] *Adv. of L., Works,* III, 367. Cf. *De aug.,* IV, 1, *Works,* IV, 373.

Primary Philosophy in Bacon's system is the logical and final outcome of applying the inductive method to the interpretation of nature, including that of man in society. When nature has been painstakingly analyzed according to the new organon and her principles established, then a philosophy can be written which will interpret the results accurately. But the philosophy which is thus formulated will be of little or no use in rhetorical practice, because the esoteric axioms and concepts of philosophy can be properly understood only by highly educated people.

Rhetoric, accordingly, even though it may seek to popularize the First Philosophy, must ultimately rely upon received philosophies and subjects of discourse. Its subject matter, broadly speaking, lies in popular opinions and manners. It finds precise, scientific knowledge of little use. In the preface to the *Novum organum*, Bacon establishes the point:

> I am far from wishing to interfere with the philosophy which now flourishes, or with any other philosophy more correct and complete than this which has been or may hereafter be propounded. For I do not object to the use of this received philosophy, or others like it, for supplying matter for disputations and ornaments for discourse,—for the professor's lecture and for the business of life. Nay, more, I declare openly that for these uses the philosophy which I bring forward will not be much available. It does not lie in the way. It cannot be caught up in passage. It does not flatter the understanding by conformity with preconceived notions. Nor will it come down to the apprehension of the vulgar except by its utilities and effects.[52]

Thus it is clear that rhetoric relies on popular truth rather than on scientific truth. The arguments employed in rhetorical address will be drawn from popular opinion, will utilize a method of disposition appropriate to this level of truth and to their persuasive function, and finally will be expressed and delivered in a manner consonant with their social function.

---

[52] *Works*, IV, 41-42. Cf. the following (112-113): "There is no reason why the arts which are now in fashion should not continue to supply matter for disputation and ornaments for discourse, to be employed for the convenience of professors and men of business; to be in short like current coin, which passes among men by consent. Nay I frankly declare that what I am introducing will be but little fitted for such purposes as these, since it cannot be brought down to common apprehension, save by effects and works only."

Rhetoric, because it deals with popular opinions and disputations and because it makes its appeal to the approbation of the multitude, is, in Bacon's mind, an inferior science. Though "excellently well laboured," and excellent in itself "truly valued . . . eloquence is doubtless inferior to wisdom. For what a distance there is between them is shown in the words spoken by God to Moses, when he declined the office assigned him on the ground that he was no speaker: 'There is Aaron, he shall be thy speaker, thou shalt be to him as God.' Yet in profit and in popular estimation wisdom yields to eloquence; for so Solomon says: 'The wise in heart shall be called prudent, but he that is sweet of speech shall compass greater things'; plainly signifying that wisdom will help a man to a name or admiration, but that it is eloquence which prevails most in action and common life." [53]

The science which discovers new knowledge is that which Bacon esteems most. All other studies must rank below it, for they can only begin their discussions when scientific research has supplied the facts and materials:

Are we the richer by one poor invention, by reason of all the learning that hath been these many hundred years? The industry of artificers maketh some small improvement of things invented; and chance sometimes in experimenting maketh us to stumble upon somewhat which is new; but all the disputation of the learned never brought to light one effect of nature before unknown. When things are known and found out then they can descant upon them, they can knit them into certain causes, they can reduce them to their principles.[54]

Yet, so far as popular arts are concerned, logic and rhetoric "rightly taken are the gravest of sciences, being the arts of arts, of the one for judgment, the other for ornament; besides they give the rule and direction how both to set forth and illustrate the subject matter." [55]

Francis Bacon's theory of rhetorical address, therefore, by virtue of its reference to the imaginative faculty of man's mind and the peculiar function of the imagination in relation to the reason and the affections is essentially social in character. Con-

---

[53] *De aug.*, VI, 3, *Works*, IV, 454–455.
[54] *Letters and Life*, I, 123-124.
[55] *Adv. of L.*, *Works*, III, 326; cf. *Works*, IV, 288.

ceived as the most effective means of communicating knowledge for persuasive ends, rhetoric at the same time carries the social obligation of helping reason to prevail over passion, of establishing, on the level of popular knowledge, the just and good cause. To this end the orator, abjuring the vain scholastical manner of utterance, should speak "soundly indeed, ordering the matter he handleth distinctly for memory, deducing and drawing it down for direction, and authorizing it with strong proofs and warrants. . . ." [56]

---

[56] *An Advertisement touching the Controversies of the Church of England, Letters and Life*, I, 91.

CHAPTER THREE

INVENTION

In those places in Bacon's works where rhetoric is alluded to incidentally, where the nature of rhetoric seems to be caught up in a phrase, a reader might well infer that Bacon conceived of rhetoric as dealing with the "ornament" or style of speech. In one instance, for example, he refers to logic and rhetoric as the "arts of argument and grace of speech," respectively.[1] Furthermore, his definition of rhetoric as the art of clothing reason in an imaginative dress seems to suggest a stylistic approach to rhetoric. Occasionally he alludes to rhetoric as the "adornment" of discourse, perhaps at the moment thinking of rhetorical address as the dressing up and ornamenting of ideas for popular appreciation. But his use of "adornment" seems to be uncritical and transitory, and probably indicates merely that he was aware of the attempt, by those contemporary rhetoricians who endeavored strictly to compartmentalize the arts, to identify rhetorical discourse with ornamental presentation. In truth, when one sees Bacon's rhetorical system in correct perspective, it is clear that he did not think of rhetorical activity as beginning only after logical processes have discovered the basic arguments; it is obvious that his emphasis is on the invention and selection of ideas with reference to a given occasion, rather than on a special and elaborate manner of composition which would involve abundant use of tropes and figures, unusual diction, and harmonious rhythms.   Fundamental to rhetoric is content and probable argument.

---

[1] *Of the Interpretation of Nature, Works,* III, 230.

Early in *The Advancement of Learning*, Bacon hastens to put the ornamental aspects of style in their proper place. He distinguishes three distempers of learning, the fantastical, the contentious, and the delicate, the first of which is characterized by an emphasis upon style rather than upon matter. Briefly he cites the forces which in the past caused men to "study words and not matter":

> . . . these four causes concurring, the admiration of ancient authors, the hate of the schoolmen, the exact study of languages, and the efficacy of preaching, did bring in an affectionate study of eloquence and copie of speech, which then began to flourish. This grew speedily to an excess; for men began to hunt more after words than matter; and more after the choiceness of the phrase, and the round and clean composition of the sentence, and the sweet falling of the clauses, and the varying and illustration of their works with tropes and figures, than after the weight of matter, worth of subject, soundness of argument, life of invention, or depth of judgment. Then grew the flowing and watery vein of Osorius, the Portugal bishop, to be in price. Then did Sturmius spend such infinite and curious pains upon Cicero the orator and Hermogenes the rhetorician, besides his own books of periods and imitation and the like. Then did Car of Cambridge, and Ascham, with their lectures and writings almost deify Cicero and Demosthenes, and allure all young men that were studious unto that delicate and polished kind of learning. . . . In sum, the whole inclination and bent of those times, was rather towards copie than weight.[2]

Bacon warns, in short, that "as substance of matter is better than beauty of words, so contrariwise vain matter is worse than vain words. . . ."[3] In the essay, *Of Studies*, occurs the familiar statement that although one of the chief uses of studies is for ornament in discourse, to use them too much for embellishment is affectation.[4]

---

[2] *Adv. of L., Works,* III, 283-284.   [3] *Ibid.,* 285.

[4] *Works,* VI, 497. Cf. ". . . words are but the images of matter; and except they have life of reason and invention, to fall in love with them is all one as to fall in love with a picture." (*Adv. of L., Works,* III, 284.) Nevertheless, Bacon would have it understood that ornamentation, in the sense of presenting ideas vividly, is not to be neglected, and his general criticism of a contemporary pamphlet reflects this opinion: ". . . surely this book is . . . of the meanest workmanship; being fraughted with sundry base scoffs and cold amplifications and other characters of despite, but void of all judgment or ornament."

In a letter to Essex, Bacon reminds him that those who aim merely at grace of speech have mistaken the end of their journey; they rest prematurely:

The true end of knowledge is clearness and strength of judgement, and not ostentation or ability to discourse; which I do the rather put your Lordship in mind of, because the most part of our noblemen and gentlemen of our time have no other use of their learning but table talk; and the reason is because they before setting down their journey's end ere they attain to it they rest, and travel not so far as they should; but God knows they have gotten little that have only his discoursing gift; for though, like empty casks, they sound loud when a man knocks upon their outside, yet if you pierce into them you shall find them full of nothing but wind.[5]

(*Certain Observations made upon a Libel Published This Present Year, 1592. Letters and Life,* I, 153.)

[5] *Letters and Life,* II, 14. Bacon's opinion of contemporaneous preaching is in point here, for his remarks, chiefly critical and advisory, boil down to this: Neither invention nor style can be neglected in the preacher's art, yet if either must be slighted, let it not be that pertaining to wise proofs and sound interpretations. Those who inveigh against lack of preaching in the Established Church need perspective: ". . . they make too easy and too promiscuous an allowance of such as they account preachers, having not respect enough to years . . . , not respect enough to their learnings in other arts, which are handmaids to divinity; not respect enough to the gift itself, which many times is none at all. For God forbid, that every man that can take unto himself boldness to speak an hour together in a Church upon a text, should be admitted for a preacher, though he mean never so well. I know there is a great latitude in gifts and a great variety in auditories and congregations, but yet so as there is *aliquid infimum* below which you ought not to descend . . . ; amongst many causes of Atheism which are miserably met in our age, as schisms and controversies, profane scoffing in holy matters, and others, it is not the least that divers do adventure to handle the word of God which are unfit and unworthy. And herein I would have no man mistake me, as if I did extol curious and affected preaching, which is as much on the other side to be disliked, and breeds atheism and scandal as well as the other (for who would not be offended at one that comes into the pulpit as if he came upon a stage to play parts or prizes?). . . ." (*Pacification and Edification of the Church, Letters and Life,* III, 118-119.) Again: "Is there no means to train up and nurse ministers (for the yield of the universities will not serve, though they were never so well governed)—to train them . . . not to preach (for that every man confidently adventureth to do), but to preach soundly, and handle the Scriptures with wisdom and judgment?" (*An Advertisement Touching the Church of England, Letters and Life,* I, 88.)

Cf. Bacon's references elsewhere to preaching: *Works,* III, 479, 480, 483-488;

After all, the discovery of that which will link a general truth, admitted by the audience, to the specific proposal urged by the speaker, is far more efficient and more to the point than is mere amplification; ". . . the invention or election of the mean is more effectual than any inforcement of accumulation of endeavours." [6]

If these citations truly state Bacon's attitude toward the content-side of prose composition, they serve to explain fully the prominence given to Invention in those parts of the *Advancement* and *De augmentis* which deal explicitly with rhetoric. Although these citations represent Bacon as putting content in the first place, it is apparent that the process of invention, as Bacon understands it, includes much of what we ordinarily allot to *manner* of writing. Invention comprehends not only the finding of bare arguments but also the discovery of effective and striking ideas whose arresting aspect may be attributed in part to the ideas as such, in part to their manner of expression. As aids to invention, for example, Bacon cites not merely topics which help in discovering arguments, nor only *antitheta* which are unadorned arguments pro and con on various subjects, but also apothegms which are "pointed speeches" or apt phrases whose deft manner of expression can scarcely be improved on. Such, for instance, is the famous apothegm, sprinkled throughout Bacon's works, which likens the progress of time to the progress of a river. "Time is like a river, which has brought down to us things light and puffed up, while those which are weighty and solid have sunk." [7] This simile might today be hastily classed as an aspect of style, but to Bacon its discovery is as much a part of the inventive process as is the finding of an argument. The apothegm is really an excellent illustration of a rhetoric whose function is to clothe reason in an imaginative dress. What Bacon means by invention, then, is the finding of any material which recommends itself to the imaginative faculty as well as the discovery of those propositions and arguments which form the irreducible content of a composition.

"Invention," writes Bacon, "is of two kinds, much differing;

Works, V, 113, 114, 115-117; *Letters and Life,* I, 76, 77, 80, 88, 92, 93; *Letters and Life,* III, 114, 115, 118, 119.

[6] *Adv. of L., Works,* III, 322.

[7] Preface to the *Great Instauration, Works,* IV, 15.

the one, of Arts and Sciences; and the other, of Speech and Arguments." [8] Bacon explains that the first type may be properly called
invention, for by invention in the strict sense of the word is meant
to discover or to find out what we do not already know, as, for example, the bringing to light of one of the unknown principles or
laws of nature. The second kind of discovery, however, cannot
legitimately be characterized as invention, for it is nothing more
than *"out of the knowledge whereof our mind is already possessed,
to draw forth or call before us that which may be pertinent to the
purpose which we take into our consideration* . . . it is no *Invention,*
but a *Remembrance* or *Suggestion,* with an application. . . ."[9]
Bacon thus regards rhetorical invention because "to him who has
little or no knowledge on the subject proposed, places of invention
are of no service; and on the other hand, he who is ready provided
with matter applicable to the point in question will, even without
art and places of invention (although perhaps not so expeditiously
and easily), discover and produce arguments. So . . . this kind of
invention is . . . but a remembrance or suggestion with an application." [10] Rhetorical invention, then, is merely the process of drawing forth matter from our general store of knowledge which may be
pertinent to the question under discussion.[11]

Although Bacon would seem to limit the use of the term invention to the discovery of what is not already known, he recognizes
that the word has been traditionally used by rhetoricians to denote
the discovery of arguments. Hence he deems it expedient to concur
in the traditional usage, providing one understands the distinction
between the usual meaning and the exact. "Nevertheless, because
we do account it a Chase as well of deer in an inclosed park as in a
forest at large, and that it hath already obtained the name, let it
be called invention: so as it be perceived and discerned, that the
scope and end of this invention is readiness and present use of our
knowledge, and not addition or amplification thereof." [12]

[8] *Adv. of L., Works,* III, 384.   [9] *Ibid.,* 389.
[10] *De aug.,* V, 3, *Works,* IV, 421-422. Bacon seems here to have taken the
Platonic doctrine that all knowledge is but a remembrance and to have restricted
it specifically to the realm of everyday argument and discourse. That he had
Plato in mind, he apparently admits. (*Letters and Life,* III, 219.)
[11] *Ibid.,* 422.   [12] *Adv. of L., Works,* III, 390.

After defining rhetorical invention, Bacon proceeds to set forth aids which the writer and speaker may employ in finding arguments and ideas to support his case. These aids or means of invention appear to be divided into two main categories: Common-places and Topics. Under the former seem to fall such aids to invention as the Colours of Good and Evil, Antitheses, Apothegms, and so-called Formularies and Elegancies. Under Topics are comprehended two classes: General Topics, and Special Topics. We must now seek, accordingly, to understand what Bacon means by Common-places and Topics, and by the species of discovery belonging to each.

There are two aids to rhetorical invention, two means to procure a ready use of knowledge. In the *Advancement,* one aid is called Preparation, the other Suggestion,[13] in the *De augmentis,* Preparation becomes the Promptuary, and Suggestion becomes *Topica.*[14] The Promptuary or the Common-place is distinguished from the Topica, as Spedding points out, in that the first is "a collection of arguments such as you are likely to want, laid up and ready for use; the other a system of directions to help you in looking for the thing you want to find." [15] Or, in Bacon's terminology, the Promptuary consists of arguments "concerning such matters as commonly fall out and come under discussion that be composed beforehand and laid up for use." [16] The Topics he describes as "the place where a thing is to be looked for may be marked, and as it were indexed." [17] They are that part of invention which *directs* us to certain places "which may excite our mind to return and produce such knowledge as it hath formerly collected, to the end we may make use thereof." [18] The distinction, then, between Common-places and Topics seems to be that which exists between the *results* of investigation and study, and the *directions* or guides for undertaking the investigation and for retrieving ideas previously discovered.

As he turns to discuss Topics, Bacon divides them first into two classes, the general and the particular. Then follows the statement that the "general has been sufficiently handled in logic, so that

[13] *Adv. of L., Works,* III, 389.
[15] *Adv. of L., Works,* III, 390n.
[17] *Ibid.*

[14] *De aug.,* V, 3, *Works,* IV, 422.
[16] *De aug.,* V, 3, *Works,* IV, 422.
[18] *Adv. of L., Works,* III, 391.

there is no need to dwell on the explanation of it." [19] Unfortunately Bacon gives no explicit information as to what general topics have been customarily handled in logic. But it is probable that he is here alluding to those traditional "places" of invention first set forth in Aristotle's *Analytics* and found in one form or another in most subsequent logical treatises down to Bacon—the topics, namely, of the Like and Unlike, Equal and Unequal, the Greater and the Less, the Subject, and the Adjunct, along with the topics suggested by such questions as What is the Cause? the Effect? the Definition? the Genus and the Species? In the sixteenth century, Peter Ramus, aiming to improve on Aristotle, still retained them as foci to which he linked his discussion of invention.[20] Ramus' logic proved tremendously popular in English schools and colleges—especially at Cambridge—during the last quarter of the century, and in some instances even displaced the Aristotelian logic. Learned men, for whom Bacon was writing, certainly knew contemporary logical theory, whether derived from Ramus or direct from the ancients. Bacon himself refers to Ramus' work as though his readers were well acquainted with it.[21] Hence the casual way in which he passes off any explication of general topics perhaps tells us as much as if he named them.

More direct information concerning their nature, however, is not lacking, and the evidence which follows leads one to suspect that the Baconian *topica* are essentially similar not only to the topics of traditional logic and dialectic but also to the topics that appear in Aristotle's *Rhetoric*.

Early in his career, Bacon wrote to Essex, asking him to aid in securing the post of King's Attorney against the other candidate, Coke. In this letter, Bacon tells Essex that the Court has apparently set aside the objections to Coke, "which if they have, it will be necessary for your Lordship to iterate more forcibly your former reasons, whereof there is such *copia* as I think you may use all the places of logic against his placing." [22] What are these "places of logic" to which Bacon here refers? Possibly they may be those

---

[19] *De aug.*, V, 3, *Works*, IV, 423.
[20] *The Logike of Ramus* (*op. cit.*, p. 11) tells the reader that he will learn to "intreate of every heade in his owne place with the ten places of invention. . . ."
[21] *De aug.*, VI, 2, *Works*, IV, 448, 453.   [22] *Letters and Life*, I, 263.

conditions for the determination of the essence of a matter, which, in the Baconian cyclopedia of knowledge, belong to the First Philosophy, but which have been traditionally treated in logic. One part of the first Philosophy must be an inquiry into logical catagories:

> It is an inquiry with regard to the Adventitious Conditions of Essences (which we may call Transcendentals), as Much, Little; Like, Unlike; Possible, Impossible; likewise Being and Not-Being, and the like. For since these do not properly come under Physic, and the logical discussion concerning them belongs rather to the laws of reasoning than to the existence of things, it is very proper that the consideration of them (wherein there is no little dignity and profit) should not be altogether neglected, but should find at least some place in the divisions of the sciences.[23]

Perhaps we have here some lines of investigation—that of degree, of comparison, of the possible and the impossible—which Bacon might admit to his rhetorical theory as General Topics.[24]

Bacon's example of a particular topic, or "Articles of Inquiry concerning Heavy and Light," also provides some assurance that the question of degree and of comparison may be named as general topics. Although seventeen of the nineteen questions are technical and would only be suggested by one acquainted with the characteristics of falling bodies, the first two inquiries ask, first, the simple question as to what bodies are susceptible to the pull of gravity; second, what bodies are not; and third, what bodies are heavier than others. This procedure, clearly exhibiting the questions of presence and absence concerning the quality investigated and the questions of comparative instances and of degree, conforms to the start of Bacon's inductive method as it appears in the *Novum organum*. The first two inquiries follow:

---

[23] *De aug.*, III, 1, *Works*, IV, 339-340; cf. *Adv. of L.*, *Works*, III, 353.

[24] Anthony Wotton's revision and amplification of Ramus' logic has this to say of "places": "Logick teacheth us to find out arguments after a generall manner, by the schewing us the places, or heades whence we are to serch the proofe, or declaration of a thing: and therefore this part of Logick, is called in Greeke by the Stoiks . . . a place." (*The Art of Logick*, ed. by Anthony Wotton, translated and amplified by his son, Samuel Wotton (London, 1626), p. 4.)

1. Inquire what bodies are susceptible of the motion of gravity, what of levity, and if there be any of an intermediate and indifferent nature. 2. After the simple inquiry concerning heavy and light, proceed to comparative inquiry; as to what bodies weigh more, what less, in the same dimensions. Likewise of light bodies, which rise quicker, which slower.[25]

In the dialogue called *An Advertisement Touching a Holy War*, Martius, one of the characters of the piece, tells how to use the argument of the possible and impossible most effectively and, in addition, how to combat it when the argument is not carried out concretely. Martius' remarks indicate also that Bacon thought the topic of the possible and impossible to be a common mode of attack in deliberative writing and speaking:

> Now I have often observed in deliberations, that the entering near hand into the manner of performance and execution of that which is under deliberation hath quite overturned the opinion formerly conceived of the possibility or impossibility. So that things that at the first show seemed possible, by ripping up the performance of them have been convicted of impossibility; and things that on the other side have showed impossible, by the declaration of the means to effect them, as by a back light, have appeared possible, the way through them being discerned.[26]

Bacon's speech in favor of general naturalization for the Scots whose country was linked to England with the accession of King James to the English throne provides some basis for deducing two more general topics and gives further evidence that the question of degree may be legitimately considered as a topic:

> All consultations do rest upon questions comparative; for when a question is *de vero*, it is simple, for there is but one truth; but when a question is *de bono*, it is for the most part comparative; for there be differing degrees of good and evil, and the best of the good is to be preferred and chosen, and the worst of the evil is to be declined and avoided. And therefore in a question of this nature you may not look for answer proper to every inconvenience alleged; for somewhat that cannot be specially answered may nevertheless be encountered and overweighed by matter of greater moment.[27]

Passing over matters of truth which are too simple to require

---

[25] *De aug.*, V, 3, *Works*, IV, 424. [26] *Works*, VII, 25.
[27] *Letters and Life*, III, 308.

topics, we observe that the speaker may frame two questions. He may ask, "Is the matter a question of goodness?" And of two contesting lines of argument concerning the good, he might well query, "Which presents the greater good?"

Although Bacon leaves the reader to infer the names of the General Topics, he does comment explicitly, if briefly, on their nature. As general aids to investigation, they are not limited solely to rhetoric, to argumentations and disputations, but may be profitably employed by anyone who contemplates any subject. This kind of Topic, as Bacon puts it, "is of use not only in argumentations where we are disputing with another, but also in meditations, where we are considering and resolving anything with ourselves. . . ." [28] The general Topic, furthermore, does not merely suggest arguments which the speaker may well use, but it also prompts questions and inquiries which will lead to new ideas and arguments. By the use of the topic, the speaker seems to uncover, by means of questions, knowledge whose existence he *anticipates*:

> Neither does it serve only to prompt and suggest what we should affirm and assert, but also what we should inquire or ask. For a faculty of wise interrogating is half a knowledge. For Plato says well, 'whosoever seeks a thing, knows that which he seeks for in a general notion; else how shall he know it when he has found it?' And therefore the fuller and more certain our anticipation is, the more direct and compendious is our search. The same places therefore which will help us to shake out the folds of the intellect within us, and to draw forth the knowledge stored within, will also help us to gain knowledge from without; so that if a man of learning and experience were before us, we should know how to question him wisely and to the purpose; and in like manner how to select and peruse with advantage those authors, books and parts of books, which may best instruct us concerning that which we seek.[29]

What we gather, as a result, from Bacon's rather meagre remarks on the general Topic is three-fold: first, it is a line of investigation applicable to any subject; second, it serves to suggest material which has already been discovered, but which does not immediately fly to present use; and lastly, it prompts an interrogation of wise

---

[28] *De aug.*, V, 3, *Works*, IV, 423.   [29] *Ibid.* Cf. *Adv. of L.*, *Works*, III, 391.

men and of books, whereby we may derive from without us facts that have heretofore escaped our observation.

In so far as the general topic comprises a method whereby the speaker may find facts and ideas that he has otherwise not known, a functional similarity is perceived between Bacon's scientific method of discovery and rhetorical topics. Both seek to invent new knowledge, and consequently the technique of discovery useful in science may, within certain limits, prove advantageous to the practical art of rhetoric. As was indicated in Chapter II, a systematic manner of recording observations in table form, such as Bacon recommends in connection with the new instrument, may lead to an increased perception of similarity and difference among facts, and thus facilitate inductive inference in any field where the system may be adopted. Hence, although only two of many general topics appear in the scientific method of investigation, the technique employed is suggestive of what the speaker might do with respect to any or all of the logical topics. It should be observed again, however, that whereas the new instrument yields knowledge new to mankind, its application to rhetorical invention gives knowledge new only to the speaker.

The Particular Topic, like the General Topic, aids the investigator or searcher by recalling to mind ideas and arguments which he had previously unearthed, and by prompting lines of inquiry which will bring forth new material appropriate to the purpose at hand. The Particular Topic, however, differs from the General Topic in that each substantive science, as distinct from the methodological sciences like logic and rhetoric, has a line of inquiry appropriate to it and to no other science. It has been seen that the general topics as treated in logic and to some extent in rhetoric constitute methods of discovery applicable to all sciences. Beyond these general methods, however, a substantive science like physics or ethics may evolve particular means of investigation and invention whose existence logic can only point out. The method of invention described in the *Novum organum*, for example, can only apply in its entirety to physics. Although the general topics of presence and absence, like and unlike, occur in the scheme, yet the subject matter of physics demands that they appear in particular questions concerning the nature of heat; thus particularized they could apply to no other science. Particular Topics, then, are "places of invention and inquiry appropriated to particular subjects and sciences . . . they are a kind of mixture of logic with the proper matter of each science." [30] Bacon therefore separates his *Topica* into the species general and particular because no one scheme of invention, no single formula, can be applied to all subjects and to all phases of their growth and development. Each science, as it pursues its special inquiries, will develop its own art of invention:

. . . he must be a trifler and a man of narrow mind who thinks that the perfect art of invention of knowledge can be devised and propounded all at once; and that it needs only to be set at work. Let men be assured that the solid and true arts of invention grow and increase as inventions themselves increase; so that when a man first enters into the pursuit of any knowledge, he may have some useful precepts of invention; but when he has made further advances in that knowledge, he may and ought to devise new precepts of invention, to lead him the better to that which lies beyond.[31]

In the realm of political action, for example, experience may suggest the utility of the particular topic of lawfulness, a topic that Bacon comments on in *An Advertisement Touching a Holy War*. The treatise intends to examine the feasibility of undertaking a war to propagate the Christian faith, and hence to a student of the law the first logical question must be, "Is such a course lawful?" This line of argument is to be handled like the general topic of impossibility or possibility. Just as "it is a loose thing to speak of possibilities without the particular designs; so it is to speak of lawfulness without the particular cases." [32] Thus it is clear that the particular topic of lawfulness derives from the special subject, politics; but that its treatment—the amassing of cases—rests on the general topic of similarity and dissimilarity. Bacon himself thought so well of the particular topic and special lines of investigation that he intended to work them out in detail for one hundred and forty separate histories[33] he intended to write, but never did: "As soon . . . as I have leisure for it, I mean to draw up a

---

[30] *De aug.*, V, 3, *Works*, IV, 424.   [31] *Ibid.*
[32] *Works*, VII, 26.
[33] *Aphorisms on the Composition of the Primary History*, *Works*, IV, 265-270.

set of questions . . . and to explain what points with regard to
each of the histories are especially to be inquired and collected
. . . , like a kind of particular Topics." [34]

What, then, is the value of the special line of inquiry to the
speaker and writer? Bacon might well reply that the technical ex-
positor should become familiar with those special classifications,
categories, and problems of analysis that are peculiar to his own
subject, partly with a view of systematizing and remembering new
knowledge that he may acquire through further investigation and
reading, and partly with an eye to their suggestive value in bringing to mind ideas that might possibly be included in any composition which he may undertake. To the speaker, especially, such
topics would prompt the memory in the extempore situation. Bacon
would doubtless urge, also, that in rhetorical address, a man may
extend his own knowledge, improve the content of his composition,
and train his memory if he is willing to master the special, even
technical, questions into which his subject may lead. The popular
persuader will not be smugly satisfied, like the poor debater, with
the apparatus of "stock issues" and worn questions of analysis
that as general topics serve to start investigation; in addition, he
will strive to understand the technical problems that lead him to
the crux of his subject. If this be Bacon's advice and if the admonition were heeded, rhetoric could not be an "empty and verbal
art."

The second main division of the Baconian aids to invention is
designated as a digest of Common-places. In the *Advancement of
Learning* and the *De augmentis*, a digest of Common-places is first
mentioned as facilitating the arrangement and classification of
knowledge, as aiding the memory, and as improving invention and
judgment. "For the *disposition* and *collocation* of that knowledge
which we preserve in writing, it consisteth in a good digest of
common-places. . . . I hold the entry of common-places to be a
matter of great use and essence in studying; as that which assureth
copie of invention and contracteth judgment to a strength." [35] The
worth of common-places is thus indicated, but here there is no
light concerning their nature.

---

[34] *Ibid.*, 263.

[35] *Adv. of L., Works*, III, 398. Cf. *De aug.*, V, 5, *Works*, IV, 435.

But from Bacon's first description of the Promptuary or Preparation—a passage which seems to be intended as a general description of the Antitheta, the Colours of Good and Evil, the Formularies and Elegancies, as well as the Promptuary—one is led to believe that "common-place" may be a class name applicable to any
idea which either recurs often, or is likely to recur often, during
a speaker's career, and whose repetition, accordingly, justifies
cataloguing it together with related ideas, for future reference.
The common-place, I take it, is *any* idea likely to recur and to
prove useful in a rhetorician's life-time. It may concern good and
evil, as do Bacon's *Colours;* it may be pros and cons on a subject,
such as the *Antitheta;* it may be a fixed part of speech—a preface
or a conclusion—general in nature, such as some of the items in the
Promus of Formularies. Following is the passage which appears to
sum up all these species of common-place:

> Preparation . . . seemeth scarcely a part of Knowledge, consisting
> rather of diligence than of any artificial erudition . . . the ancient
> writers of rhetoric do give it in precept, that pleaders should have the
> Places whereof they have most continual use ready handled in all the
> variety that may be; as that, to speak for the literal interpretation of
> the law against equity, and contrary; and to speak for presumptions and
> inferences against testimony, and contrary. And Cicero himself, being
> broken unto it by great experience, delivereth it plainly, that whatso-
> ever a man shall have occasion to speak of . . . he may have it in effect
> premeditate, and handled *in thesi;* so that when he cometh to a particu-
> lar, he shall have nothing to do but to put to names and times and places,
> and such other circumstances of individuals. We see likewise the exact
> diligence of Demosthenes; who, in regard of the great force that the
> entrance and access into causes hath to make a good impression, had
> ready framed a number of prefaces for orations and speeches.[36]

---

[36] *Adv. of L., Works,* III, 390. In a letter of doubtful authorship, that
Spedding declares to be "very Baconian in matter and manner," the author
attempts to distinguish common-places from epitomes. In so doing, he seems
to make common-places synonymous with the entries in any careful, logical
analysis and arrangement of facts. Both the epitome and the common-place,
in the example which follows, relate to biography or history, the first being
merely the grouping of various accidents and facts under appropriate but
unessential heads, the second apparently being much more analytical and
grouping the facts under essential heads. "He that will out of Curtius or
Plutarch make an epitome of the life of Alexander, considers but the number

As an illustration of the common-place idea which is sufficiently general so that the speaker "when he cometh to a particular, he shall have nothing to do but to put to names and places and times," a brief passage may be quoted from the piece called "Pacification and Edification of the Church." Progress in ecclesiastical as in all matters, Bacon writes, does not come about by following custom and tradition. To progress is to think independently of custom and usage. This point is handled, as Bacon himself says, by the common-place which likens time to the flow of a stream, and the man of independent thought to one who rows against the current:

. . . who knoweth not that time is truly compared to a stream, that carrieth down fresh and pure waters into that salt sea of corruption which environeth all human actions? And therefore if man shall not by his industry, virtue, and policy, as it were with the oar row against the stream and inclination of time, all institutions and ordinances, be they never so pure, will corrupt and degenerate. But not to handle this matter commonplace-like. . . .[37]

The first species of common-place which Bacon notices is the Colour of Good and Evil, whose nature is perhaps suggested by the heading to the first collection of the *Colours* published in 1597. The fragment is entitled: "A table of colours or appearances of good and evil, and their degrees, as places of persuasion and discussion, and their several fallaxes, and the Elenches of them." [38] Immediately following this caption is Bacon's first sentence of the preface to the *Colours:* "In deliberatives the point is, what is good and what is evil, and of good what is greater, and of evil what is

---

of years he lived, the names of places he conquered, the humors and affections he had, and the variety of accidents he met withal in the course of his life. But he that will draw notes out of his life under heads will show, under the title of a Conqueror, that to begin in the strength and flower of his age; to have a way made to greatness by his father; to find an army disciplined, and a council of great captains; and to procure himself to be made head of a league against a common enemy, whereby both his quarrel may be made popular and his assistance great; are necessary helps to great conquests." (*Letters and Life*, II, 23-24.)

[37] *Letters and Life*, III, 105. This analogy occurs in Bacon's works no less than six times.

[38] The edition of 1597 is found in the *Works*, VII, 73-92.

the less." [39] It is apparent, consequently, that in deliberative speaking the *Colours* find their chief application.

The collection contains examples of the Colours, both "simple and comparative," each colour consisting of a statement apparently true, but not really so, concerning the nature of good and evil, followed by a refutation of the fallacy which underlay the colour. The character of the collection, in the form in which it finally appears in the *De augmentis*, may be sufficiently indicated by citing one of its twelve sophisms:

Sophism

What men praise and honour is good; what they dispraise and condemn is evil.

Answer

This Sophism deceives in four ways; by reason of ignorance, of bad faith, of party spirit and factions, of the natural dispositions of those who praise and blame. By reason of ignorance; for what is popular judgment worth as a test of good and evil? Better was Phocion's inference, who when the people applauded him more than usual, asked whether he had done wrong. By reason of bad faith, because in praising and blaming, men are commonly thinking of their own business, and not speaking what they think. . . . And again; 'It is naught, it is naught (says the buyer); but when he is gone his way, he will vaunt.' By reason of factions; for any man may see that men are wont to exalt those of their own party with immoderate praises, and depress below their desert those of the contrary. By reason of natural disposition; for some men are by nature formed and composed for servile adulation, while others on the contrary are crabbed and captious; so that in praising and blaming they do but gratify their own dispositions, with little regard to truth. [40]

The illustration, it should be observed, makes a statement concerning good and evil, that is *apparently* true, but not really so. Bacon, therefore, correctly designates it as a sophism, for it has the appearance of wisdom but not the reality. [41] The illustration, moreover, is simple in degree, rather than comparative. In this respect

---

[39] *Of the Colours of Good and Evil, Works,* VII, 77.

[40] *De aug.,* VI, 3, *Works,* IV, 459.

[41] One passage in the *Advancement* makes "Colour" synonymous with hypocrisy: "Colour is when men make a way for themselves to have a construction made of their faults or wants as proceeding from a better cause, or intended for some other purpose. . . ." *Works,* III, 464.

it differs from some of the sophisms in the collection; a few, dealing with degrees of good and evil, are comparative in nature. Such, for example, is the statement that *the evil which a man brings on himself by his own fault is greater; that which is brought on him by external causes, is less.*[42]

Bacon intends that the sophisms should serve two purposes. They are, in the first place, to constitute a means of argument, both direct and refutative. By bringing together current, popular aphorisms and their fallacies, the speaker has invented, ready for use, their refutation. This, of course, is in line with Bacon's wish that rhetoric should aid reason rather than suppress it:

> . . . to make a true and safe judgment, nothing can be of greater use and defence to the mind, than the discovering and reprehension of these colours, shewing in what cases they hold, and in what they deceive: which as it cannot be done, but out of a very universal knowledge of the nature of things, so being performed, it so cleareth man's judgment and election, as it is the less apt to slide into any error.[43]

As direct arguments, Bacon seems to suggest that sophisms may be used to sway men's judgment where "true and solid reasons" do not suffice; he says, ". . . the persuader's labour is to make things appear good or evil, and that in higher or lower degree; which as it may be performed by true and solid reasons, so it may be represented also by colours, popularities and circumstances, which are of such force, as they sway the ordinary judgment either of a weak man, or of a wise man not fully and considerately attending and pondering the matter."[44] Finally, Bacon points out that a very important use of the *Colours*—a use that Aristotle overlooked—lies in their power to impress and move the hearer: ". . . they . . . quicken and strengthen the opinions and persuasions which are true: for reasons plainly delivered, and always after one manner, especially with fine and fastidious minds, enter but heavily and dully: whereas if they be varied and have more life and vigour put into them by these forms and insinuations, they cause a stronger apprehension, and many times suddenly win the mind to a resolution."[45]

---

[42] *De aug.*, VI, 3, *Works*, IV, 464. [43] *Colours, Works,* VII, 77.
[44] *Colours, Works,* VII, 77.
[45] *Ibid.* A letter from Bacon to Lord Mountjoy and headed "Mr. Francis Bacon of the colours of good and evil, to the Lord Mountjoye," definitely

A second collection of common-places which are valuable as aids
to invention comprises what Bacon calls *antitheta*, or ideas which
develop the pros and cons of a subject likely to prove useful in
rhetorical address:

> *Antitheta* are Theses argued *pro* et *contra;* wherein men may be more
> large and laborious; but (in such as are able to do it) to avoid prolixity
> of entry, I wish the seeds of the several arguments to be cast up into
> some brief and acute sentences; not to be cited, but to be as skeins or
> bottoms of thread, to be unwinded at large when they come to be used;
> supplying authorities and examples by reference.[46]

Antitheses, it appears, are similar in nature and in form to the
modern affirmative and negative briefs which, taken in conjunction,
develop the possible and probable arguments on both sides of the
question. Antitheses are general storehouses of argument from

---

acknowledges Aristotle's precedent in framing the sophisms: "I . . . do freely
acknowledge that I had my light from him; for where he gave me not matter
to perfect, at the least he gave me occasion to invent." (*Works*, VII, 70.)
But from what portion of Aristotle's works Bacon took the idea is not easy to
establish. Neither the form nor the precise content of Bacon's twelve Colours
corresponds to anything in Aristotle. Indeed, Bacon himself establishes this in
the Mountjoy letter: ". . . some that shall compare my lines with Aristotle's
lines, will muse by what art, or rather by what revelation, I could draw these
conceits out of that place." (*Ibid.*) Doubtless Spedding is right in suggesting
that the inspiration for *Colours* came from Aristotle's *Rhetoric*, I, 6-7, where
the nature and the degrees of the good are discussed. In the *De augmentis*,
Bacon again links Aristotle with the colours, and in calling them the "Sophisms
of Rhetoric" appears to refer directly to the *Rhetoric:* "Aristotle . . . began to
make a collection of *the popular signs or colours of apparent good and evil*,
both simple and comparative; which are really the sophisms of rhetoric. . . .
But the labours of Aristotle regarding these colours are in three points
defective; one, that he recounts a few only out of many; another, that he does
not add the answers to them; and the third, that he seems to have conceived
but a part of the use of them. For their use is not more for probation than for
affecting and moving." (VI, 3, *Works*, IV, 458.) This passage is accurately
descriptive of chapters six and seven of the *Rhetoric*, save for the statement
that Aristotle handled but "a few only out of many." Actually Aristotle offers
a fairly extensive, if compact and practical account of the good. But perhaps
Bacon's lapse in judgment here is offset by the accuracy of his observation to
Mountjoye, *i.e.*, that Aristotle had merely given him "occasion to invent."
There is but slight analogy between his *Colours* and their ancestor; in fact, only
two of Bacon's colours find exact counterparts in the *Rhetoric* of Aristotle.

[46] *Adv. of L., Works*, III, 413.

which the rhetorician may draw ideas that comprise the logical structure of any particular speech. From the *De augmentis* it is learned, furthermore, that antitheses should be made for all kinds of rhetorical productions—the deliberative, the judicial, and the demonstrative. Bacon testifies to the universal utility of antitheses:

The second Collection which belongs to the *Promptuary* or Preparatory Store, is that to which Cicero alludes . . . where he recommends the orator to have common-places ready at hand, in which the question is argued and handled on either side; such as 'for the letter of the law,' 'for the intention of the law,' etc. But I extend this precept to other cases; applying it not only to the judicial kind of oratory, but also to the deliberative and demonstrative. I would have in short all topics which there is frequent occasion to handle (whether they relate to proofs and refutations, or to persuasions and dissuasions, or to praise and blame) studied and prepared beforehand; and not only so, but the case exaggerated both ways with the utmost force of the wit, and urged unfairly, as it were, and quite beyond the truth. And the best way of making such a collection, with a view to use as well as brevity, would be to contract those common-places into certain acute and concise sentences; to be as skeins or bottoms of thread which may be unwound at large when they are wanted. Some such piece of diligence I find in Seneca, but in hypotheses or cases. A few instances of the thing, having a great many by me, I think fit to propound by way of example. I call them *Antitheses of Things.*[47]

Bacon includes in the *De augmentis* forty-seven different theses with their pros and cons. Most of them, as Bacon himself points out, reflect his youth and thus are "in the moral and demonstrative kind, but in the deliberative and judicial very few."[48] It is probable, in fact, that in content the collection reflects not only Bacon's younger days but also the Elizabethan school-boy's practice of writing and declaiming moral essays somewhat after the manner of Seneca's *suasoriae.*[49] For the antithetical aspect of the collection he took the hint from Seneca's *controversiae.* The Antithesis concerning learning seems a fair specimen:

---

[47] *De aug.*, VI, 3, *Works*, IV, 472.   [48] *De aug.*, VI, 3, *Works*, IV, 492.
[49] Consult the author's "Rhetorical Exercises in Tudor Education," *Quarterly Journal of Speech*, XXII (February, 1936), 28-51.

LEARNING

For	*Against*
If books were written about small matters, there would be scarce any use of experience.	In colleges men learn to believe.
In reading a man converses with the wise, in action generally with fools.	What art ever taught the seasonable use of art?
Sciences which are of no use in themselves are not to be deemed useless, if they sharpen the wit and put the thoughts in order.	To be wise by rule and to be wise by experience are contrary proceedings; he that accustoms himself to one unfits himself for the other.
	Art is often put to a foolish use, that it may not be of no use at all.
	Almost all scholars have this —when anything is presented to them, they will find in it that which they know, not learn from it that which they know not.[50]

In this antithesis, as in Bacon's other examples, the "antithetical" element, strictly speaking, is lacking. The concise common-places on either side of a question are not opposed to each other in sense, as black is to white. They are not contraries, nor, for that matter, are they contradictories. They are simply arguments for and against a proposition, jotted down as they occurred to Bacon. The same example, in addition, affords an illustration of "exaggerating both ways with the utmost force of the wit"—advice which perhaps is intended to encourage the student in stretching his inventive powers. The assertion that "art is often put to a foolish use, that it may not be of no use at all" is perhaps "quite beyond the truth." But because it is extreme, it may provoke the intellect to inspection, analysis, and qualification; thus it may bring a tenable and fresh line of thought to consciousness.

How useful *antitheta* were to Bacon's own composition has been splendidly demonstrated in E. A. Abbott's edition of the Essays. In 1625 the Lord Verulam published fifty-eight essays in their

---

[50] *De aug.,* VI, 3, *Works,* IV, 483.

final form. From the long list of *antitheta* in the *De augmentis,*
published in 1623, Abbott shows that at least twenty-three of those
skeins of thread became the essential theme, more or less qualified,
of as many Essays. A somewhat smaller proportion of pros and
cons, in relation to the number of essays, is evident in the Essays of
1597 and of 1612. When one remembers that Bacon began to collect common-places at least as early as 1595, the date of the first
entries in his *Promus,* and that he was ever interested in the formulation of aphorisms for "moralls" and "policie," as well as for
natural history, it seems probable that the generic idea of an
antitheta served to prompt and suggest related lines of thought
and their amplification.

Antitheta and Colours, then, are to be regarded as kinds of common-places. They are aids to invention in two ways: first, they supply a storehouse of ideas which may prompt the composer's mind
to activity; second, the practice of compiling such collections sys-
tematizes ideas and aids the retentive and associative faculties.
Antitheta apply to all types of discourse; the Colours relate only
to the deliberative variety. The first may deal with any type of
subject matter; the second is restricted to topics of good and evil.
And finally, the one constitutes a supply of arguments which may
be used in direct argument; the other includes refutative arguments only.

Besides *antitheta* and the *Colours of Good and Evil,* Bacon has
other aids to rhetorical invention, the next in order being what he
refers to in the *Advancement* as Formulae, in the *De augmentis* as
Lesser Forms. In the two works mentioned, enough is said about
Formulae to indicate that they are small parts of a speech, fully
composed and ready for use; they are phrases or sentences—a
ready introductory phrase or a stock transitional sentence—such
as there is frequent occasion to employ. In form, they differ from
antitheta and the *Colours* in that they are completely made up;
they do not admit of re-wording to suit the time, place, and occasion, as do other common-places:

I do resume . . . that which I mentioned before touching Provision or
Preparatory store for the furniture of speech and readiness of inven-

tion; which appeareth to be of two sorts; the one in resemblance to a shop of pieces unmade up, the other to a shop of things ready made up; both to be applied to that which is frequent and most in request; the former of these I will call *Antitheta,* and the latter *Formulae.*[51]

Formulae, Bacon explains, give to a rhetorical production finish and ornament:

The third Collection, which belongs to the Promptuary, or Preparatory Store, and is likewise deficient, is that of what I call *Lesser Forms.* I mean those parts of speech which answer to the vestibules, back doors, ante-chambers, withdrawing-chambers, passages, etc., of a house; and may serve indiscriminately for all subjects. Such are prefaces, conclusions, digressions, transitions, intimations of what is coming, excusations, and a number of the kind. For as in buildings it is a great matter both for pleasure and use that the fronts, doors, windows, approaches, passages, and the like be conveniently arranged, so also in a speech these accessory and interstitial passages (if they be handsomely and skilfully fashioned and placed) add a great deal both of ornament and effect to the entire structure. . . .[52]

If arguments constitute the skeins or bottoms of thread, then the Lesser Forms, binding together the grosser elements and giving to the pattern smoothness and finish, render the tapestry as a whole readily perceptible and interesting.

The two passages cited comprise all of Bacon's remarks on the theory of the *Formulae.* For further information concerning this particular aid to invention, one turns to an early Baconian composition, the *Promus of Formularies and Elegancies,* a collection in which, despite its miscellaneous nature, we find a few entries that fit the description of Formulae as set forth in the *Advancement of Learning.* The following statements, occurring in the *Promus,* are undoubtedly terse conclusions which could be employed in any deliberative or forensic speech:

I leave the reasons to the party's relation and consideration of them to your wisdom.

Wishing you all, etc., and myself occasion to do you service.[53]

---

[51] *Adv. of L., Works,* III, 412-413.

[52] *De aug.,* VI, 3, *Works,* IV, 492. Cf. *Adv. of L., Works,* III, 413.

[53] "Extracts from the Promus of Formularies and Elegancies," *Works,* VII,

Such an entry, "The difference is not between you and me, but between your profit and my trust," [54] may possibly serve as a deft
transition which, besides harking back to an examination of alleged differences, states the real issue and foreshadows its development. Finally, we select from the *Promus* an admirable example of
an "excusation": "I wish one as fit as I am unfit." [55]

Besides transitions, excusations, and conclusions, the *Promus*
affords us examples of the repartee that is fully composed and
ready for use in a speech. There are a number of expressions which
appear to be retorts such as might prove very useful in forensic
debate and Parliamentary discussions. From his own experience in
the law courts, in the House of Commons, and in managing con-
ferences on political matters for Elizabeth and James, Bacon had
apparently invented or adopted various retorts which opened a line
of attack on his opponent. When Bacon jotted down the entry, "no
wise speech, though easy and voluble," he evidently had in mind a
definite situation. When in conference or in deliberative debate, a
speaker, by his volubility and ease in speech, has given the impression of speaking wisely, one may retort immediately that the
speech, in spite of its manner, is not wise. If a speech digresses, you
reply, "this goeth not to the end of the matter"—a rejoinder
which, from the final phrase of the entry in the *Promus*, Bacon had
evidently taken from the practice of contemporary lawyers.[56]

Occasionally the *Promus* yields repartees that have a sharp sting-
ing quality, and suggest that Bacon may have found them useful
in the conflicts of the law-courts. They are aimed to meet the attack
of an opponent. When one's adversary declares, "you go from the
matter," you reply: "But it was to follow you." When he demands
that "you come to the point," you answer: "Why, I shall not find
you there." If he says, "You take more than is for granted," you
retort: "You grant less than is proved." These examples make it

---

198. The abrupt, telegraphic aspect of the entries in the collection points to the
true character of the *Promus*. Bacon is apparently using the term, "Promus," in
the sense of multiply, generate, and create (*De aug.*, VII, 2, Works, V, 10-11).
Hence, each entry stands for a line of thought that is to be applied and
amplified upon occasion, either in speech or in writing.

[54] *Ibid.*, 199.   [55] *Ibid.*

[56] The complete entry reads: "Of speeches digressive: This goeth not to the end
of the matter . . . from the lawyers." (*Works*, VII, 198.)

clear that Bacon as lawyer and Parliamentarian had found certain set retorts very practical, perhaps as introductions to short refutative rejoinders.

One other aid to invention is mentioned in Bacon's works. Besides the *Colours, Antitheta,* and *Formulae,* Bacon sees considerable utility in a collection of Apothegms, or "pointed speeches"— words which are as goads, words with an edge or point, that cut and penetrate the knots of business and affairs.[57] Bacon felt that as former occasions are continually returning, and what served once will serve again; whether produced as a man's own or cited as an old saying."[58] Hence, Bacon himself by way of example, made a collection of the deft repartees attributed to famous persons, always supplying enough of the narrative to give the clever rejoinder point. Here is one of Bacon's examples, the apothegm being underlined:

Alcibiades came to Pericles, and stayed a while ere he was admitted. When he came in, Pericles civilly excused it, and said: *I was studying how to give my account.* But Alcibiades said to him: If you will be *ruled by me, study rather how to give no account.*[59]

Concerning the use of the apothegms, Bacon declares that "you may extract the salt out of them and sprinkle where you will."[60] Also "they may serve to be interlaced in continued speech," or upon occasion they may be cited by themselves.[61] Although if an ancient authority is attached to them they may gain in effect, Bacon feels that they are most useful if "you take the kernel of them, and make them your own."[62] Perhaps this opinion accounts for those nimble, keen-edged speeches in the *Promus,* jotted down without their setting:

Those are great with yow that are great by yow.
It may be well last for it hath lasted well.[63]
It is not the first untruth I have heard reported nor
it is not the first truth I have heard denied.[64]

---

[57] *De aug.,* II, 12, *Works* IV, 314.   [58] *Ibid.*
[59] *Apophthegmes, New and Old, Works,* VII, 130.
[60] Bacon's preface to the *Apophthegmes, Works,* VII, 123.
[61] *Ibid.*   [62] *Ibid.*
[63] "Extracts from the *Promus," Works,* VII, 207.   [64] *Ibid.,* 206.

If by common-place Bacon means *any* idea likely to recur and to prove useful in the speaker's lifetime, then we must allow one more class of common-place material that Bacon as rhetorician would probably advise the professional writer and speaker to collect. This includes the analogy, a category that is not comprehended under the Colours, the Antitheta, Formulae, and Apothegms. Literary critics have often remarked on Bacon's fondness for the comparison, and the prevalence of them in his completed works may point to a systematic attempt to collect them. In the *Promus* we find many analogies, not fully developed in language, as though their phraseology were left to the occasion of their use. Such, for example, are the following:

Speech that hangeth not together nor is concludent: Raw silk; sand.

Speech of good and various weight but not nearly applied: A great vessel that cannot come near land.[65]

On many occasions the lawyer or parliamentarian would find it convenient to compare incoherent speech with raw silk or sand, or to characterize a weighty speech without point as a great vessel unable to make land. Just how useful the common-place analogy was to Bacon is strikingly indicated by the repetition in various works of the metaphor which compares Time to a river, and the independent thinker to the man who rows against the current.

That Bacon was profoundly concerned with the analogy is evident, also, from the pains he took with *The Wisdom of the Ancients*. This interpretation of fables and myths, so Spedding asserts,[66] he worked over, revised, and enlarged until he thought it worthy of appearing in its final form in a volume to be called *Opera moralia et civilia*. Furthermore, his exposition of the hidden meanings of the fables makes use of analogy exclusively. In the myth of "Endymion: or the Favorite," for instance, Bacon sees Endymion as the prince's favorite, and the moon as the prince. Endymion's cave becomes the favorite's house, and the increase of

---

[65] *Ibid.*, 198.
[66] *Works*, VI, 607.

his flock, the prince's bounty. It is such an identity of relationship between two unlike contexts that Bacon finds in each of the thirty-one myths he analyzes.

One of the distinctive aspects of Bacon's theory of rhetorical address, then, is the recognition of the common-place as a practical tool for the speaker who must upon occasion produce or invent ideas. The collecting of ideas that are likely to recur in popular deliberations, whether the ideas represent popular conceptions of good and evil, pros and cons on persistent questions, or striking analogies and apothegms, furnishes a storehouse to which the speaker may resort. The Colours, Antitheta, and Apothegms assist in the discovery or recall of content—the first two pertaining especially to deliberative speaking, with the Apothegms and possibly the Antitheta pertaining more to the clash of forensic rhetoric. Formulae and analogies may be regarded as aids to expression, the first constituting those "interstitial passages" that make clear the structure of the speech and at the same time lend it grace, the second contributing directly to the task of recommending reason to imagination.

As prompters to thought and invention and as forms of expression that help to recommend reason to the imagination, common-places were so highly regarded by Bacon that he made his own collections. The *Promus*, to which reference has been made, is in all probability a common-place book in which Bacon jotted down, from time to time, all kinds of matter—formulae, words and phrases, repartees, proverbs, and *antitheta*—which he had himself invented or gathered from his reading. He evidently regarded the *Promus* as his private storehouse of ideas and phrases, for never in his lifetime did he publish it or indicate any intention of making it public. We must remember that he completed only a fraction of his proposed writings, and it is probable, therefore, that he valued the *Promus* as a note-book from which, were it not for his sudden illness and death, he would have continued to derive elegancies and "skeins and bottoms of thread." The relation of the *Promus* to the *antitheta* and the *Colours* as we find them in the *De augmentis* supplies further evidence of the common-place character of Bacon's note-book, for it contains the earliest instances of the pros and cons and the sophisms concerning good and evil that were later amplified in the text of the *De augmentis*.[67]

Up to this point in the exposition of the Baconian inventive process, there have been set forth what Bacon understands by invention—particularly rhetorical invention—and what aids the speaker and writer may utilize in discovering that which he wishes to communicate. Now there is to be considered what advice Bacon gives to the student of rhetoric who is interested in compiling materials and common-places for future use. Although such an inquiry may at first sight seem pedagogical only, it actually strikes at the core of the entire problem of invention, whether pursued in science, in formulating a theory of rhetoric, or in gathering ideas for any given speech. For we must note that all the aids to invention are either compilations, as in the case of common-places, or methods of discovery or recall, as in the case of Topics. The fundamental question still remains: from what sources does the student collect the materials upon which he will direct his question-topics? Bacon himself points out that a scheme of inquiry is not very useful unless one has some knowledge toward which to direct it. He would, accordingly, refer the student of rhetoric—or any investigator—to three primary sources: nature or human beings in action, books, and conversation. From these sources knowledge is derived by observing, studying, and listening.

Bacon's first piece of advice for the collection of common-places is to observe. The special value inhering in observation as a method of gathering information lies, according to a letter of doubtful authorship, in understanding the causes of things, the search for which constitutes the goal of Bacon's inductive method: "The use of observation is in noting the coherence of causes and effect, counsels and successes, and the proportion and likeness between nature and nature, force and force, action and action, state and state, time past and time present. The philosopher did think that all

---

[67] Mrs. Henry Pott in the preface of her edition of *Bacon's Promus of Formularies and Elegancies* (London, 1883) holds, among other things, that the *Promus* constituted a common-place book. For interesting suggestions concerning the growth of some of Bacon's works, notably the *Essays*, from ideas first occurring in the *Promus*, see E. Abbott, *Francis Bacon*, especially pp. 436–437. Cf. James Nichol, *Francis Bacon, His Life and Philosophy*, II, 138.

knowledge doth much depend on the knowledge of causes. . . ." [68]
Bacon values observation highly, because he believes that the general is implicit in the particular. Hence a habit of observing particular instances and of studying special cases has a practical value beyond the single example upon which attention is centered. The point is made in writing of the art of Negotiating:

> . . . there is a wisdom of counsel and advice even in private causes, arising out of an universal insight into the affairs of the world; which is used indeed upon particular cases propounded, but is gathered by general observation of causes of like nature. For so we see in the book which Q. Cicero writeth to his brother . . . although it concerned a particular action then on foot, yet the substance thereof consisteth of many wise and politic axioms, which contain not a temporary but a perpetual direction in the case of popular elections.[69]

Not only does the observation of particular cases lead to an understanding of fundamental causes and to the formulation of general laws, but it also leads the student to perceive the *similarity* of events, which to Bacon constitutes an important source of rhetorical proof:

> The observation of proportion or likeness between one person or one thing and another, makes nothing without example, nor nothing new; and although *exempla illustrant non probant,* examples may make things plain that are proved, but prove not themselves; yet when circumstances agree, and proportion is kept, that which is probable in one case is probable in a thousand, and that which is reason once is reason ever.[70]

Finally, in observation lies the best ground for judging the utterances of others. A letter to the Earl of Essex, signed by Anthony Bacon but actually composed by his brother Francis,[71] urges Essex

---

[68] From a series of three letters of advice addressed to the Earl of Rutland on his travels, and signed supposedly by Essex. Spedding, however, maintains that Bacon was the author. Letter I, *Letters and Life,* II, 14.

[69] *Adv. of L., Works,* III, 448.

[70] Letter I to the Earl of Rutland, *Letters and Life,* II, 14.

[71] Bacon's docket to this and another letter is: "Two letters framed by Sir Francis Bacon. The one is in the name of Mr. Anthony Bacon, his brother, to the Earl of Essex; the other is the Earl's answer thereunto." (*Letters and Life,* II, 196.)

"to consider of these reasons which I have collected; and to make judgment of them, neither out of the melancholy of your present fortune, nor out of the infusion of that which cometh to you by others' relation (which is subject to much tincture), but *ex rebus ipsis*, out of the nature of the persons and actions themselves, as the trustiest and least deceiving grounds of opinion." [72]

Bacon's second piece of advice to the student is to converse. "He that questioneth much shall learn much." [73] He ought, however, to confer only with expert men, and he should "apply his questions to the skill of the persons whom he asketh." [74] Conference and discourse are particularly valuable to one who already has gained some information, and for this reason a letter to the Earl of Rutland, probably written by Bacon, places conference as a help to knowledge second in order, but first in expedition and profit:

I make conference the second help to knowledge in order, though I have found it the first and greatest in profiting, and I have so placed them because he that hath not studied knows not what to doubt nor what to ask: but when the little I had learned had taught me to find out mine own emptiness, I profited more by some expert man in half a day's conference, than by myself in a month's study.[75]

In spite of the utility of conversation, however, one must be not too eager to believe. Some private discourse, like some books, is only to be tasted, not swallowed. "In conference be neither superstitious, nor believing all you hear . . . nor too desirous to contradict. For of the first grows a facility to be led into all kind of error; since you shall ever think that he that knows all that you know, and somewhat more, hath infinite knowledge, because you cannot sound or measure it. Of the second grows such a carping humour, as you shall without reason censure all men, and want reason to censure yourself." [76] Bacon, it should be observed, set enough store by conversation that he deliberately sought to arrange discussions. In the memoranda written in the summer of 1608 and representing some of his projects, Bacon jotted down: "To have particular occasions, fitt and gratefull and continuall, to

---

[72] *Letters and Life,* II, 198. [73] *Of Discourse, Works,* VI, 456.
[74] *Ibid.* [75] *Letters and Life,* II, 13.
[76] *Ibid.*

maintain pryvate speech wth every ye great persons and sometimes drawing more than one of them together, Ex Imitation Att. This specially in publicke places and wth out care or affectation." [77]

Bacon advises the student, in the third place, to study. Anyone who seeks knowledge of men and affairs, particularly knowledge of politics and government, should realize that "all men that live are drawn either by book or by example, and in books you . . . shall find (in what course soever you propound to yourself) rules prescribed by the wisest men, and examples left by the wisest men that have lived before us." [78] To the statesman Bacon recommends sources that may well constitute the materials and learning of the political orator:

> I debar him not studies nor books, to give him store and variety of conceit, to refresh his mind, to cover sloth and indisposition, and to draw to him from those that are studious respect and commendation. But let him beware lest they possess not too much of his time, that they abstract not his judgment from present experience, nor make him presume upon knowing much to apply the less. . . . If to make the prince happy he serves, let the instructions to employed men, the relations of ambassadors, the treaties between princes, and actions of the present time, be the books he reads: let the orations of wise princes or experimented counsellors in council or parliament, and the final sentences of grave and learned judges in weighty and doubtful causes, be the lectures he frequents. Let the holding of affection with confederates without charge, the frustrating of the attempts of enemies without battles, the entitling of the Crown to new possessions without show of wrong, the filling of the prince's coffers without grudging, the appeasing tumults and seditions without violence, the keeping of men in appetite without impatience, be the inventions he seeks out. Let the policy and matter of state be the chief, and almost the only thing he intends. . . .[79]

The student must seek, moreover, to gain broad general knowledge; he must "have the grounds of learning, which are the liberal arts; for without them you shall neither gather other knowledge easily, nor make use of that you have." [80] Above all other books, Bacon

---

[77] *Commentarious Solutus or Transportata, Letters and Life,* IV, 93.

[78] To the Earl of Rutland, Letter I, *Letters and Life,* II, 12.

[79] From the Statesman's speech in Bacon's device for the Queen's day, *Letters and Life,* I, 381-382.

[80] Letter to the Earl of Rutland, *Letters and Life,* II, 12.

recommends "the Histories, for they will best instruct you in matter moral, military, and politic, by which and in which you must ripen and settle your judgment." [81] If we may again accept, with Spedding, a letter of doubtful authorship, histories are indeed deemed most profitable to a study of humanity, and of these Bacon thinks "Tacitus simply the best; Livy very good; Thucydides above any of the writers of Greek matters; and the worst of these, and divers others of the ancients, to be preferred before the best of our moderns." [82] Poets, according to the same letter, Bacon cannot commend, and as for the orators, if he must choose any, "it shall be Demosthenes, both for the argument he handles, and for that his eloquence is more proper for a statesman than Cicero's." [83] Bacon reminds the student, then, that whatever the books read the objects of study are always two, "the first to conceive or understand; the second to lay up or remember. . . . To help you to conceive, you may do well in those things which you are to read to draw yourself to read with somebody that may give you help. . . . To help you to remember, you must use writing, or meditation, or both; by writing I mean making of notes and abridgements of that which you would remember." [84]

Bacon's concluding admonition to the student concerns not the sources of common-places but rather the manner of gathering them —whether or not they may be collected by deputy. Bacon holds that "one man's notes will little profit another, because one man's conceit doth so much differ from another's; and also because the bare note is nothing so much worth as the suggestion it gives the reader." [85] In the essay *Of Studies*, Bacon writes that "some books . . . may be read by deputy, and extracts made of them by others; but that would be only in the less important arguments, and the meaner sort of books. . . ." [86] If material is to be gathered by deputy let it be ideas that support only particular

---

[81] *Ibid.*

[82] *Letters and Life*, II, 25. This is from a letter which Essex is supposed to have written Sir Foulke Greville upon his entrance to Cambridge. Spedding, however, feeling that it is "very Baconian in matter and manner," holds that Bacon is the real author.

[83] *Ibid.*   [84] Letter to Rutland, *Letters and Life*, II, 13.

[85] Letter to Sir Foulke Greville, *Letters and Life*, II, 25.

[86] *Works*, VI, 498.

points in a speech; the general plan and structure of a persuasive effort must be one's own:

> ... I do confess I would have you gather the chiefest things and out of the chiefest books yourself, and to use your other collectors in gathering arguments and examples to prove or illustrate any particular position or question. For they should like labourers bring stone, timber, mortar, and other necessaries to your building. But you should put them together and be the master-workman yourself; and instruction is easilier given and will be better followed in one point than in many.[87]

Bacon seems particularly anxious that the speaker or writer should dominate his composition and give to it the mark of originality. To this end, he cautions students against the accepted methods of compiling common-places and against the slavish use of phrase books already made up. For a century the young grammar-school pupil had been required to write orations in English and in Latin. To aid the invention of matter, students had to keep note-books in which significant ideas and well-turned expressions were jotted down from their perusal of classical authors.[88] Under such a system, it is natural that phrase-books and volumes of common-places should appear in circulation, and thus make it unnecessary for the pupil to read widely.[89] It is to this system that Bacon objects. The continued use of such phrase-books makes orations smack of him who compiled the book, and compositions tend to become stereotyped in content. Bacon feels, moreover, that the

---

[87] Letter to Sir Foulke Greville, *Letters and Life*, II, 26.

[88] Foster Watson, in *The English Grammar Schools to 1660*, states that while reading classical authors, "the pupil was expected to have his note-book at hand into which he transcribed all phrases and information likely to be of use for the need of conversation and of written exercises." [(Cambridge, 1908), 6.] Charles Hoole's *New Discovery of the Old Art of Teaching School* (1660) directs the pupil "to have a large common-place book, in which they should write at least those heads which Mr. Farnaby had set down in his Index Rhetoricus, and then busy themselves to collect the short Histories out of Plutarch, Valerius, Maximus, Caesar, Lucius, Florus, Livy, Pliny, Pareus, *Medulla Historiae*, Aelian." (Cited by Watson, p. 455.)

[89] "It would seem that these elaborate phrase-books were likely to defeat their own ends—for the boys must have been relieved to a great extent from collecting phrases in a Common-place book—an exercise on which, at any rate, Hoole, as we have seen, laid great stress. They could, by these phrase-books, usually find what they wanted, or, at any rate, what would serve, without themselves collecting from classical authors." (Watson, *op. cit.*, 462.)

same effect is obtained even though the student does his own reading. For the schools of the time each had their favorite classical authors; hence, the student's note-book bore the "face of a school." Bacon prefers that the student observe Nature, and from her derive his common-places:

> ... of the *methods* of common-places that I have seen, there is none of any sufficient worth; all of them carrying merely the face of a *school,* and not of a *world;* and referring to vulgar matters and pedantical divisions without all life or respect to action.[90]

For this reason, too, Bacon explicitly bids the preacher to forego the current common-place books that assemble the arguments pro and con on controversial texts of Scripture, and those books which aim to present a system of divinity. Such works are likely to be biased in their choice of issues or in their species of theology—to carry, in other words, the face of a school. The proper course is to look at the Scriptures unhampered by pre-judgments and as a result of observation, to jot down in aphoristic form the interpretation that one arrives at:

> In perusing books of divinity, I find many books of controversies; and many of common places and treaties; a mass of positive divinity, as it is made an art; a number of sermons and lectures, and many prolix commentaries upon the Scriptures, with harmonies and concordances: but that form of writing in divinity, which in my judgment is of all others most rich and precious, is positive divinity collected upon particular texts of Scriptures in brief observations; not dilated into common places, not chasing after controversies, not reduced into method of art. . . .[91]

Bacon, it is clear, fully appreciates the limitations of any schemes and rules of invention. There is no substitute for hard study. To employ any procedure in a cut-and-dried, rule-of-thumb manner can only result in a product which reflects its mechanical construction. Consequently, Bacon never hesitates to point out that the basis of fertile invention is broad and deep knowledge, for it is "but a counterfeit thing in knowledges to be forward and

---

[90] *Adv. of L., Works,* III, 398.
[91] *Ibid.,* III, 487.

pregnant, except a man be deep and full. . . ." [92] To employ common-places alone, furthermore, makes for a sterotyped product,
lacking variety and individuality. Bacon's tract, *In felicem
memoriam Elizabethae*, in one passage clearly implies that common-place observations do not impart individuality to that to
which they are applied. They should be supplemented by further
study:

> . . . if I should enter into her praises, whether moral or political, I
> should either fall into certain commonplace observations and com-
> memorations of virtues, which would be unworthy of so rare a princess;
> or in order to give them a lustre and beauty peculiar and appropriate, I
> should have to run into the history of her life.[93]

In the essay *Of Discourse*, Bacon does not hesitate to criticize those
who "have certain common-places and themes wherein they are
good, and want variety; which kind of poverty is for the most part
tedious, and when it is once perceived, ridiculous." [94] The speaker
who relies too early upon his common-place book, moreover, im-
peaches his own dignity and renders rhetoric contemptible:

> Scholars in universities come too soon and too unripe to logic and
> rhetoric; arts fitter for graduates than children and novices; for these
> two, rightly taken, are the gravest of sciences; being the arts of arts,
> the one for judgment, the other for ornament; and they be the rules and
> directions how to set forth and dispose matter; and therefore for minds
> empty and unfraught with matter, and which have not gathered that
> which Cicero calleth *sylva* and *supellex*, stuff and variety, to begin with
> those arts (as if one should learn to weigh or to measure or to paint the
> wind), doth work but this effect, that the wisdom of those arts, which is
> great and universal, is almost made contemptible, and is degenerate

---

[92] *Adv. of L., Works*, III, 398. Amusing testimony as to value that Elizabethans placed upon common-place collections comes from one of John Weever's
epigrams. A suitor of Florella's arguing for a substantial dowry, brings her
friends and relatives

> . . . strait within his studie doore,
> And there he shew'd them old Orations,
> A common place-booke of ten quire and more,
> Latines, Verses, Theames and Declamations;
> He swore these cost four hundred pound at least. . . .

    —*Epigrammes in the Oldest Cut, and newest fashion* (London, 1599).
[93] *Works*, VI, 318.   [94] *Ibid.*, 455.

into childish sophistry and ridiculous affectation. And further, the untimely learning of them hath drawn on by consequence the superficial and unprofitable teaching and writing of them, as fitteth indeed to the capacity of children.[95]

It is apparent from the foregoing pages that Bacon's conception of the inventive process is a broad one; it embraces not merely the finding of thoughts and ideas, pure and simple, but also includes the invention of striking analogies and sentences which may be dropped into a speech *in toto*. Invention means also a system of gathering and cataloguing material that it may be easier recovered upon any given occasion. It means, furthermore, a series of questions or topics, the answers to which uncover new knowledge pertinent to the question in hand. In brief, invention denotes, in Bacon's system of rhetorical address, discovering and recovering, the emphasis being placed on the second process.

---

[95] *Adv. of L., Works,* III, 326. Identical passage in the preface to the King, preceding *De aug.,* II, *Works,* IV, 288.

CHAPTER FOUR

LOGICAL PROOF

One of the characteristics of Bacon's thought is its emphasis upon the reasoning process of the individual as distinguished from the emotional and affective states. Bacon's activity as a lawyer, his natural logical bent, and his desire to reform scientific inference account, in part, for the exaltation of reason above emotion. But whatever the forces at work, the entire body of Bacon's utterances exhibits a logical mind in action. Not only is the reader conscious of a controlling intellect manifesting itself in masterly analysis and arrangement of ideas, but many a passage expressly declares the glory of rational thought. Further evidence of Bacon's respect for reason is implicit in the value assigned to philosophy as one of the three divisions of knowledge. Because it addresses itself to the reasoning faculty, philosophy, to Bacon's way of thinking, is far superior to poetry and history, for these utilize, the one merely the imagination, the other the memory. But perhaps the best indication of Bacon's emphasis on reason lies in the utility and nature of the four Intellectual Arts. Rational in character, they constitute a methodology for all other departments of knowledge. Every knowledge, whether it be science or politics or ethics, in order to pursue its proper end of investigation, persuasion or instruction, must utilize the arts of invention, of judgment, of memory, and of delivery or communication. In other words, the intellectual arts taken as a whole really comprise logic and rhetoric—two activities which Bacon describes as the "arts of all arts"—one being the science of reason, the other the art of applying reason.

In view of the logical character of Bacon's mind and of the value set upon reason, it is not surprising that when Bacon comes to talk of rhetorical proof, he declares argument or rational inference to be the outstanding method of proof open to the speaker.

Bacon's works show two points of view in respect to the problem of proving or disproving logically a given judgment. First, induction is the *great* method of reasoning, and is especially appropriate to scientific investigation; deduction can be of real service only in the social sciences and the humanities. Second, whether deduction or induction be employed, the greatest obstacle to the formulation of correct judgments lies in the errors inherent in the human mind; man cannot reason accurately until he learns to recognize the false idols to which he has unwittingly paid obeisance. The first observation is, of course, well known. The second, however, needs stress, because it explains why Bacon defines the function of rhetoric as applying and recommending the dictates of reason to imagination, and why, in the *Advancement* and the *De augmentis*, he gives so much space to the Colours or sophisms of rhetoric and to the Idols or errors of reasoning, devoting little time to formal methods of proof. Rhetoric, we recall, is the agency which wins the imagination from the affections and applies it on the side of reason; thus it guards man against the side of his nature that is prone to error. In the realm of communication the reign of reason is subject to tumults and seditions:

. . . the government of reason is assailed and disordered in three ways; either by the illaqueation of sophisms, which pertains to Logic; or by the juggleries of words, which pertain to Rhetoric; or by the violence of the Passions, which pertains to Ethics. For as in negotiations with others, men are usually wrought either by cunning, or by importunity, or by vehemency; so likewise in this negotiation within ourselves, we are either undermined by fallacies of arguments, or solicited and importuned by assiduity of impressions and observations, or agitated and transported by violence of passions.[1]

It is necessary, then, to know about the errors and abuses of reason that we may guard against them, and the speaker, whether he be engaged in public address or private conversation, must know thoroughly the customary errors and deceits in order that he may

---

[1] *De aug.*, VI, 3, *Works*, IV, 455.

avoid error himself or detect the mistakes of others. "For abuses of arts only come in indirectly, as things to guard against, not as things to practice." [2] Hence there appear in the *Essays* discourses on cunning, on simulation and dissimulation.

With the exception of a detailed description of the inductive process in the *Novum organum,* Bacon describes the types of logical proof in what he calls the "Art of Judgment." Here he sets forth the inferential processes which underlie all arts and sciences. They are two: induction and deduction, with enthymemes and examples as abridgments of these two. "The art of judging," Bacon explains, ". . . handles the nature of proofs and demonstrations. In this art (as indeed it is commonly received) the conclusion is made either by induction or by syllogism. For enthymems and examples are but abridgements of these two." [3]

The ways of inference may be conveniently discussed, Bacon continues, by dividing the art of Judgment "into Analytic, and the doctrine concerning *Elenches,* or detection of fallacies; whereof the one proceeds by way of direction, the other by way of caution." [4] Or, stated in other words, "Analytic sets down true forms of consequences in argument; from which if there be any variation or deflexion, the conclusion is detected to be faulty; and this contains in itself a kind of detection, or refutation; for the straight . . . indicates what is not straight as well as what is. And yet it is safest to employ Elenches, as monitors, for the better detection of fallacies by which the judgment would otherwise be ensnared." [5] Discussion of the inferential process would, of course, belong to Analytic. Pertaining to the Elenches are the doctrine concerning sophistical fallacies, fallacies of interpretation, and the doctrine of false appearances or idols. Finally, Bacon suggests that an appendix to the art of judging would consider the appropriateness of the types of demonstration to the various sciences.

The twofold classification of proofs into induction and deduction would seem to be contradicted by a passage in which Bacon remarks that there are four kinds of demonstration: "immediate consent and common notions," induction, syllogism, and "that which Aristotle rightly calls *demonstration in circle*—(that is, not from

---

[2] *Ibid.,* 456.   [3] *De aug.,* V, 4, *Works,* IV, 428.
[4] *Ibid.,* 429.   [5] *Ibid.*

things higher in the order of nature, but as it were from the same level)." [6] But his statement follows a distinction between the demonstrations of mathematicians and the persuasions of orators, and is followed by the assertion that "there are certain subjects and matters in science wherein each of these demonstrations respectively does well. . . ." [7] Hence the species of proof known as demonstrations is to be taken as limited to the sciences, and the terms induction and syllogism, referred to here as kinds of demonstration, are to be understood as the absolute or demonstrative induction and syllogism of science.[8]

The kind of demonstration called "immediate consent and common notions" may in part be explained by reference to Divination and Fascination, two appendices to the faculties of the mind. The former has two divisions, Artificial and Natural. The Artificial, we note, "makes prediction by argument, concluding upon signs and tokens; Natural forms a presage from an inward presentiment of the mind, without the help of signs." [9] In other words, Natural divination and immediate consent may be identical with that rational proces which is today described as "immediate inference."

By the fourth item, "demonstration in circle," Bacon refers to that method of scientific inference that is called in the *De augmentis*, Learned Experience, or inference in which one moves from experiment to experiment, example to example, within a single genus or species or class. Inference here does not proceed from the general to the specific (deduction) or from specific instances to the general law ((induction), but merely remains on a single level. When, for example, "in things already known an experiment has scarcely been tried except in a certain kind of matter," one may repeat the experiment in other kinds of material sufficiently similar to the original to suggest the possibility of obtaining the same re-

---

[6] *Ibid.*, 434.

[7] *Ibid.*

[8] Concerning the syllogism and induction in science Fowler writes: "The syllogism . . . was indeed incompetent to establish the first principles from which it reasons, but, when these were once firmly established by induction on the basis of experience, it was perfectly competent to reason correctly from them. When the higher axioms have been constituted by induction, they should be developed deductively into all their consequences, and then ultimately, if they admit of it, applied to practice." [*Bacon* (New York, 1881), 197.]

[9] *De aug.*, IV, 3, *Works*, IV, 399.

sults, as "the manufacture of paper has been only tried in linen, not in silks . . . nor yet in hair stuffs. . . ." [10] Actually, the inference involved, then, is an abbreviated induction which does not rise to the level of the scientific axiom.

In sum, the basic classification of inference into induction and deduction seems not to be altered by the recognition of the four kinds of demonstration unless we wish to admit "immediate inference" as a species of reasoning distinct from the inductive and the deductive. In speaking of the demonstration, Bacon is using the term, as did Aristotle, to designate the inferences and proofs of science; in alluding to the enthymeme and the example he is naming the two modes of inference as they appear in rhetorical discourse; and in referring induction and deduction to "Analytic," he is regarding the two forms of inference as general instruments of thought that are employed in any field, not in science nor in rhetoric merely. Accordingly, Bacon looks at the modes of logical proof as general tools that not only are used by every discipline, but in use are somewhat changed and adapted to meet the conditions of a special subject. His position may be represented schematically:

General View of Inference
   I. Analytic
      A. Induction
      B. Deduction: the syllogism
         1. Reduction direct and reduction inverse
            a. *Ostensive proof*
            b. *Reductio ad absurdum*
  II. Elenches or Refutation
      A. Sophistical fallacies
      B. Fallacies of Interpretation
      C. Idols

Modes of Inference in Special Fields
   I. In Science
      A. For direct proof
         1. The New Induction
         2. Syllogism

---

[10] *De aug.,* V, 2, *Works,* IV, 413. In *Works,* IV, 413-421, Bacon classifies the various "methods" of experimenting.

3. Immediate Inference
4. Demonstration in Circle

B. For prevention of error
1. Sophistical fallacies
2. Fallacies of Interpretation
3. Idols

II. In Rhetorical Discourse

A. For direct proof
1. Enthymeme: rhetorical syllogism
   a. Ostensive proof
   b. *Reductio ad absurdum*
2. The Example
   a. Parabolical (hypothetical)
   b. Historical (actual)

B. For prevention of error and circumvention of prejudice
1. Sophistical fallacies
2. Fallacies of Interpretation
3. Idols

It is not necessary here to undertake an exposition of all the species of inference indicated above. It will be sufficient merely to suggest how these types of logical proof may be applicable to rhetorical situations.

Although reasoning as a general process is evident in all studies and all activities, not all types of it work equally well under all conditions. Bacon recognizes the truth of this statement in his description of the Appendix to the Art of Judging. The art, he says, "treats of the application of the differing kinds of proofs to the differing kinds of matters or subjects; and may be called the doctrine of the judgment of judgments." [11] Bacon sees, for example, a marked difference between the proofs proper to scientific investigations and those adequate in the realm of popular opinion. The *Novum organum* notes the distinction by contrasting the method of inference termed "interpretation of nature" with what is quaintly called "anticipations of nature": "The conclusions of human reason as ordinarily applied in matter of nature, I call for the sake of distinction *Anticipations of Nature* (as a thing rash or

---

[11] *De aug.*, V, 4, *Works*, IV, 434.

premature). That reason which is elicited from the facts by a just
and methodical process, I call *Interpretation of Nature*." [12] Anticipations, Bacon points out, constitute grounds sufficiently firm for
winning consent. Indeed, for the securing of assent, they may be
superior to scientific, esoteric proof:

> . . . anticipations are far more powerful than interpretations; because
> being collected from a few instances and those for the most part of
> familiar occurrence, they straightway touch the understanding and fill
> the imagination; whereas interpretations on the other hand, being
> gathered here and there from very various and widely dispersed facts,
> cannot suddenly strike the understanding; and therefore they must
> needs, in respect of the opinions of the time, seem harsh and out of tune;
> much as the mysteries of faith do.[13]

The *De augmentis* also remarks on the appropriateness of proof to
subject matter by commending Aristotle for rightly observing
"that we ought not to require either demonstrations from orators
or persuasions from mathematicians." [14]

If we may not require demonstrations from orators, what, then,
may we expect? If the inductive process or the "Interpretation of
Nature" works especially well in science, what forms of logical
proof are particularly useful in rhetorical endeavor? Bacon re-
plies that the received methods of proof, the syllogism and the
example, constitute the main types of inference open to the orator.

Bacon distinguishes the induction by example from the rhetorical
syllogism by describing the action of the mind engaged in each.
In induction, the inference is immediate. Whether one is inventing
or discovering material by means of induction, or whether one is
testing or proving a conclusion inductively, yet "the same action
of the mind which discovers the thing in question judges it; and
the operation is not performed by help of any middle term but
directly, almost in the same manner as by the sense. For the sense
in its primary objects at once apprehends the appearance of the
object, and consents to the truth thereof." [15] In the syllogism,
however, there are two mental operations. One consists in electing
the mean which lies between the two extremes; the other consists in

---

[12] *Nov. org.*, aphorism 26, *Works*, IV, 51.

[13] *Ibid.*, aphorism 28, *Works*, IV, 51-52.

[14] *De aug.*, V, 4, *Works*, IV, 434.   [15] *Ibid.*, 428.

recognizing this mean as an essential step in reaching the conclusion. The proof, in syllogistic reasoning, "is not immediate, but by mean. And therefore the invention of the mean is one thing, and the judgment of the consequence is another; for the mind ranges first, and rests afterward." [16]

Beyond describing the action of the mind in syllogistic and in inductive inference, Bacon discourses briefly but explicitly on the nature of syllogistic proof. The art of judging by the syllogism "is but the *reduction of propositions to principles in a middle term:* the Principles to be agreed by all and exempted from argument; the Middle Term to be elected at the liberty of every man's invention. . . ." [17] In other words, the speaker, in arranging his argument deductively gains acceptance for his proposition if he can bring it within ideas or principles that are already held by his audience. Bearing in mind the audience's beliefs and opinions, he himself is at liberty to select the middle term or bridge which will connect his proposition with that already believed.

Bacon points out, moreover, that deductive inference or the reduction of propositions to principles in a middle term may be carried on in two ways, direct or inverted. The one is "when the proposition is reduced to the principle, which they term *Probation ostensive;* the other when the contradictory of the proposition is reduced to the contradictory of the principle, which is that which they call *per incommodum,* or *pressing an absurdity.* . . ." [18] This undoubtedly means that the speaker presents his argument in the customary deductive form by directly bringing his proposition within accepted, general principles, or that he proves his proposition indirectly by showing that the contradictory of the proposition, when linked by a middle term to its appropriate generalization, derives from a principle that is exactly opposite to what the audience believes. It is thus absurd for the audience to deny the speaker's original proposition and to affirm its contradictory.

The exact nature of rhetorical induction, as Bacon comprehends it, is hard to determine. Concerning induction by example Bacon is nowhere as explicit as with the syllogism. As it pertains to science

---

[16] *De aug.,* V, 4, *Works,* IV, 428.
[17] *Adv. of L., Works,* III, 392-393.　　　　　　[18] *Ibid.,* 393.

and to the interpretation of nature, induction is treated at length in the *Novum organum,* but in the *Advancement* and the *De augmentis* Bacon does little more than mention it by name. We are not, however, left entirely in the dark. In one instance the example is called the "abridgement" of inductive inference,[19] and in another, inductive inference in the realm of the contingent is said to differ from scientific induction in that it proceeds "from a few instances and those for the most part of familiar occurrence." [20] Bacon thus apparently takes for granted the congruity of the example and stresses its acceptability to the persons addressed.

Having considered briefly the nature of induction and deduction as they function in rhetoric, it may be well to inquire, before passing on to the fallacies of reasoning, what value Bacon set upon the two forms of inference. The answer is what might be expected from a philosopher who believed that all accurate knowledge is derived from specific instances. The syllogism is a perpetual source of error, because it cannot examine the first principles from which it reasons. "The syllogism consists of propositions, propositions consist of words, words are symbols of notions. Therefore if the notions themselves . . . are confused and over-hastily abstracted from the facts, there can be no firmness in the superstructure. Our only hope therefore lies in a true induction." [21] Hence, although Bacon is here referring to scientific inference, it seems obvious that the accuracy of judgment in popular knowledge is also enhanced by the use of specific instances, by referring the general to the explicit. Accordingly the speaker and the writer who desire to be accurate, whether in invention or presentation, will endeavor to think in terms of concrete situations. But besides a gain in accuracy, the use of the example in rhetorical productions is particularly effective. In the first place, examples will prove a given proposition more quickly than will precepts and rules. In a speech to Sir William Jones, Bacon declares in the introduction that he will not delay business, but "will lead you the short journey by examples, and not the long by precepts." [22] And again, in a letter

---

[19] *De aug.,* V, 4, *Works,* IV, 428. [20] *Nov. org.,* aphorism 28, *Works,* IV, 51.
[21] *Nov. org.,* aphorism 14, *Works,* IV, 49. Cf. "Plan of the Work," a part of the preface of the *Great Instauration, Works,* IV, 24.
[22] *Letters and Life,* VI, 205.

to his friend Toby Matthew, occurs Bacon's statement that "I am of opinion that rules without examples will do little good . . . but that there is such a concordance between the time to come and the time past, as there will be no reforming the one without informing of the other." [23] If one is to urge a future change, in other words, specific examples drawn from knowledge of past events are employed to great advantage. Finally, examples not only produce a sense of continuity of time, but if they concern men better than the ordinary, flatter people's conceit. Bacon remarks on this effect in a dedicatory epistle to Bishop Andrewes, which prefaces the *Advertisement Touching an Holy War*, and although he speaks particularly of consoling men in grief, yet the allusion seems sufficiently general in application to be included in his rhetorical theory:

. . . amongst consolations, it is not the least, to represent to a man's self like examples of calamity in others. For examples give a quicker impression than arguments; and besides, they certify us, that which the Scripture also tendereth for satisfaction, *that no new thing is happened unto us.* This they do the better, by how much the examples are liker in circumstances to our own case; and more especially if they fall upon persons that are greater and worthier than ourselves. For as it savoureth of vanity, to match ourselves highly in our own conceit; so on the other side it is a good sound conclusion, that if our betters have sustained the like events, we have the less cause to be grieved.[24]

In concluding this discussion of rhetorical induction, mention of two species of example must not be omitted, the parable and the historical example. Both of these make their appearance in Bacon's advice on collecting specific instances for future use, whether for public address or for private conversation. Parables are hypothetical instances which illustrate abstractions. In ancient times, Bacon states, "as men found out any observation that they thought was good for life, they would gather it and express it in parable or aphorism or fable." [25] In times past and present, parables and fables have been utilized to veil meaning, but their real and proper function lies in making clear obscure generalizations and new ideas.

---

[23] *Letters and Life*, II, 63.   [24] *Works*, VII, 11.

[25] *Adv. of L., Works*, III, 453.

They were employed historically as illustrations, and as such they legitimately function. They are means of exposition:

> . . . inventions that are new and abstruse and remote from vulgar opinions may find an easier passage to the understanding. On this account it was that in the old times, when the inventions and conclusions of human reason . . . were as yet new and strange, the world was full of all kinds of fables, and enigmas, and parables, and similitudes: and these were used not as a device for shadowing and concealing the meaning, but as a method of making it understood. . . . For as hieroglyphics came before letters, so parables came before arguments. And even now if any one wish to let new light on any subject into men's minds, and that without offence or harshness, he must still go the same way and call in the aid of similitudes.[26]

Though Bacon thus points out the value of the parable and sanctions its use in didactic discourse, he prefers, whether in teaching or in private negotiation and conversation, the historical example. Its events have really happened. Fables, after all, "were vicegerents and supplies where examples failed; now that the times abound with history, the aim is better when the mark is alive." [27] The individual searching for means of supporting his argument he will find that "the form of writing which of all others is fittest for . . . variable argument of negotiation and occasions is that which Machiavel chose wisely and aptly for government; namely, *discourse upon histories or examples.*" [28] Examples drawn from history, furthermore, produce their effect by themselves; they do not need the added tag of some recognized authority. Finally, instances derived from history, better than those from philosophy and poetry, are closely allied to action, and hence are especially fitted for the moving of men:

> History of all writings deserveth least taxation, as that which holdeth least of the author, and most of the things themselves. Again, the use which it holdeth to man's life, if it be not the greatest, yet assuredly is the freest from any ill accident or quality. For those which are conversant much in poets, as they attain to great variety, so withal they be-

---

[26] Bacon's preface to the *Wisdom of the Ancients, Works,* VI, 698. Cf. *Adv. of L., Works,* III, 344; *De aug.,* II, 13, *Works,* IV, 317.

[27] *Adv. of L., Works,* III, 453.

[28] *Ibid.*

come conceited; and those that are brought up in philosophy and sciences do wax (according as their nature is) some of them too stiff and opinionate, and some others too perplexed and confused. Whereas History possesseth the mind of the conceits which are nearest allied unto action, and imprinteth them so, as it doth not alter the complexion of the mind neither to irresolution nor pertinacity.[29]

In spite of Bacon's marked preference for the historical example, he interposes two words of caution concerning its selection. First, "the rule of imitation and examples is, to consider not only which are the best, but which are the likest, and to choose the best of the likest. . . ." [30] Second, the most accurate examples are those which, set down in some detail, determine the inferences and interpretations to be drawn from them, rather than existing merely for the sake of the ideas that they support. Or, in Bacon's words, "it hath much greater life for practice when the discourse attendeth upon the example, than when the example attendeth upon the discourse." [31] Bacon explains that the position of the example depends upon its content:

. . . this is no point of order, as it seemeth at first, but of substance. For when the example is the ground, being set down in an history at large, it is set down with all circumstances, which may sometimes control the discourse thereupon made and sometimes supply it, as a very pattern for action; whereas the examples alleged for the discourse's sake are cited succinctly and without particularity, and carry a servile aspect toward the discourse which they are brought in to make good.[32]

To sum up, the logical means of persuasion in the Baconian rhetoric are the example and the rhetorical syllogism, the latter having two forms, the ostensive and *reductio ad absurdum*. Both means of persuasion are forms of reasoning proper to the realm of the contingent, the province to which rhetoric belongs. The famed Baconian method of induction, being reserved for the Interpretation of Nature, is on a higher level of validity and has, therefore, no essential application in rhetoric. Sufficient for the winning

---

[29] Preface to the *History of King Henry VII, Works*, VI, 18.
[30] *Pacification and Edification of the Church, Letters and Life*, III, 108.
[31] *Adv. of L., Works*, III, 453.
[32] *Adv. of L., Works*, III, 453. Cf. *De aug.*, VIII, 2, *Works*, V, 56.

of consent is a less perfect kind of induction, whose conclusion is based on a few examples drawn from popular opinions.

Bacon is not content with pointing out merely the positive lines of proof open to the orator and writer, or, for that matter, to the scientist. He indicates in addition the pitfalls and errors against which all discourse must guard. The scientist cannot interpret nature accurately without recognizing the idols or errors of the intellect; the speaker and the writer cannot insure the government of reason, cannot "apply and recommend the dictates of reason to imagination" for the proper influencing of the will without being keenly aware of those sophisms and juggleries of words which undermine reason. Hence it is that Bacon is interested in examining those errors to which man's sense and man's intellect are inherently or adventitiously prone.

Bacon groups the errors to which the human mind is susceptible under the general caption of "fallacies," a study which appears to have a doctrine of its own. It has three parts: "detection of *sophistical* fallacies, of fallacies of *interpretation*, and of *false appearances* or Idols." [33] Bacon's classification, however, does not appear to be mutually exclusive, for the fallacies of interpretation are, in one sense at least, merely a species of sophistical fallacies. This is evident, I think, from Bacon's own explanation of them.

From Bacon's point of view, sophistical fallacies are inferences which on the surface appear correct, but upon examination do not prove to be so. Sometimes the errors are so gross that, though the reasoning seems sound, we immediately suspect a trick beneath. "The grosser kind of fallacies," Bacon writes, "is well compared by Seneca to the feats of jugglers, in which though we know not how the thing is done, yet we know well it is not as it seems to be." [34] Sometimes the error is so subtle that it utterly confounds our judgment. "The more subtle sophisms not only put a man beside his answer, but many times seriously confound his judgment." [35]

Such a description of the nature of sophisms would clearly embrace not only those fallacies due to faulty analysis, but also those errors due to the ambiguous use of words. Actually, however, Bacon elevates the mistakes caused by ambiguous terminology into a class

---

[33] *De aug.,* V, 4, *Works,* IV, 430.   [34] *Ibid.*
[35] *Ibid.*

by themselves. He calls them the fallacies of Interpretation, and refers to them as "the sophisms of sophisms":

For common and general notions enter necessarily into every discussion; so that unless care be taken to distinguish them well at the outset, all the light of disputations will be strangely clouded with darkness by them, and the matter end in disputes about words. For equivocations and false acceptations of words (especially of this sort) are the sophisms of sophisms.[36]

If fallacies of interpretation are really a species of sophism, it is pertinent to inquire why Bacon gave them a special division. The answer, though it be somewhat hypothetical, seems worth attempting, for it serves to bring into relief the distinction between the sophism and its species, the fallacy of interpretation. In the first place, Bacon, by his use of the phrase "sophisms of sophisms," clearly indicates that ambiguous words comprise the most fundamental and perhaps the most frequent device of those who reason trickily. Because the fallacies of interpretation are so fundamental, he thinks it "better that the treatment of them should be made a part by itself, than that it should either be included in Summary Philosophy or Metaphysic, or placed partly under Analytic; as has been done by Aristotle confusedly enough."[37] Secondly, Bacon may have wished the errors of interpretation to be restricted to *words* only, while the sophistical fallacies may pertain chiefly to the mistakes of inference caused by poor analysis. For example, the Colours of Good and Evil, which Bacon terms the sophisms of rhetoric, are propositions whose fallacies for the most part rest on faulty induction and faulty causal connections, rather than on ambiguity of words. Finally, the species may differ from the genus by the *intent*, or lack of intent, exhibited by the reasoner. Ambiguous phraseology happens whether we will or no, whereas

---

[36] *Ibid.*, 431. Compare: " . . . the great sophism of all sophisms being equivocation or ambiguity of words and phrase, specially of such words as are most general and intervene in every inquiry, it seemeth to me that the true and fruitful use (leaving vain subtilties and speculations) of the inquiry of majority, minority, priority, posteriority, identity, diversity, possibility, act, totality, parts, existence, privation, and the like, are but wise cautions against ambiguities of speech." (*Adv. of L., Works,* III, 394.)

[37] *De aug.,* V, 4, *Works,* IV, 431. Bacon here refers to Aristotle's *De sophisticis elenchis.*

sophistical reasoning is usually deceitful; it deliberately carries the appearance of wisdom without the reality. This is the Aristotelean meaning of sophistic, and it is certain that Bacon was well aware of it.

In closing his remarks on sophistical and interpretative fallacies, Bacon cautions the student concerning their study and use. A knowledge of fallacies is valuable only for their refutation. Such knowledge, of course, can be turned to a corrupt use, but in the long run is not worth the trouble:

> ... although we have said that the use of this doctrine is for redargution, yet it is manifest the degenerate and corrupt use is for caption and contradiction; which passeth for a great faculty, and no doubt is of very great advantage: though the difference be good which was made between orators and sophisters, that the one is as the greyhound, which hath his advantage in the race, and the other as the hare, which hath her advantage in the turn, so as it is the advantage of the weaker creature.[38]

Bacon's third kind of fallacy is the Idols. These differ from the other fallacies in that the error is due to the fallibility of the human mind in receiving and reporting impressions:

> ... Idols are the deepest fallacies of the human mind. For they do not deceive in particulars, as the others do, by clouding and snaring the judgment; but by a corrupt and ill-ordered predisposition of mind, which ... perverts and infects all the anticipations of the intellect. For the mind of man ... far from being a smooth, clear, and equal glass (wherein the beams of things reflect according to their true incidence), is rather like an enchanted glass, full of superstition and imposture.[39]

"The mind," Bacon explains, "when it receives impressions of objects through the sense, cannot be trusted to report them truly, but in forming its notions mixes up its own nature with the nature of things." [40]

Four classes of Idols occur in Bacon's works. They are called the Idols of the Tribe, Idols of the Cave, Idols of the Market-

---

[38] *Adv. of L., Works*, III, 393-394. Cf. *De aug.*, V, 4, *Works*, IV, 430.

[39] *De aug.*, V, 4, *Works*, IV, 431. Cf. *Adv. of L., Works*, III, 394-395.

[40] "Plan of the Work"; part of preface to the *Great Instauration, Works*, IV, 27.

Place, and Idols of the Theatre. The first two come about in the functioning of the human mind itself, when it improperly combines the impression which it receives; the last two are imposed upon the mind from without. In Bacon's terminology, the Idols of the Tribe and Cave are *innate;* the Idols of the Market-Place and Theatre are adventitious.[41]

The Idols of the Tribe inhere in the very nature of the human mind. The intellect, for example, quite fallaciously considers, that "the sense of man is the measure of things." [42] In fact, however, the senses not only give false information, but many details escape their observation.[43] The mind errs, moreover, by yielding to positive assertions more often than to negative: ". . . *to the nature of the mind of all men it is consonant for the affirmative or active to affect more than the negative or privative:* so that a few times hitting or presence, countervails ofttimes failing or absence. . . ." [44] This error is closely linked to another of the mind's mistakes: the tendency to rationalize beliefs that are already held. Thus the *Novum organum* points out that "the human understanding when it has once adopted an opinion (either as being the received opinion or as being agreeable to itself) draws all things else to support and agree with it." [45] The mind, furthermore, tends to believe what it wants to believe, or, in terms of Bacon's faculty psychology, "the human understanding . . . receives an infusion from the will and affections; . . . for what a man had rather were true he more readily believes." [46] This tendency of the understanding to rationalize may be due in a measure to the human being's desire to avoid the unpleasantness of doubt, and this is in itself another source of error:

Another error is an impatience of doubt, and haste to assertion without due and mature suspension of judgment. For the two ways of contemplation are not unlike the two ways of action commonly spoken of by the ancients; the one plain and smooth in the beginning, and in the

---

[41] *Works,* IV, 27. In the *Advancement* and the *De augmentis* the Idols are not discussed as fully as in the later *Novum organum.* The Idols are also referred to in *The Interpretation of Nature,* and in the "Plan of the Work," part of the preface to the *Great Instauration.*

[42] *Nov. org., Works,* IV, 54.

[43] *Works,* IV, 26. [44] *Adv. of L., Works,* III, 395.

[45] *Works,* IV, 56. [46] *Nov. org., Works,* IV, 57.

end impassable; the other rough and troublesome in the entrance, but
after a while fair and even. So it is in contemplation; if a man will begin
with certainties, he shall end in doubts; but if he will be content to
begin with doubts, he shall end in certainties.[47]

The Idols of the Cave differ from those of the Tribe in that the
former arise from the nature of man's mind in general; whereas
the latter derive from the individual as determined by his peculiar
mental equipment and as conditioned by his environment. These
"false appearances imposed upon us by every man's own individual
nature and custom" may be conveniently illustrated, writes Bacon
in the *Advancement*, in that feigned supposition that Plato made
of the cave:

> . . . certainly if a child were continued in a grot or cave under the
> earth until maturity of age, and came suddenly abroad, he would have
> strange and absurd imaginations; so in like manner, although our
> persons live in the view of heaven, yet our spirits are included in the
> caves of our own complexions and customs; which minister unto us
> infinite errors and vain opinions, if they be not recalled to examination.[48]

Such complexions and customs, the *Novum organum* explains,
"take their rise in the peculiar constitution, mental or bodily, of
each individual; and also in education, habit, and accident. . . ."[49]
And ". . . every one . . . has a cave or den of his own, which refracts
and discolours the light of nature; owing either to his own proper
and peculiar nature; or to his education and conversation with
others; or to the reading of books, and the authority of those whom
he esteems and admires; or to the differences of impression, accordingly as they take place in a mind preoccupied and predisposed or
in a mind indifferent and settled. . . ."[50]

The two remaining Idols, those of the Market-Place and of the
Theatre, are distinguished from the Idols of the Tribe and the
Idols of the Cave by being imposed upon men, not by the nature
of men in general nor by the nature of an individual's mental
equipment and training, but by the conditions upon which their
social existence depends. In a word, men are deceived by the
very words that comprise the chief medium of their discourse and

---

[47] *Adv. of L., Works*, III, 293.
[48] *Ibid.*, 396.   [49] *Nov. org., Works*, IV, 59.   [50] *Nov. org., Works*, IV, 54.

by philosophical systems which they accept on authority. The first deception Bacon terms the Idols of the Market-Place; the second, the Idols of the Theatre.

The Idols of the Market-Place are most troublesome, according to Bacon, because they "have crept into the understanding through the tacit agreement of men concerning the imposition of words and names." [51] The trouble arises because words, which comprise the ordinary medium of communication among men, "are generally framed and applied according to the conception of the vulgar, and draw lines of separation according to such differences as the vulgar can follow." [52] When men of more than ordinary intelligence make profound discoveries and draw fine distinctions they have at hand, for purposes of communication, only the language of the ordinary man. In such circumstances, "words rebel"; they cannot convey adequately the ideas of wise men. Errors and misunderstandings result, which are almost impossible to conquer. "It is almost necessary," Bacon writes in the *Advancement*, "in all controversies and disputations to imitate the wisdom of the Mathematicians, in setting down in the very beginning the definitions of our words and terms, that others may know how we accept and understand them, and whether they concur with us or no." [53] But in spite of this care in definition, Bacon adds in the *De augmentis*, still "the juggleries and charms of words will in many ways seduce and forcibly disturb the judgment. . . ." [54]

The last class of Idols—those of the Theatre—come about from ideas "which have immigrated into men's minds from the various dogmas of philosophies, and also from wrong laws of demonstration." [55] Philosophers, instead of investigating patiently according to the method of the true induction, have "taken for the material of philosophy either a great deal out of a few things, or a very little out of many things; so that on both sides philosophy is based on too narrow a foundation of experiment and natural history, and decides on the authority of too few cases." [56] Any individual, in believing a traditional system of philosophy, is giving credence to no more than a stage play. For, in Bacon's judgment, "all the

---

[51] *De aug.*, V, 4, *Works*, IV, 423.
[53] *Adv. of L.*, *Works*, III, 396-397.
[55] *Nov. org.*, *Works*, IV, 55.

[52] *De aug.*, V, 4, *Works*, IV, 433.
[54] *De aug.*, V, 4, *Works*, IV, 434.
[56] *Ibid.*, 63.

received systems are but so many stage-plays, representing worlds of their own creation after an unreal and scenic fashion." [57]

The received philosophies Bacon describes as of three types: the Sophistical, the Empirical, and the Superstitious. The first type, mostly of the Rational School, errs by snatching "from experience a variety of common instances, neither duly ascertained nor diligently examined and weighed, and leaves all the rest to meditation and agitation of wit." [58] The sophistical philosopher places too much reliance upon his own inventive reason:

> Another error hath proceeded from too great a reverence, and a kind of adoration of the mind and understanding of man; by means whereof men have withdrawn themselves too much from the contemplation of nature and the observations of experience, and have tumbled up and down in their own reason and conceits. Upon these intellectualists, which are notwithstanding commonly taken for the most sublime and divine philosophers, Heraclitus gave a just censure, saying, *Men sought truth in their own little worlds, and not in the great and common world;* for they disdain to spell and so by degrees to read in the volume of God's works; and contrariwise by continual meditation and agitation of wit do urge and as it were invocate their own spirits to divine and give oracles unto them. . . .[59]

To believe the empirical philosophers, Bacon suggests, is to believe those, "who having bestowed much diligent and careful labour on a few experiments, have thence made bold to educe and construct systems; wresting all other facts in a strange fashion to conformity therewith." [60] Such philosophers commit the error which Bacon calls "the over-early and peremptory reduction of knowledge into arts and methods":

> But as young men, when they knit and shape perfectly, do seldom grow to a further stature; so knowledge, while it is in aphorisms and observations, it is in growth; but when it once is comprehended in exact methods, it may perchance be further polished and illustrated, and accommodated for use and practice; but it increaseth no more in bulk and substance.[61]

---

[57] *Ibid.,* 55.

[58] *Ibid.,* 63-64.

[59] *Adv. of L., Works,* III, 292.

[60] *Nov. org., Works,* IV, 64.   [61] *Adv. of L., Works,* III, 292.

Perhaps the real cause of this premature systematizing of knowledge consists in mistaking the true end of knowledge:

> . . . the greatest error of all the rest is the mistaking or misplacing of
> the last or furthest end of knowledge. For men have entered into a desire
> of learning and knowledge, sometimes upon a natural curiosity and in-
> quisitive appetite; sometimes to entertain their minds with variety and
> delight; sometimes for ornament and reputation; and sometimes to
> enable them to victory of wit and contradiction; and most times for
> lucre and profession; and seldom sincerely to give a true account of
> their gift of reason, to the benefit and use of men. . . .[62]

The third type of the Idols of the Theatre arise when we accept
the dogmas of the Superstitious philosophers—"those who out of
faith and veneration mix their philosophy with theology and traditions; among whom the vanity of some has gone so far aside as to
seek the origin of sciences among spirits and genii." [63]

These philosophies, then,—the Sophistical, the Empirical, and
the Superstitious—seem like stage-plays. They miss reality, because their authors err in their method of investigation, in formulating a comprehensive theory upon too few facts, and in mixing
philosophy and theology. They constitute a very fertile source of
error, for the philosophers themselves not only pay obeisance to the
habits and traditions of their own calling, but the rank and file of
men bow to their authority and pay tribute to their wisdom.

Bacon holds that the conventional treatment of Analytic is the
main guide for the speaker, but he emphasizes as the most suitable
type of proof the example, especially the historical example. He
accepts the conventional treatment of fallacies, but marks out for
the speaker's attention errors of interpretation. He contributes,
finally, the doctrine of idols.

The utility of the idols in rhetoric, however, requires some
clarification. It can hardly be maintained that Bacon would expect
the speaker to beware of the idols and be prepared to expose them,
as he might sophisms or ambiguities. The idols of the tribe, of the
market-place, and of the theatre have all a wide currency and are
with utmost difficulty counteracted even by the scientist. How then
can they be overcome by the orator, who on the whole must deal

---

[62] *Ibid.*, 294.   [63] *Nov. org., Works*, IV, 64.

with the public as he finds it, in order to effect the particular change that he advocates? Bacon would answer that the analysis of idols is the equivalent on the intellectual side to the study of character on the ethical. The orator must know human nature and allow for it if he is to change it even in the slightest. In a similar way, the speaker who deals with an individual, a judge, or a monarch, must take into account the idols of the den. The lore of idols, then, is useful to the orator in a way different from the lore of sophisms, for sophisms are to be exposed whereas idols must be circumvented. Only thus can the speaker "second reason and not oppress it."

CHAPTER FIVE

PATHOS AND ETHOS

IN

RHETORICAL DISCOURSE

Out of his system of ethics emerge Bacon's views of what rhetoricians call emotional proof or pathetic appeal. Ethics or moral knowledge is that study "which respects and considers the will of man." [1] The will, according to Bacon, is that aspect of mind which operates as the efficient cause of all human action, but which does not impel activity without itself being influenced by man's reason, his character, and his passions. By character Bacon means "original disposition," a quality beyond man's control, and immutable. By affection or passion Bacon denotes a *disease* or perturbation of the mind, also immutable. Thus in every individual there are postulated characters which are intrinsically staid and temperate, and affections which are to character what tempests are to the sea:

For as the ancient politicians in popular states were wont to compare the people to the sea, and the orators to the winds; because as the sea would of itself be calm and quiet, if the winds did not move and trouble it; so the people would be peaceable and tractable if the seditious orators did not set them in working and agitation; so it may be fitly said, that the mind in its own nature would be temperate and staid; if the affections as winds, did not put it into tumult and perturbation. [2]

---

[1] *De aug.*, VII, 1, *Works*, V, 3.   [2] *De aug.*, VII, 3, *Works*, V, 23.

Moral knowledge accepts the unalterable elements of the individual, studies them, and seeks to cure the diseases:

. . . in the culture of the mind and the cure for its diseases three things are to be considered: the different characters of dispositions, the affections, and the remedies; just as in the treatment of the body three things are observed; the complexion or constitution of the sick man, the disease, and the cure; but of these three, only the last is in our power, the two former are not. Yet the inquiry into things beyond our power ought to be as careful as into those within it; for the exact and distinct knowledge thereof is the groundwork of the doctrine of remedies, that they may be more conveniently and successfully applied; and we cannot fit a garment, except we first take measure of the body.[3]

Ethical science, consequently, is a physician to human nature. By studying the passions, ethics seeks to reduce them to a condition of equilibrium in which they operate as checks upon each other.

Such a conception of "moral knowledge" is profoundly significant to rhetoric, because it reveals the peculiar way in which pathetic appeal may be employed by both the orator and the writer. In Bacon's view, ethics and rhetoric share the same end—the moving of men to action by influencing the will. Rhetoric differs from ethics principally in the medium employed and in the peculiar relationship of the speaker to his audience. It follows that rhetoric, like ethics, must consider men's original natures or dispositions and must examine human affections and passions. It follows, moreover, that the rhetorician makes the same assumption concerning human action as does the moralist. Just as the instructor in moral knowledge assumes that human conduct is intrinsically good if the passions do not interfere, so the rhetorician supposes that man will act upon reason, providing the passions do not usurp his judgment. In studying human nature and affections, therefore, the orator regards them as means of gaining acceptance for his arguments; direct address to the emotions, by itself and exclusive of argument, is no legitimate means of persuasion. The speaker, consequently, employs his knowledge of human nature in two ways: he renders his audience capable of perceiving his argument by allaying the affections of the mind which would other-

---

[3] *Ibid.*, 20-21.

wise make perception impossible; and he wins approval for his argument by relating it to the dispositions of his hearers. Emotional appeal, pure and simple, is outlawed from the Baconian rhetoric.

That Bacon intends the speaker to dispel the diseases of the mind, to make reason, rather than passion, the arbiter of conduct is manifest also from the function that he assigns to the imagination as it relates to reason in rhetorical discourse. The imagination, we recall, is that faculty which the orator seeks to win from the passions, in order to employ it in the service of reason. If the passions dominate the imagination, they usurp all authority to themselves, and as a result pervert conduct. But if the imagination is wooed from the passions to the side of reason, then directed and rational action follows the dictates of judgment.

That Bacon intends the orator to refrain from using emotional appeal for its own sake is apparent from the strong ethical color that Bacon gives to rhetoric. The speaker at his best seeks a *good* end which he tries to effect by rational means. Bacon does not permit the speaker to gain his end by any means; he particularly debars emotional appeal and any attempt at making the worse appear the better reason. In fact, when insisting, in the *Advancement*, that physicians should be judged by their *acts* rather than their success, Bacon implies that all speaking, as well as the forensic variety, is to be appraised by its methods and intentions, not by its effects: ". . . almost all other arts and sciences are judged by acts or masterpieces[4] . . . not by the successes and events. The lawyer is judged by the virtue of his pleading,[5] and not by the issue of the cause. . . ."[6]

That Bacon expects the orator to make his argument acceptable by harmonizing it with the listener's disposition will be apparent if we refer once again to the function of rhetoric. In "applying reason to imagination" rhetoric not only ornaments argument with vivid phrases, but it also seeks to bring its arguments within the experience of the auditor. Arguments concerning good and evil, for

---

[4] The corresponding passage in the *De augmentis* reads "by their powers and functions."

[5] The *De augmentis* reads "his pleading and speaking."

[6] *Adv. of L., Works,* III, 371.

example, address themselves to man's disposition to act rightly; hence, "they are of . . . use to quicken and strengthen the opinions and persuasions which are true: for reasons plainly delivered, and always after one manner, especially with fine and fastidious minds, enter but heavily and dully; whereas if they be varied and have more life and vigour put into them by these forms and insinuations (i.e., by the Colours of Good and Evil), they cause a stronger apprehension, and many times suddenly win the mind to a resolution." [7] The end of rhetoric, Bacon reminds us, "is to fill the imagination with observations and images, to *second* reason, and not to oppress it." [8]

If the speaker is to control the "perturbations" of his auditors, if he is to handle his arguments so as to make them emotionally acceptable to the listener, he must obviously be acquainted with the aims and dispositions of men, with their motives and drives. The rhetorician ought, therefore, to inspect human ends and desires as Bacon understands them.

The investigation seems to fall into two divisions, the first dealing with the nature of the individual and his relation to society at large, the second concerning the individual's behavior as a member of an audience or crowd. Material for the first investigation derives principally from Bacon's ethical notions and from his essays; material for the second division is garnered from incidental comments in various works and letters. With the first we shall now deal.

Bacon believes that the good which is inherent in the human being exhibits a double nature: the good as it relates solely to a self-centered individual, seeking his own ends; and the good as it pertains to a social individual, recognizing a necessary relation between his own conduct and the demands of society. Of the two goods, the last is superior. "There is formed in everything," writes Bacon, "a double nature of good: the one, as everything is a total or substantive in itself; the other, as it is a part or member of a greater body; whereof the later is in degree the greater and worthier, because it tendeth to the conservation of the more general form." [9]

---

[7] Preface to the *Colours of Good and Evil, Works,* VII, 77.

[8] *De aug.,* VI, 3, *Works,* IV, 456.   [9] *Adv. of L., Works,* III, 420.

Corresponding to the two types of good are duty and virtue, the dutiful individual being one whose rational and emotional natures are "well disposed" towards others, the virtuous person being one whose rational and affective elements are well balanced within himself. Duty and virtue, however, are not mutually exclusive; neither quality of conduct is fully present without the other: ". . . the term of Duty is more proper to a mind well framed and disposed towards others, as the term of Virtue is applied to a mind well formed and composed in itself; though neither can a man understand Virtue without some relation to society, nor Duty without an inward disposition." [10]

Duty, Bacon states, has two parts: one is "the common duty of every man" as a member of a state; the other treats of "the respective or special duties of every man, in his profession, vocation, rank and character." [11] Man's highest duty, accordingly, lies in subordinating his own interests to those of society, and hence if he has to choose between saving his own life and sacrificing it for the state, he selects the latter course. Man's next highest duty lies in fulfilling his obligations to his work and to his family, for these are the cardinal bonds which make society possible:

. . . unto . . . respective duty, do . . . appertain the mutual duties between husband and wife, parent and child, master and servant; so likewise the laws of friendship and gratitude, the civil bonds of companies, colleges, neighbourhood, and the like; but it must ever be kept in mind, that they are here handled, not as they are parts of civil society (for that is referred to policy), but as to the framing and predisposing of the minds of particular persons towards the preservations of those bonds of society.[12]

The doctrine of the good as it relates primarily to the individual is considered in two parts, active and passive. Human beings have two main appetites: the active urge "to multiply and propagate themselves," and the "passive" desire "to preserve or continue themselves." [13] The former is the stronger and more worthy:

For in the universe, the heavenly nature is mostly the agent, the earthly nature the patient; in the pleasures of living creatures, that of

---

[10] Ibid., 428.
[12] Ibid., 18.
[11] De aug., VII, 2, Works, V, 15.
[13] Ibid., 10-11.

generation is greater than that of food; in divine doctrine, "It is more blessed to give than to receive," and in common life, there is no man's spirit so soft and effeminate but esteems the effecting of somewhat that he has fixed in his desire more than any pleasure or sensuality. And this preeminence of the active good is infinitely raised by the consideration that the condition of man is mortal, and exposed to the blows of fortune; for if we might have a certainty and perpetuity in our pleasures, the certainty and continuance of them would advance their price.[14]

In other words, active good consists in making and creating according to the individual's ends and desires—providing, of course, that his ends are consonant with those of society. From such activity man derives the highest type of pleasure. Passive good, on the other hand, consisting entirely of acts which preserve or continue the individual, affords only sensuous pleasure:

> There is . . . another important preeminence of the active good, produced and upheld by that affection which is inseparable from human nature; the love of novelty and variety; which in the pleasures of the sense . . . is very confined. . . . But in enterprises, pursuits and purposes of life there is much variety; whereof men are sensible with pleasure in their inceptions, progressions, rests, recoils, reintegrations, approaches and attainings to their ends; so as it was well said, "Life without a purpose is unsettled and languid." [15]

Such a brief sketch of Bacon's ethical system reveals at once how fundamental is the notion of good. It remains to be seen how the good is useful to rhetoric.

If it is true, as we originally suggested, that Bacon sees rhetoric and ethics sharing a common end, and that what ethics can reveal concerning the nature of man is of practical utility in gaining the public acceptance of arguments, then it follows that arguments

---

[14] *Ibid.*, 11.

[15] *Ibid.* Bacon's opinions on ethics contain an interesting observation on an ethical tenet of Aristotle's. Bacon asserts that the active life is a greater good than the comtemplative, because it conforms with the idea that the greatest good is the good of society. And this highest good, the welfare of society, "decides the question touching the preferment of the contemplative or active life, and decides it against Aristotle. For all the reasons which he brings for the contemplative respect private good, and the pleasure or dignity of a man's self. . . . Men must know that in this theatre of man's life it is reserved only for God and Angels to be lookers on. . . ." (*De aug.*, VII, 2, *Works*, V, 8.)

which establish the good or which are linked to the good are likely to win credence and to move the listener ultimately to action. Thus we discover why Bacon says with point that the purpose in all "deliberatives" is to establish the good, and that the use of the Colours of Good and Evil lies in *moving* as much as in proving. And thus we perceive the force of Bacon's suggestion to James when urging him to call a Parliament: "The subject of the Parliament must have three properties. The first is that which I always begin with, that it be *de vero* good, *bonum in se;* and not speculatively or commonplace-like good, but *politicly* good; that is, apt and agreeable for the state of the King and Kingdom." [16] The political orator, in short, does well to appeal to the "highest good"—the welfare of society. We may perhaps take this as a statement of one of Bacon's own rhetorical expedients in addressing Parliament.

The orator, however, does not stop with arguments and appeals concerning the social good. He may proceed to deduce appeals in line with what is *privately* good, either on the "active" or "passive" side of the individual's nature. On the active side, we note that it is good for man to attain the ends that he sets for himself in the "enterprises, pursuits, and purposes of life." In the achievement of his goal, he finds pleasure. Hence, the speaker may advantageously identify his recommended course of action with the desires of the audience, or with the means necessary to achieve those desires. In this respect, what holds of character-shaping holds also of rhetorical persuasion: "the surest key to unlock the minds of men, is by searching and thoroughly understanding either their natures and characters, or their intentions and ends." [17] The speaker, moreover, will try to discover, not merely a variety of ends to which he can appeal, but the more important and more practical *controlling* or ultimate ends of human conduct. In many cases, these will represent professional or vocational interests: "Nor is it enough to inform ourselves only of the variety of men's natures and ends simply; but we should also examine them comparatively,

---

[16] *Letters and Life*, V, 189.

[17] *De aug.*, VIII, 2, *Works*, V, 62. Cf. " . . . the most noble and effectual to the reducing of the mind unto virtue, and placing it in the state nearest to perfection . . . is the electing and propounding unto a man's self good and virtuous ends of his life and actions; such as may be in a reasonable sort within his compass to attain." (*De aug.*, VII, 3, *Works*, V, 28.)

and find what it is that predominates and directs the rest." [18] In at least one instance, futhermore, we discover that Bacon so respects the persuasive value of ends that he has for the moment, at any rate, recognized them as the mark distinguishing persuasion from "leading," or "awing," or "governing" a man into action. The passage occurs in the essay *Of Negociating:* "If you would work any man, you must either know his nature and fashions, and so lead him; or his ends, and so persuade him; or his weakness and disadvantages, and so awe him; or those that have interest in him, and so govern him." [19]

On the passive side of the human being, where good is either "perfective" or "conservative," man strives to perfect or to conserve himself. He is possessed by ambitions and desires purely individual in character. They drive him to realize all that he is potentially capable of becoming, as a discreet, not a social, individual. To preserve himself man needs food and sleep; "the love of life . . . is the predominant feeling in the individual. . . ." [20] There are, moreover, many self-centered motives:

> The delight which men have in popularity, fame, honour, submission and subjection of other men's minds, wills, or affections (although these things may be desired for other ends), seemeth to be a thing in itself, without contemplation of consequence, grateful and agreeable to the nature of man. . . . The best temper of minds desireth good name and true honour: the lighter, popularity and applause: the more depraved, subjection and tyranny; as is seen in great conquerors and troublers of the world; and yet more in arch heretics; for the introducing of new doctrines is likewise an affection of tyranny over the understandings and beliefs of men. [21]

It is manifest, therefore, that the speaker may profitably render his arguments acceptable and mollify the perturbations that defeat the rule of reason by relating the logical aspect of his speech to appropriate motives, or, as Bacon terms them, types of good. To

---

[18] *De aug.,* VIII, 2, *Works,* V, 63.

[19] *Works,* VI, 493-494.   [20] *De aug.,* VII, 1, *Works,* V, 7.

[21] *Sylva sylvarum,* Century X, *Works,* II, 672. "All men are drawn into actions by three things,—pleasure, honour, and profit." So Bacon advises James to mould his course for persuading emigrants to Ireland, on these three motives, but particularly the last two. (*Discourse on the Plantation in Ireland, Letters and Life,* IV, 120.)

control the passions and desires, however, to put the hearers into a favorable state of mind is a special duty of the speaker. He, like the ethical teacher who instructs privately, accepts human nature as he finds it. Its disturbing emotional elements, being basic, persistent, and immutable, can only be controlled and directed. Hence, the speaker, like the ethical teacher, draws upon those ideas which can control human nature:

Now we come to those points which are within our own command, and have force and operation upon the mind to affect the will and appetite and to alter manners; wherein they ought to have handled *custom, exercise, habit, education, example, imitation, emulation, company, friends, praise, reproof, exhortation, fame, laws, books, studies* . . . of these are such receipts and regiments compounded and described, as may seem to recover or preserve the health and good estate of the mind. . . .[22]

Bacon has observed in particular that men revere custom and tradition; "it is true that with all wise and moderate persons custom and usage obtaineth that reverence, as it is sufficient matter to move them to make a stand and to discover and take a view; but is no warrant to guide or conduct them; a just ground . . . of deliberation, but not of direction." [23] Finally, Bacon holds that the orator, if he is to control "the perturbations and distempers of the affections," must learn the principle of allopathic medicine, and smother one bothersome passion by besetting it with its opposite. He suggests that society itself is held together by this principle. Accordingly, the special use in moral and civil matters of a knowledge of human emotions is "to set affection against affection, and to master one by another . . . upon which foundation is erected that excellent use of *praemium* and *poena*, whereby all civil states consist; employing the predominant affections of *fear* and *hope*, for the suppressing and bridling the rest." [24]

---

[22] *Adv. of L., Works*, III, 438.

[23] *Pacification and Edification of the Church, Letters and Life*, III, 105. Note that by "direction" Bacon means guidance to *new* knowledge. Deliberation, on the other hand, takes place on the level of generally accepted ideas.

[24] *Adv. of L., Works*, III, 438. Cf. *De aug.*, VII, 3, *Works*, V, 24. Cf. also one of Bacon's great moral precepts: "The third precept shall be that which Aristotle mentions by the way. 'To bear ever with all our strength, so it be without vice, towards the contrary extreme of that whereunto we are by nature in-

So far, all of Bacon's notions concerning men's natures and the ideas which one can utilize in controlling them have been sketchy and abstract. Beyond these abstract ideas the *De augmentis* and the *Advancement* do not go. For specific information on human nature we turn to the Essays which, for the most part, seem to be to Bacon's ethical notions what Book II of the *Novum organum* is to Book I, what the "Article of Inquiry concerning Heavy and Light" in the *De augmentis* is to the general explanation of the doctrine of special topics. The second part of the *Novum organum* is a specific example, though incomplete, of the general principles of the new scientific method of interpreting nature which Bacon lays down in the first part. The outline of the new scientific method Bacon first suggested in a small tract, *Of the Interpretation of Nature*. The Inquiry concerning Heavy and Light is merely a specific illustration of the doctrine of special topics, a doctrine that was first enunciated in the *Advancement of Learning*. Bacon, then, early in his career, set himself the task of surveying human knowledge and marking its deficiencies. In leisure snatched from affairs of state, he gradually supplied models and examples of what ought to be done if ever the deficiencies were to be removed. Such is the nature of the second half of the *Novum organum;* such is the nature of the "Article of Inquiry concerning Heavy and Light"; and such seems to be the real nature of most of Bacon's *Essays.* As both Crane and Zeitlin have observed, most of them were apparently undertaken to satisfy some of the deficiencies that are noted in the *Advancement*.[25] A passage already quoted is significant enough to repeat:

Now we come to those points which are within our own command, and have force and operation upon the mind to affect the will and appetite and to alter manners; wherein they ought to have handled *custom, exercise, habit, education, example, imitation, emulation, company, friends, praise, reproof, exhortation, fame, laws, books, studies* . . . of

clined'; as when we row against the stream, or straighten a wand by bending it contrary to its natural crookedness." (*De aug.*, VII, 3, *Works*, V, 25.)

[25] R. S. Crane, "The Relation of Bacon's 'Essays' to his Program for the Advancement of Learning," *Schelling Anniversary Papers* (New York, 1923); Jacob Zeitlin, "The Development of Bacon's Essays—with Special Reference to the Question of Montaigne's Influence upon them," *Journal of English and Germanic Philology*, XXVII (October, 1928), 496-519.

these are such receipts and regiments compounded and described, as may seem to recover or preserve the health and good estate of the mind, as far as pertaineth to human medicine. . . .[26]

When one turns to the first edition of the *Essays*, published in 1597, one observes that the deficiency cited concerning books and studies has been partially met in the treatise *Of Studies;* that concerning friends, in the essay *Of Followers and Friends.*[27] The deficiency concerning fame is perhaps supplied in part by a fragmentary, undated essay *On Fame.* Examination of the *Essays* published in 1612 reveals that still more of the insufficiencies remarked in 1605 in the *Advancement* have been removed. Here there appear *Of Custom and Education, Of Praise, Of Ambition, Of Great Place, Of Nobilitie,* and *Of Friends.* Finally, in the edition of 1625 Bacon has written on the title-page, "Counsels Civil and Moral." An inspection of their titles or their content demonstrates that many of them are related directly to ethics.

Of Truth	Of Revenge	Of Adversity
Of Simulation and Dissimulation	Of Parents and Children	Of Marriage and Single Life
Of Envy	Of Love	Of Great Place
Of Boldness	Of Goodness, and Goodness of Nature	Of Nobility
Of Seditions and Troubles	Of Atheism	Of Superstition
Of Cunning	Of Seeming Wise	Of Friendship
Of Suspicion	Of Ambition	Of Nature in Men
Of Custom and Education	Of Fortune	Of Youth and Age
Of Beauty	Of Deformity	Of Followers and Friends
Of Suitors	Of Faction	Of Praise
Of Vain Glory	Of Honour and Reputation	Of Anger

---

[26] *Adv. of L., Works,* III, 438.

[27] It is true, of course, that the first edition of the *Essays* appeared eight years before the publication of the *Advancement*. Spedding conjectures, however, that Bacon had in mind the plan of the work "much earlier."

In brief, only twenty-five of the fifty-eight essays in the edition of 1625 do not immediately suggest an analysis of character or of conduct. When one links this circumstance with Bacon's comment to his brother Anthony in the preface of the first edition—namely, that he supposes the essays may prove "medicinable"—it seems highly probable that many of the essays represent his attempt to supply the deficiencies of which he was aware.[28]

Other circumstances, moreover, point in a similar direction. From the *Novum organum*, it is clear that Bacon's famous method of investigation can, in some instances, be applied to sciences other than the physical:

> It may also be asked . . . whether I speak of natural philosophy only, or whether I mean that the other sciences, logic, ethics, and politics, should be carried on by this method. Now I certainly mean what I have said to be understood of them all; and as the common logic, which governs by the syllogism, extends not only to natural but to all sciences; so does mine also, which proceeds by induction, embrace everything. For I form a history and tables of discovery for anger, fear, shame, and the like; for matters political; and again for the mental operations of memory, composition, and division, judgment and the rest. . . .[29]

It is probable, therefore, that the Essays represent Bacon's attempt to apply his method to the observations of human nature, and to summarize, in more or less aphoristic style, the results of his observations. The piece *Of Anger* may very well be the final form of "a history and tables of discovery for anger." [30]

---

[28] The *De augmentis* is somewhat more specific than the *Advancement* in suggesting the nature and purpose of those deficiencies of both "Morality and Policy" that Bacon would see remedied by special treatises. The new treatises would deal with systematic observations on men's *"natures and dispositions,"* not only as they are influenced by nature, but also as they are imposed "by sex, by age, by region, by health and sickness, by beauty and deformity, and the like; and again, those which are caused by fortune, as sovereignty, nobility, obscure birth, riches, want, magistracy, privateness, prosperity, adversity, and the like." The treatises, too, will deal with men's *"affections and perturbations"* and "other particularities of this kind" that are of "special use in moral and civil matters. . . . " See *De aug.*, VII, 3, *Works*, V, 21 ff.

[29] *Nov. org.*, *Works*, IV, 112.

[30] In writing of the development, from 1597 to 1625, of the content and tone of the Essays, Zeitlin observes: "We find his ideas tending increasingly toward

To conceive of the Essays as part of Bacon's ethical system holds profound importance to any study of his theory of public address. If rhetoric and ethics share a common end and differ only in their medium and means of operation, then it is hard to escape the inference that Bacon, if he had fully constructed a rhetorical system, would certainly have included in it his essays on character, perhaps in much the same manner that Aristotle has sketched human character in his *Rhetoric*. Some, such as the essays *Of Anger, Of Praise, Of Youth and Age, Of Faction,* would teach the speaker to use pathetic appeal and to allay feelings that are hostile to his cause; others, such as those on *Cunning, Of Simulation and Dissimulation,* and *Of Honor and Reputation,* would help him to make his own character look right, and to make himself acceptable as an authority.

Up to this point there has been considered Bacon's position with regard to the function of pathetic appeal. Considered, also, has been how the use of pathetic proof depends upon a knowledge of human character, and how such knowledge is broadly outlined in Bacon's treatment of ethics, and then particularized in the *Essays*. But a study of Bacon's rhetorical remarks reveals, further, some practical suggestions for handling various types of audiences, whether the group be large, as on public occasions, or small, as in private conversation and conference. Most of these hints were

---

the communication of practical advice . . . and observing a *strict neutrality* of judgment. . . ." (*Op. cit.,* 514; italics mine.) Some of the Essays, like that *Of Envy,* are little more than a group of aphorisms on which is imposed some semblance of structure; accordingly, they seem to represent Bacon's attempt to apply his own "Method" of aphorisms (*De aug.,* VI, 2) to moral philosophy. They do not seem intended to influence the reader's belief, nor his action. Other Essays, such as *Unity in Religion,* are less aphoristic in style. Frequently didactic, they may reflect Bacon's use of his Magistral or of his Initiative "Method" of disposition.

As aphorisms, the Essays represent observations which direct the reader to a keener appreciation of their subject matter. In conjunction with his own knowledge and experience, the reader is to weigh them and arrive at his own conclusions; indeed, he functions like a scientist whose object of observation is not direct experience, but the current aphorism. Bacon advised the expressing of scientific observations in an aphoristic style, because only in this manner could they be free of the author's bias and hence be suitable as bases for subsequent inference. If this interpretation is correct, then, the Essays concerning human character were to be to Bacon's scheme of ethics what the Axioms were to his scheme of natural philosophy.

doubtless prompted by Bacon's own experience as a lawyer, a Parliamentarian, and a diplomat.

If one wants to rouse to action large bodies, such as Parliament or the country as a whole, argument proves of little avail. This is especially true when the action desired is of international scope. In the reign of Henry VII when France desired England's aid, Bacon remarks that "the Parliament was . . . moved with the point of oppression; for although the French seemed to speak reason, yet arguments are ever with multitudes too weak for suspicions." [31] What holds of Parliament holds usually of large groups: ". . . nothing pleases the many unless it strikes the imagination, or binds the understanding with the bands of common notions. . . ." [32] Bacon observes, moreover, that "the vulgar people are sometimes led with vain and fond prophecies. . . ." [33] Another effective means of securing action on a large scale is to tie one's project to a famous personality, an expedient to which Bacon calls the King's attention at a time when England was endeavoring to encourage emigrant settlers in Ireland:

. . . the more strongly and fully your Majesty shall declare yourself in it, the more shall you quicken and animate the whole proceeding. For this is an action, which as the worthiness of it doth bear it, so the nature of it requireth it to be carried in some height of reputation; and fit in my opinion for pulpits and parliaments and all places to ring and resound of it.[34]

The passage reveals, incidentally, that Bacon well understands the influence wielded by pulpit and Parliament in promoting national action.

A very useful method of winning favor for one's argument is to praise the auditors for their past virtuous actions or for their commendable beliefs. Usually, however, in order to avoid vain and vulgar flattery, it is best to praise the offices and professions of men, rather than their characters.[35] The speaker, moreover, should

---

[31] *History of King Henry VII, Works,* VI, 81.
[32] *Nov. org., Works,* IV, 76.
[33] "Charge on Opening the Court of the Verge," *Letters and Life,* IV, 271.
[34] *Discourse on the Plantation in Ireland, Letters and Life,* IV, 120.
[35] For general discussion of this idea, see the essay *Of Praise, Works,* VI, 501-503. It is with monotonous regularity that Bacon's letters to men of position

remember that the praise acceptable to the multitude often displeases the discerning and disgusts men in authority. To this matter Bacon refers in a commentary on the tactics of a Puritan pamphleteer: ". . . though I observe in him (a libeller) many glosses, whereby the man would insinuate himself into their favours, yet I find it to be ordinary, that many pressing and fawning persons do misconjecture of the humours of men in authority, and many times . . . they seek to gratify them with that which they most dislike." [36]

Bacon has a few remarks that indicate the worth of humour in handling hostile audiences and quieting their perturbations:

> . . . when you have anything to obtain of present despatch, you entertain and amuse the party with whom you deal with some other discourse; that he be not too much awake to make objections. I knew a counsellor and secretary, that never came to Queen Elizabeth of England with bills to sign, but he would always first put her into some discourse of estate, that she mought the less mind the bills.[37]

But wit and humor, though for the most part good, can be carried too far. If not appropriate, it defeats its purpose: "as for jest, there be certain things which ought to be privileged from it; namely, religion, matters of state, great persons, any man's present business of importance, and any case that deserveth pity." [38] Bacon urges that those who speak and converse exercise care in determining the essence of true wit. Wit may be aptly termed the "salt" of speech, but if it be a bitter salt, it may do more harm to the speaker than good: ". . . there be some that think their wits have been asleep, except they dart out somewhat that is piquant, and to the quick . . . men ought to find the difference between saltness and bitterness. Certainly, he that hath a satirical vein, as he maketh

---

commence with commendations and praises that strike the 20th century reader as vulgar flattery. Because of this many a critic has called Bacon obsequious and servile, whereas a careful reading of the essay *Of Praise* reveals that Bacon probably was only conforming to Elizabethan practice: "Some praises come of good wishes and respects, which is a form due in civility to kings and great persons, *laudando praecipere;* when by telling men what they are, they represent to them what they should be." (*Works*, VI, 502.)

[36] *An Advertisement Touching the Controversies of the Church of England, Letters and Life*, I, 78.

[37] *Of Cunning, Works*, VI, 429.   [38] *Of Discourse, Works*, VI, 455.

others afraid of his wit, so he had need be afraid of others' memory." [39] Such are the few special comments on pathetic proof which one finds in Bacon. Some of the essays, notably *Of Cunning* and *Of Simulation and Dissimulation,* discuss in greater detail the expedients which the speaker may employ to attain his end. Much of the information appearing in these essays, however, deals chiefly with the *ethos* of an author or with matters of strategy that relate to disposition, and hence we shall deal more appropriately with their content later.

Bacon's conception of pathetic appeal does not rest entirely upon a knowledge of character-types. He suggests that the art of influencing others is above all dependent upon fairly complete knowledge of the *particular* person or definite audience with which one is confronted. All general knowledge of character and conduct goes wasted unless the speaker keenly analyses his immediate audience, because particular knowledge in conjunction with general truths is the only union which permits correct deduction. Humanity is not uniform in character, and to know men at large merely enables one to frame rough generalizations. One can say, for example, that "most men love honor and reputation." But the practical result which may be obtained from such a proposition depends entirely on whether the special person or special audience under observation really values honor and reputation and really falls within the class of "most men." To influence action effectively is to appraise correctly the rhetorical situation that confronts one. The basis for inventing pathetic proof—and for that matter ethical and logical proof—is to look into the "window" of the heart:

> This window we shall obtain by carefully procuring good information of the particular persons with whom we have to deal; their natures, their desires and ends, their customs and fashions, their helps and advantages, with their principal means of support and influence; so again their weaknesses and disadvantages, where they lie most open and obnoxious; their friends, factions, patrons and clients; their enemies, enviers, and competitors; their moods and times; lastly their principles, fashions, prescribed rules, and the like: and this not only

---

[39] *Ibid.,* 455-456.

of particular persons, but also of the particular actions which are on foot from time to time, and as it were under the anvil; how they are directed and succeed, by whom promoted or opposed, what is their weight and importance, what consequences they involve, and the like. . . . These informations of particulars touching persons and actions, are as the minor propositions in every active syllogism; for no truth or excellence of observations or axioms (whence the major political propositions are drawn) can suffice to ground a conclusion, if there be error in the minor proposition.[40]

"Persuasion," Aristotle writes, "is achieved by the speaker's personal character when the speech is so spoken as to make us think him credible."[41] Bacon, like Aristotle, also entertains the notion that the speaker and writer, whether in the ordinary affairs of business and private conversation or in public discourse, ought, by his language, to render his own character acceptable to his audience. His language ought to be so handled that it is credible not merely because of inherent logical validity, but because his audience believes that he is telling the truth as he sees it. In short, an author through what he says in any given composition is his own character witness.

But where Aristotle seeks to exclude from the rhetorical art the effect of the popular reputation which the speaker has already established, Bacon refuses to make this limitation; for him, ethical proof is not confined to the impression of good character that a speaker may convey in a single speech before a given audience. The speaker, like any man, should realize that his popular reputation is always an important factor in the audience's estimation of his character. What he has done and what he has said in the past constitute his popular character. His *ethos,* as perceived in any speech, affects his reputation on any subsequent occasion. He in effect constructs his own reputation through cumulative utterance. Accordingly, Bacon holds that an author has two tasks: to create his own character through what he says; and once his public character is established—whether it be his real nature or exist through

---

[40] *De aug.,* VIII, 2, *Works,* V, 59-60.

[41] *De Rhetorica,* tr. by W. Rhys Roberts; Book I, Chapter 2. In *The Works of Aristotle Translated into English,* ed. by W. D. Ross (Oxford, 1924), XI, 1356 a 4-5.

popular hearsay or both—to preserve and to defend that character.

Any man, whether he engages in private conversation or in public discourse, should of course know his own nature thoroughly. It is not enough, however, for a man merely to know himself: "he should consider also of the best way to set himself forth to advantage; to disclose and reveal himself; and lastly, to turn and shape himself according to the occasion." [42] Since we see nothing more usual than for the worse man to make the better external show, the good and wise man, if he is to compete with the venal and mischievous, must not neglect self-revelation:

. . . it is therefore no unimportant attribute of prudence in a man to be able to set forth to advantage before others, with grace and skill, his virtues, fortunes, and merits (which may be done without arrogance or breeding disgust); and again, to cover artificially his weaknesses, defects, misfortunes, and disgraces; dwelling upon the former and turning them to the light, sliding from the latter or explaining them away by apt interpretations, and the like.[43]

To set one's self out to advantage obviously requires considerable art, "lest it become wearisome and contemptible." But the political orator, in particular, ought not to refrain from remarks that demonstrate a good character, because "ostentation, though carried to the first degree of vanity, is rather a vice in morals than in policy." [44] It can be managed unobtrusively in most affairs:

. . . if this self-display whereof I am speaking be carried with decency and judgment, as with a natural, candid, and ingenious bearing; or if it be employed in times of danger, as by military persons in time of war, or at times when others are most envied; or if what a man says in his own praises appears to drop carelessly and unintentionally, without being dwelt upon too long or too seriously; or if a man at the same time that he praises does not refrain from ridiculing and finding fault with himself; or if he do it not spontaneously, but appears provoked and challenged to it by the reproaches and insolence of others, it adds greatly to his reputation.[45]

Thus the technique of self-portraiture lies in the art of appear-

[42] De aug., VIII, 2, Works, V, 66. [43] Ibid.
[44] Ibid., 67. [45] Ibid.

ing natural, candid, and ingenuous. But beyond this, Bacon's advice to the speaker who desires to make his character look right seems to be nicely stated in the essay *Of Honour and Reputation*. Here the winning of honor is but "the revealing of a man's virtue and worth without disadvantage." [46] One of the best means of appearing to advantage relates not to a direct statement of virtue, but to the preservation of "a sound and wise mediocrity" in declaring or concealing one's intention in the action that one urges. Let the speaker state the ends and aims of the conduct that he urges on others. Though secrecy and dissimulation, effecting everything by "dark arts and methods," are often useful, yet frequently dissimulation "breeds errors which ensnare the dissembler himself. Whence we see that the greatest and most noted politicians have not hesitated to declare freely and undisguisedly the objects which they had in view." [47]

Two aspects of delivery—movement and bold bearing—Bacon looks at as they contribute to the speaker's authoritativeness:

It is a trivial grammar-school text, but yet worthy a wise man's consideration. Question was asked of Demosthenes, *what was the chief part of an orator?* he answered, *action:* what next? *action:* what next again? *action.* He said it that knew it best, and had by nature himself no advantage in that he commended. A strange thing, that that part of an orator which is but superficial, and rather the virtue of a player, should be placed so high, above those other noble parts of invention, elocution, and the rest; nay almost alone, as if it were all in all. But the reason is plain. There is in human nature generally more of the fool than of the wise; and therefore those faculties by which the foolish part of men's minds is taken are most potent. Wonderful like is the case of Boldness, in civil business; what first? Boldness: what second and third: Boldness. And yet boldness is a child of ignorance and baseness, far inferior to other parts. But nevertheless it doth fascinate and bind hand and foot those that are either shallow in judgment or weak in courage, which are the greatest parts; yea and prevaileth with wise men at weak times.[48]

Even boldness of advocates—evidently a studied practice on the

---

[46] *Works*, VI, 505.
[47] *De aug.*, VIII, 2, *Works*, V, 69.
[48] *Of Boldness, Works*, VI, 401-402.

part of seventeenth-century lawyers—sometimes influences staid judges, as Bacon indicates in his essay *Of Judicature*.[49]

To Bacon the preserving and maintaining of one's character is largely a matter of covering up defects in one's nature, and hence most of Bacon's remarks pertaining to ethos constitute *cautionary* advice to the speaker and writer. Bacon seems keenly aware of the delicate relationship which obtains between popular reputation once established and that revealed by words. An established character is a priceless asset to a man's influence, but it is easily harmed, even destroyed, by inadvertent speech. Hence Bacon seems to hold up as a general rule that "speech of a man's self ought to be seldom and well chosen." [50]

Defects of character may be covered up in three ways: by caution, by colour, and by confidence. Caution is apparent "when men discreetly avoid those things to which they are not equal," [51] and the speaker, therefore, should avoid undertaking what is beyond his ability. Colour is manifest "when men warily and skilfully make and prepare a way for themselves, for a favourable and convenient construction of their faults or wants; as proceeding from a better cause, or intended for some other purpose, than is commonly imagined." [52] If a man, for instance, were to conceal vice, "he must take care to borrow the mask and colour of the neighboring virtue that shadows it; as if he be dull, he must affect gravity." [53] But perhaps the most effectual remedy for concealing defects of character is confidence, or the impudence that manifests itself whenever a man professes to depreciate what he cannot obtain.

Bacon holds that any of these three ways of concealing unfavorable characteristics may be practised in three degrees. A man may hide and veil his true self, first, by Closeness and Secrecy, as "when a man leaveth himself without observation, or without hold to be taken, what he is." [54] In a speech this would be possible only if the speaker never revealed his true intent. The second degree of concealment is by Dissimulation, as "when a man lets fall signs and arguments, that he is not that he is"; the third degree is by

---

[49] *Works*, VI, 508.   [50] *Of Discourse, Works*, VI, 456.

[51] *De aug.*, VIII, 2, *Works*, V, 68.   [52] *Ibid.*   [53] *Ibid.*

[54] *Of Simulation and Dissimulation, Works*, VI, 387-388.

Simulation, as "when a man industriously and expressly feigns and pretends to be that he is not." [55] Actually, however, the technique of concealment involves only simulation and dissimulation, for secrecy can only be perfectly preserved when men are thrown off the trail. To be utterly silent means that a man is hiding something, and this invites inquiries. And to equivocate is scarcely better, for "equivocations or oraculous speeches . . . cannot hold out long." [56]

The specific ways by which one may simulate and dissimulate Bacon sets forth mainly in the essays *Of Cunning, Of Seeming Wise*, and in the *De augmentis*, Book VIII. Some of these ways have already been marked. Of more concern now is Bacon's attitude toward the use of Simulation. The essay on that subject, in so far as it expresses a positive opinion, seems clear. Simulation and Dissimulation are of advantage in three ways: first, they serve to preclude opposition, for "where a man's intentions are published, it is an alarum to call up all that are against them." [57] Second, they make it possible for a speaker—especially a Parliamentarian—to keep open a means of retreat, for "if a man engage himself by a manifest declaration, he must go through or take a fall." [58] Third, they enable a converser or debater better to sound out the mind of an opponent, for to the speaker "that opens himself men will hardly shew themselves adverse; but will . . . let him go on, and turn their freedom of speech to freedom of thought." [59] On the other hand, certain disadvantages of dissembling offset its advantages. Dissembling, if suspected by an audience, weakens its confidence in the speaker's character: "it depriveth a man of one of the most principal instruments for action; which is trust and belief." [60] Then, too, simulation often alienates those in the audience who would be favorable to the speaker's proposal, for "it puzzleth and perplexeth the conceits of many, that perhaps would otherwise coöperate with him; and makes a man walk almost alone to his own ends." [61] Finally, the speaker, finding it exceedingly difficult not to betray his tactics, almost always makes a "shew of fearfulness":

[55] *Ibid.*   [56] *Ibid.*   [57] *Ibid.*, 389.
[58] *Ibid.*   [59] *Ibid.*   [60] *Ibid.*
[61] *Ibid.*

It is hard to find any man so skilled and perfect in the art of dissimulation, or any countenance so controlled or commanded . . . as to sever from a feigned and dissembling tale all these marks (i. e. involuntary movements and slips of speech) and prevent the style from being either more careless, or more adorned, or more tedious and wandering, or more dry and hard, than usual.[62]

On the whole, Bacon's real position seems to be that stated early in the essay *Of Simulation and Dissimulation*. Dissembling is only necessary when a speaker lacks either the wisdom to know when to tell the truth or the courage to speak the truth if he perceives it. The weaker set of politicians are the dissemblers:

. . . if a man have that penetration of judgment as he can discern what things are to be laid open, and what to be secreted, and what to be shewed at half lights, and to whom and when, (which indeed are arts of state and arts of life, as Tacitus well calleth them,) to him a habit of dissimulation is a hindrance and a poorness. But if a man cannot obtain to that judgment, then it is left to him generally to be close, and a dissembler. For where a man cannot choose or vary in particulars, there it is good to take the safest and wariest way in general; like the going softly, by one that cannot well see.[63]

The passage quoted from makes fairly evident Bacon's position concerning the whole doctrine of covering up defects of character. He finds that only fools and men of poor judgment dissemble; they possess inferior judgment and they can hardly do otherwise. Merely because a majority of Bacon's comments on *ethos* pertain to what Aristotle would call sophistry is no valid reason for believing that Bacon condones dissembling and urges it as a general practice. In reality "though some persons of weaker judgment and

---

[62] *De aug.*, VIII, 2, *Works*, V, 61.

[63] *Of Sim. and Dissim.*, *Works*, VI, 387. An interesting sidelight on dissembling is shown by Bacon's advice to Essex when that Earl was seeking the Queen's favor: "The third impression is of a popular reputation; which because it is a good thing in itself, being obtained as your Lordship obtaineth it, that is *bonis artibus;* and besides, well governed, is one of the best flowers of your greatness both present and to come; it would be handled tenderly. The only way is to quench it *verbis* and not *rebus.* And therefore to take all occasions, to the Queen, to speak against popularity and popular courses vehemently; and to tax it in all others; but nevertheless to go on in your honourable commonwealth courses as you do." Letter to Essex, *Letters and Life*, II, 44.

perhaps too scrupulous morality may disapprove" of the art of en-
hancing a man's virtues by conscious self-portraiture, "yet no one
will deny that we ought at least to take care that virtue be not
undervalued and unduly debased through neglect." [64] Indeed the
real reasons for Bacon's paying such attention to the tricks and
deceits of character are made amply clear in the De augmentis.
First, moral theorists have in the past largely neglected this side
of moral doctrine, and second, only by perceiving vice can it be
avoided. Precisely the same two reasons account for the care
bestowed on the Colours of Good and Evil. The De augmentis
reads:

> There belongs further to the handling of this part, touching the
> respective duties of vocations and professions, a relative or opposite
> doctrine touching the frauds, cautions, impostures, and vices of every
> profession; for corruptions and vices are opposed to duties and vir-
> tues. And it is true that these are not altogether passed over, but there
> are many treatises and writings in which they are touched upon at
> least in passing; but how? rather in a satire, and cynically after the
> manner of Lucian, than seriously and wisely. For men have rather
> sought by wit to traduce much that is good or useful in professions, and
> expose it to ridicule, than to discover and sever that which is vicious
> and corrupt. But Solomon says well, 'A scorner seeks wisdom, and
> finds it not, but knowledge offers itself unto him that is desirous
> thereof'; for he who comes to seek after knowledge with a mind to
> scorn and censure will be sure to find matter enough for his humor,
> but very little for his instruction. But the serious handling of this
> argument with integrity and sincerity ought, as it appears to me, to
> be reckoned among the best fortifications for honesty and virtue. For
> as the fable goes of the basilisk, that if he see you first, you die for it, but
> if you see him first, he dies; so it is with deceits, impostures, and evil
> arts, which, if they be first espied, they lose their life, but if they
> prevent, they endanger. . . .[65]

After all, Bacon writes, "the politician, as such, must study
human nature as it is, its vices with the rest, and take things as
they are, not as they ought to be."

Perhaps there is no better testimony concerning the value which
Bacon attaches to ethical proof and to the preservation of the

---

[64] De aug., VIII, 2, Works, V, 67.   [65] Works, V, 17.

speaker's reputation and authority than his condemnation of invective. "Speech of touch towards others should be sparingly used; for discourse ought to be as a field, without coming home to any man." [66] The effect of invective, in debates especially, is that no man comes off with a good character. In a speech relative to the undertakers in Ireland, Bacon declares: "if ye fret and gall one another's reputation, the end will be, that every man shall go hence, like coin cried down, of less price than he came hither." [67] The same attitude is apparent in Bacon's criticism of those Puritan preachers and Anglican ecclesiastics who, in the latter part of Elizabeth's reign, carried on a pamphlet war. He commends the tactics of one bishop who refrained from attacking his opponent's character: ". . . I do much esteem the wisdom and religion of that bishop which replied to the first pamphlet of this kind, who remembered that *a fool was to be answered, but not by becoming like unto him;* and considered the matter that he handled, and not the person with whom he dealt." [68]

Not only does invective tarnish reputation, but inconsiderate and untimely speech is just as effective in destroying authority. This holds true particularly of preaching and of the clergy whose chief claim to authority rests on the implicit identification by which laymen habitually refer the preacher to the ultimate divine authority. To break down this habit of identification on the part of one's parishioners is to lose the chief source of religious persuasion. Bacon perceived this, and his diagnosis of the ills which beset the established church in the latter part of the sixteenth century comes down to one chief cause: the loss of authority and reputation on the part of the Anglican clergy. By entering into ill-considered controversy, by setting themselves up as authorities in their own right, and by rhetorical displays which endeavored to cater to the fashion of the time, the Anglican Church had in effect destroyed its birthright:

Concerning the occasion of controversies, it cannot be denied that the imperfections in the conversation and government of those which have chief place in the church have ever been principal causes and

---

[66] *Of Discourse, Works,* VI, 456.   [67] *Letters and Life,* V, 44.
[68] *An Advertisement Touching the Controversies of the Church of England, Letters and Life,* I, 77.

motives of schisms and divisions. For whilst the bishops and governors of the church continue full of knowledge and good works; whilst they feed the flock indeed; whilst they deal with the secular states in all liberty and resolution, according to the majesty of their calling, and the precious care of souls imposed upon them; so long the church *is situate as it were upon an hill;* no man maketh question of it, or seeketh to depart from it. But when these virtues in the fathers and leaders of the church have lost their light, and that they wax worldly, *lovers of themselves,* and *pleasers of men,* then men begin to grope for the church as in the dark; . . . they can never speak *tanquam auctoritatem habentes;* as having authority, because they have lost their reputation in the consciences of men, by declining their steps from the way which they trace out to others.[69]

Perhaps a fitting conclusion to this discussion of pathetic and ethical "proof" would consist in a statement of the sources to which Bacon would send the speaker or the rhetorician who sought to inform himself on characters and dispositions. Two general sources of information are available: men in action, and books. For all knowledge of men "may be derived and obtained in six ways; by their countenances and expressions, their words, their actions, their dispositions, their ends, and lastly by the reports of others." [70]

As far as observation is concerned, Bacon advises the speaker to disregard the old adage, "Trust not to a man's face," for "though this may not be wrongly said of the general outward carriage of the face and action, yet there are some more subtle motions and labours of the eyes, mouth, countenance, and gesture, by which . . . the 'door of the mind,' is unlocked and opened." [71] The speaker must, above all, observe the actions and speech of men that he may perceive *"the different characters of natures and dispositions."* [72] By this Bacon means that observation is not to be limited solely to men's virtues and vices, their disorders and passions which block the rule of reason, but also those characters which are determined by the vocation a man follows. A student of human nature, furthermore, must observe those characters "which are imposed on the mind by sex, by age, by religion, by health and sickness, by

---

[69] *Ibid.,* 80.   [70] *De aug.,* VIII, 2, *Works,* V, 60.
[71] *Ibid.*   [72] *Ibid.,* VII, 3, *Works,* V, 21.

beauty and deformity, and the like; and again, those which are caused by fortune, as sovereignty, nobility, obscure birth, riches, want, magistracy, privateness, prosperity, adversity, and the like." [73]

The gathering of knowledge by observation, however, has its drawbacks. One is likely to see only particulars and to miss the general laws which would enable him to meet with facility any rhetorical situation:

. . . it is one thing to understand persons, and another thing to understand matters; for many are perfect in man's humours, that are not greatly capable of the real part of business; which is the constitution of one that hath studied men more than books. Such men are fitter for practice than for counsel; and they are good but in their own alley: turn them to new men, and they have lost their aim. . . .[74]

Consequently, books constitute the best source of knowledge on characters. In the *Advancement of Learning* Bacon approves of some writings of the Stoics, such as those on anger, adverse accidents, and tenderness of countenance. Poets and history writers, however, are better authorities, for in their compositions the affections are mirrored in life:

. . . we may find painted forth with great life, how affections are kindled and incited; and how pacified and refrained; and how again contained from act and further degree; and how they disclose themselves, how they work, how they vary, how they gather and fortify, how they are inwrapped one within another, and how they do fight and encounter one with another, and other the like particularities. . . .[75]

The best source of all, so Bacon believes, are the wiser sort of historians, "not only from the commemorations which they commonly add on recording the deaths of illustrious persons, but much more from the entire body of history as often as such a person enters upon the stage; for a character so worked into the narrative gives a better idea of the man, than any formal criticism and review can. . . ." [76]

---

[73] *Ibid.*, 22.
[74] *Of Cunning, Works*, VI, 428.
[75] *Adv. of L., Works*, III, 438.
[76] *De aug.*, VII, 3, *Works*, V, 21.

CHAPTER SIX

THE STRUCTURE

OF

RHETORICAL COMPOSITION

In the endeavor earlier to present Bacon's general view of communication by language,[1] this study set forth his opinions on prose structure. Then, in keeping with Bacon's intent that the "Method" or disposition of a composition should not be wound up in the skirts of dialectic and rhetoric, it seemed improper to apply and adapt his ideas on order and arrangement to any one class of discourse, whether scientific prose or rhetorical address. Taking the hints that he affords in his general account of the Methods of Discourse and employing the allusions that his works contain elsewhere, we shall now sketch his views on the structure and arrangement of rhetorical prose, specifically.

Bacon's ultimate purpose in compiling his Methods of Discourse is to center attention on the conditions and form of expository discourse necessary to advance learning. If learning and knowledge are to progress and grow, then the form of communicating knowledge must serve that end. Through an examination of various forms Bacon suggests that the arrangement of ideas suitable to this purpose is the progressive or aphoristic method. But although he examines his methods with an eye to their appropriateness for the advancement of learning, some of the methods are applicable to the disposition of a rhetorical composition.

[1] Chapter I, 17-24.

The common and accepted methods of discourse Bacon merely names; they are the "Analytic, Systatic, Diaeretic . . . Cryptic, Homeric, and the like." [2] The newer methods of managing discourse he discusses at some length. First, there are the *Magistral* and the *Initiative* methods, the former aiming to teach, the latter to examine and criticize:

> The magistral method teaches; the initiative intimates. The magistral requires that what is told should be believed; the initiative that it should be examined. The one transmits knowledge to the crowd of learners; the other to the sons, as it were, of science. The end of the one is the use of knowledges, as they now are; of the other the continuation and further progression of them.[3]

Second, there are the *Exoteric* and the *Acroamatic* methods. The first uses a way of arrangement more open than is usual, the second a way more secret. Indeed, the Acroamatic method "seems to be by obscurity of delivery to exclude the vulgar (that is the profane vulgar) from the secrets of knowledges, and to admit those only who have either received the interpretation of the enigmas through the hands of teachers, or have wits of such sharpness and discernment as can pierce the veil." [4] Third, there are the schemes called *aphorisms*, and *methods*, the second being a plan of composition that was familiar to educated Elizabethans and used by Bacon himself in the less compact and impersonal essays. "It has become the fashion to make, out of a few axioms and observations upon any subject, a kind of complete and formal art, filling it up with some discourses, illustrating it with examples, and digesting it into method." [5] The method of aphorisms, on the other hand, is compact and condensed; like the essay *Of Studies*, the composition stands without benefit of examples, description, elucidation, and connectives; "there is nothing left to make the aphorisms of but some good quality of observation." Fourth, there are the methods of *assertions with proofs* and of *questions with determinations*. Both aim to establish a case, not merely by using positive or constructive proof, but by placing considerable emphasis upon refutation. Still another method of composition is that whose form

---

[2] *De aug.*, VI, 2, *Works*, IV, 452.
[3] *Ibid.*, 449.   [4] *Ibid.*, 450.   [5] *Ibid.*

is governed by the subject matter handled. Here Bacon perceives that structure is to special subject matter as *special* topics or lines of investigation are to invention. Finally, Bacon recognizes a method of discourse that is markedly influenced by the prejudices and attitudes of the audience addressed.

We may well inquire whether the Magistral and the Initiative methods and their counterparts, the "methods" of continuous discourse and the aphoristic method, relate to the art of influencing conduct by public address. Obviously the Initiative or Progressive method is outside the province of persuasion. The speaker whose thoughts fit this method has the attitude of a critical thinker who, in his speech, not only presents the reasoned judgments that he may have reached, but also exhibits the methods and processes by which he was led to them—all in order that critical listeners may form further judgments of their own. The attitude is made plain by Bacon himself in the preface to the *Great Instauration*, where, referring to the purpose of his great program he says: "I have not sought . . . nor do I seek to force or ensnare men's judgments, but I lead them to things themselves and the concordances of things, that they may see for themselves what they have, what they can dispute, what they can add and contribute to the common stock." [6] Such a speaker has for his purpose to explain, and his work is beyond the province of a rhetoric whose function is the application of reason to imagination for the better moving of the will. Similarly, the aphoristic method, since it aims to explain specialized matter to a special audience, is inappropriate to rhetoric. On the other hand, the speaker who takes the results of critical thought and looks to their practical application and use among men, clearly demonstrates at bottom a persuasive attitude. Though his ostensible and immediate purpose may be to instruct, he is ultimately motivated by a desire to have knowledge prevail and to manifest itself in conduct. He has the attitude toward knowledge that Bacon attributes to rhetoricians, that ". . . howsoever governments have several forms, sometimes one governing, sometimes few, sometimes the multitude; yet the state of knowledge is ever a *Democratie*, and that prevaileth which is most agreeable to the senses and conceits of people." [7] The magistral method, therefore, falls within the

----

[6] *Works*, IV, 19.   [7] *Of the Interpretation of Nature, Works*, III, 227.

scope of rhetoric, and the speaker will employ the customary arrangements of connected discourse in so far as they accord with
his persuasive purpose.

The method of "assertions and proofs" manifestly is a form of
procedure planned expressly for influencing belief and action. The
procedure by "questions and answers," however, probably refers to
the method used by scholars who examine a problem exhaustively.
The aim is to evaluate and explain, with no intention of influencing
belief directly.

With respect to the Exoteric and the Acroamatic kinds of disposition, it is clear that the former, aiming to employ a manner
of discourse more open than usual, may often prove useful to the
speaker when addressing an audience of limited intelligence or information. But the affected obscurity of arrangement that is
characteristic of the acroamatic method can hardly be applicable
to practical rhetoric. Designed to set forth esoteric matters to a
very special group, its end is chiefly expository. In writing his
essay *Of the True Greatness of Britain,* Bacon avowedly seeks to
avoid the Acroamatic method. Because he intends to present history in a true, steady light, he declares that "I will use no hidden
order, which is fitter for insinuations than sound proofs, but a
clear and open order. . . ." [8]

Even the method determined by the subject matter that is presented has its application to rhetoric. A textbook in mathematics,
Bacon points out, is set forth far differently from a textbook in
political theory, and hence he recognizes that there must be particular methods for transmitting knowledge, just as there are
particular topics for invention. It follows, therefore, that if
rhetoric may be held to have as its subject matter the received
opinions of men, then the disposition of a speech, obviously enough,
depends to some extent upon the forms which men use in discussing
everyday affairs. Perhaps the simplest form of disposition, then,
will be the Aristotelean formula: state the case, and prove it.
Such a formula is not irrelevant to Bacon's observation that "those
whose conceits are seated in popular opinions need only but to
prove or dispute." [9] In deliberative speeches, arrangement and
order are influenced often by arguments of degree, because "in de-

[8] *Works,* VII, 48.   [9] *Adv. of L., Works,* III, 406.

liberatives the point is, what is good and what is evil, and of good what is greater, of evil what is the less." [10]

The procedure that is determined by the anticipations, presuppositions, and knowledge of the audience, obviously has its rhetorical bearing, though Bacon discusses it in relation to the dissemination of scientific learning. The rhetorician, like the scientist, is confronted with an audience that holds preconceived opinions, and to succeed in his purpose must not only select ideas judiciously but also form the pattern of the entire speech so as to circumvent the attitudes or "idols" of the audience. Bacon suggests, also, that the speaker must always consider to what extent his listeners are familiar with the subject of the address. A speaker who wishes to communicate specialized knowledge to a popular group, it is suggested, will have to use a method distinguished by parables and similitudes. The preacher, for example, depends upon frequent parables and tropes in his effort to convey divine meanings.

The method of imposture, a manner of presentation evident in an author who makes a show and ostentation of learning, pertains to rhetoric, we may suppose, in so far as Bacon would exhort the speaker to abstain from sophistry. In general Bacon's theory of rhetoric requires a sincere man who places matter before manner. Hence Bacon would have both orator and writer avoid those species of imposture to which the *Meditationes Sacrae* refer:

There are three kinds of speech, and as it were styles of imposture. The first kind is of those who, as soon as they get any subject-matter, straightway make an art of it, fit it with technical terms, reduce all into distinctions, thence educe positions and assertions, and frame oppositions by questions and answers. Hence the rubbish and pother of the schoolmen. The second kind is of those who through vanity of wit, as a kind of holy poets, imagine and invent all variety of stories and examples, for the training and moulding of people's minds: whence the lives of the fathers, and innumerable figments of the ancient heretics. The third kind is of those who fill everything with mysteries and highsounding phrases, allegories and allusions: which mystic and Gnostic style of discourse a number of heretics have adopted. Of these kinds, the first catches and entangles man's sense and understanding, the second allures, the third astonishes; all seduce it.[11]

_____

[10] *Colours, Works,* VII, 77.   [11] *Works,* VII, 250-251.

Finally, some of those methods that Bacon alludes to as "vulgar and received" and as having been customarily used in continuous discourse are manifestly appropriate to the ordering of rhetorical compositions. Doubtless Bacon would have described them had he fully treated of rhetorical structure. The two complimentary methods, the Analytic and the Systatic, could be employed by any speaker or writer. If he used the former, he would proceed from particular statements and examples to their general implications, probably stopping short of explicitly enunciating his general conclusion or theme. Thus he would lead his audience to think somewhat critically and speculatively with him. If he adopted the Systatic or synthetic arrangement, he would start out his composition with an explicit statement of the generalizations that underlie his theme, and then proceed to explain and to deduce their application to his theme. His discourse, in other words, would unfold like a formal syllogism, or a series of syllogisms, in which the major premise first is made clear, is next followed by the minor or particular premise, which, after being adequately discussed, is in turn followed by a complete statement of the conclusion or "point." All parts thus go together to make a neat, deductive whole, sometimes described by the logicians as progressive or compositive, which the hearer tends to accept or reject as a unit, rather than to ruminate over its parts and to discover implications for himself.[12]

---

[12] Exactly what Bacon means by the Analytic and Systatic methods we do not know. The interpretation attempted here is colored by the modern logician's conception of them. If we could be certain that Bacon, as a rhetorician, were more of a medievalist than a modern, his understanding of the two methods would be nearer that of Hemmingsen who admittedly leaned upon Melanchthon. Hemmingsen's explanation of the Analytic and Systatic orders is nearly the reverse of that set forth above: "The Sintheticall exposition is when we begin, with those things that go before the matter, and by little and little, by certain steppes and degrees do put them together, and lay them on a heape, until all those thinges do seeme to be gathered, which are sufficient to discusse the nature of the thing. . . . On this wise Synthesis doth followe the order of nature, and findeth out, expoundeth, proueth and confirmeth all those questions that naturally go before, and doth by contraries, examples, similitudes and dissimilitudes, exemplifye them." (*The Preacher*, 33-34.) The "Analyticall Kind" of progression, on the other hand, is "when wee begin from the whole, or from the ende, and afterwards finde out the partes, and those thinges which are rendered to the ende by an order, cleane contrary to the former. . . ." (*Ibid.*, 34) Apparently

The speaker or the writer might make use of another traditional pattern of arrangement, the Diaeretical. Although this method is held to be especially appropriate to expository discourse, particularly to the explanation of scriptural meanings, it may be readily adapted to rhetorical discourse. In applying the Diaeretical method, an author would start out with a general definition or a general principle, to be succeeded immediately with its divisions or its partition into the several heads or points. He would then amplify his discussion by pointing out the causes and the effects of the general principle, after which he would turn to treat of the ways in which the theme applies to the lives of his hearers. As the last step, he would discuss what the general theme did not mean, by developing its logical contrary.[13]

Rhetorical address may make use of one more traditional arrangement. It is the great "Methode" that had come to be identified as Ramean. Although its dependence upon dichotomy renders it dangerous for the exact scientist who is passing on his knowledge to another scientist, the scheme may be justly applicable to popular discourse. In pursuing it, the speaker or the writer moves through successive steps in division, from his most general proposition to his special details; and simultaneously, as he funnels down to the special, he progresses from what is clearest and most evident to his audience, to what is new, obscure, and least evident. Among the logics of the sixteenth century, probably Wotton's translation of Ramus contains the best short statement of the procedure:

The methode is a disposition by the which amonge many propositions of one sorte, and by their disposition knowen, that thing which is absolutely most cleare is first placed, and secondly that which is next:

Hemmingsen means that a writer starts with his definition or with the final conclusion that he wishes his audience to accept; thus, it is his general definition or his explicit theme that is the "whole" or "ende." He then follows Melanchthon's "order" by amplifying the theme with further definitions, with references to causes or "reasons why," along with division and sub-division into other "partes" and "duties."

[13] Hemmingsen concedes that the development of the contrary meaning is not usually restricted to a separate and distinct part of a sermon: "Contraryes haute not certain place, neither in this Methode, nor in others, but are to be dispersed heare and there, for illustration and amplifications sake. For Rhetoricians do thinck that nothing maketh a thing so plaine and easye, as the conferring of thinges which are contrary." (*Preacher*, 33.)

and therfore it contynually procedethe from the most generall to the
speciall and singuler. By this methode we proceade from the ante-
cedent more absolutely knowen to proue the consequent, which is not
so manifestly knowen. . . .

The chiefe examples of the methode are found in artes and sciences:
in the which although the rules be all generall, yet they are distinct
by there degres: for euery thing as it is more generall is first placed.
The most generall therefore shalbe first placed: then next shall
followe these which be immediatly contained under the general, euery
one orderly unto the most speciall which shalbe last disposed. The
definition therefore as most generall, shalbe first placed: next fol-
loweth the distribution, which yf it be manifold, and of diuers sortes
shalbe first diuided into his integrall partes, next unto his formes and
kindes. And euery part and forme shalbe placed and described in the
same order & place which he had in his diuision.[14]

Wotton declares that Ramus's *Dialectic* conscientiously conformed to such an arrangement; and it is not uninteresting to observe that Bacon himself, though deprecating the method in
scientific exposition, employs it in the second book of the *Advancement of Learning*. Seeking to win the support of the King and of
all learned men, the work is essentially rhetorical, and Bacon seems
to have felt that he could utilize the Ramean method with pro-
priety. His hierarchy of learning, accordingly, is presented by dividing and sub-dividing the introductory generalization. After
opening with the general position that both human and divine learning consist of History, Poesy, and Philosophy, corresponding to
man's Memory, Imagination, and Reason, he divides each subject
into its species, sub-species, and appendices, in order that each in
its proper place may be discussed even unto its particularities.
Nevertheless, in adopting the Ramean method for the second part
of his persuasive document, he does not let it "press" and warp the
subject as did the strict Rameans who, "when a thing does not
aptly fall into those dichotomies, either pass it by or force it out
of its natural shape." [15] He allows his categories to overlap, and
thus modifies the method wherever it interferes with convenience
and truth.

That the structure of rhetorical prose is a function of the cir-

---

[14] *The Logike of P. Ramus*, 94.   [15] *De aug.*, VI, 2, *Works*, IV, 448.

cumstances of address Bacon is almost self-consciously aware, particularly in his letters and speeches. Many of these not only draw attention to the method of disposition he himself is using at the moment, but at the same time they remark upon the method in such a way as to suggest the inevitable relationship between the *selection* of what is to be said to a particular audience, and the order and form in which it is presented.

The problem of selection forever confronts both the speaker and the writer; indeed, so Bacon suggests in *Short Notes for Civil Conversation,* "to desire in discourse to hold all arguments, is ridiculous, wanting true judgment. . . ." [16] Furthermore, selection is accomplished with one eye on one's audience, an undertaking that Bacon, in writing the *Articles Touching the Union of the Kingdoms,* was conscious of:

> . . . my purpose is only to break this matter of the Union into certain short articles and questions; and to make a certain kind of anatomy or analysis of the parts and members thereof. Not that I am of opinion that all the questions which I now shall open were fit to be in the consultation of the Commissioners propounded. For I hold nothing so great an enemy to good resolution as the making of too many questions; especially in assemblies which consist of many.[17]

In a speech before the House of Commons Bacon refers to both the process of selection and to one of its criteria: "And for my part I mean to observe the true course to give strength to this cause, which is by yielding those things which are not tenable, and keeping the question within the true state and compass; which will discharge many popular arguments, and contract the debate into less room. . . ." [18] Finally, in advising Mr. Phillips how to handle the Earl of Essex, Bacon is concerned with the selection of content and its manner of expression:

> I send you the copy of my letter to the Earl touching the matter between us proposed. You may perceive what expectation and conceit I thought good imprint into my Lord both of yourself and of his par-

---

[16] *Works,* VII, 109.   [17] *Letters and Life,* III, 219.

[18] Speech concerning the King's right to Impositions, *Letters and Life,* IV, 191. This speech affords a fine example of excluding the untenable and irrelevant.

ticular service. . . . The more plainly and frankly you shall deal with my Lord, not only in disclosing particulars, but in giving him *caveats* and admonishing him of any error which in this action he may commit (such is his Lordship's nature) the better he will take it.[19]

That the arrangement and sequence of what the speaker has elected to say is influenced by the audience and occasion is compellingly indicated by Bacon's various bits of advice for the proper handling of special groups and situations. Out of his own practice he points out that speaking to the Commons assembled is not the same as speaking in committee, for "speech in the House is fit to persuade the general point, and particularity is more proper and seasonable for the committee." [20] Yet, to speak to the general point, Bacon admonishes, is often done at the expense of perspicuity and simplicity; "if we speak in general, it will be temptation to lead men to ingratiate themselves, sometimes for favor, often for fame . . . and to speak as orators only, and not as lawmakers." [21] Consequently, he advises the political orator to employ a formal partition of his points and to order the entire speech strictly.[22]

Many of the methods of discourse which Bacon names, then, are seen to have specific applications to rhetorical address, and might be described as rhetorical plans constituting the main order or pattern of a composition. But what is more important to rhetoric than the applicability of speech plans to rhetorical situations is the basic principle of rhetorical form which may be derived from the *Wisdom of Transmission*. It has been seen that Bacon's conception of the method or form of discourse is essentially functional, *i.e.*, order, pattern, and arrangement are controlled by the purpose of communication. As a result, it may be expected that Bacon's conception of speech form will be also functional in character. The end of rhetoric is to move men, and the form of the speech will be that which accomplishes that purpose—a purpose, it must

---

[19] Letter to Mr. Phillips, *Letters and Life,* I, 252.

[20] Speech on the Subsidy Bill, 1598, *Letters and Life,* II, 86.

[21] From notes by R. Cotton of Bacon's speech on November 25, 1606, *Letters and Life,* III, 303.

[22] *Ibid.* If we may accept Cotton's report of the speech, Bacon acted on his own advice. (*Ibid.,* 304.)

be observed, that implicitly and necessarily takes into consideration an audience. Such a form, called into being by a persuasive
end, is organically related to the audience, the occasion, and the
speaker.

Bacon realizes that the attitudes and prejudices of an audience
will influence disposition. Where a group is hostile, for example,
an indirect order and method of procedure is often best: "In things
that are tender and unpleasing, it is good to break the ice by some
whose words are of less weight, and to reserve the more weighty
voice to come in as by chance. . . ." [23] Bacon knew one man who,
when confronted with an unfavorable situation and "came to have
speech, he would pass over that that he intended most; and go
forth, and come back again, and speak of it as of a thing that
he had almost forgot. . . ." [24] Bacon seems to feel, moreover, that
most audiences are to be dealt with in the way that he urges the
practical teacher of ethics to correct conduct:

. . . the mind is brought to anything with more sweetness and happi-
ness, if that whereunto you pretend be not first in the intention, but
be obtained as it were by the way while you are attending to something else; because of the natural hatred of the mind against necessity
and constraint.[25]

Whenever the speaker thinks that the audience holds objections
to his proposed course, it is probably best to deal with the objections at the outset of the speech, or at least near the beginning.
To this arrangement Bacon alludes (in a tract which advises James
to call a Parliament), saying that ". . . because it is first in nature
to remove impediments and then to use advantages, I will speak
first of the impediments or errors, and then of the advantages." [26]
A speech which does not anticipate objections and seek to meet
them is, to Bacon, little better than a speech which is entirely
refutative in character: "A long continued speech, without a good
speech of interlocution, sheweth slowness; and a good reply, without a good set speech, showeth shallowness and weakness." [27] The
reasoning power of an audience and its ability to judge strictly on

[23] *Of Cunning, Works,* VI, 429.   [24] *Ibid.*
[25] *De aug.,* VII, 3, *Works,* V, 25. Cf. *Adv. of L., Works,* III, 439-440.
[26] *Letters and Life,* V, 177.
[27] *Short Notes for Civil Conversation, Works,* VII, 110.

the matter at issue may also determine whether the order and
sequence of a speech is loose or well-articulated. Of this point
Bacon reminds the King in advising him concerning the conduct
of Somerset's trial; he insists that the evidence must be "well spun
and woven together. For your Majesty knoweth it is one thing to
deal with a jury of Middlesex and Londoners, and another to deal
with the Peers; whose objects perhaps will not be so much what
is before them in the present case . . . but what may be hereafter." [28]
Sometimes even the station in society of the speaker himself will
determine the form of presentation most appropriate on a given
occasion. When Bacon and Archbishop Whitgift collaborated in
writing for Elizabeth a brief defense of her ecclesiastical settlement, Bacon held that narration better suited the monarch than
argument, and according he writes to Whitgift:

> I have considered the objections, perused the statutes, and framed
> the alterations, which I send; still keeping myself within the brevity
> of a letter and form of a narration; not entering into a form of argu-
> ment or disputation: For in my poor conceit it is somewhat against
> the majesty of princes' actions to make too curious and striving apolo-
> gies; but rather to set them forth plainly, and so as there may appear
> an harmony and constancy in them, so that one part upholdeth an-
> other.[29]

The functional nature of rhetorical form is suggested, also, by
Bacon's discussion of the introduction and conclusion as parts
of a composition. He clearly appreciates that these two speech
divisions are made necessary by the audience and the occasion, and
hence influence the structure of a rhetorical utterance. His position
here emerges from his criticism of contemporary speakers who
have over-valued the introduction. He censures those who "study
more diligently the prefaces and inducements than the conclusions
and issues." [30] He seems to minimize the value of introductions because they prevent one from coming speedily to the argument:
"Prefaces and passages, and excusations, and other speeches of
reference to the person, are great wastes of time; and though they
seem to proceed of modesty, they are bravery." [31] But though he

---

[28] *Letters and Life,* V, 231.   [29] *Letters and Life,* I, 96.
[30] *De aug.,* VIII, 2, *Works,* V, 41.   [31] *Of Dispatch, Works,* VI, 435.

may appreciate that an introduction hinders dispatch, the speaker must "beware of being too material when there is any impediment or obstruction in men's wills; for pre-occupation of mind ever requireth preface of speech; like a fomentation to make the unguent enter." [32] Conclusions, on the other hand, so advance the speaker's business that they should be carefully prepared in advance. They may relate to the matter in hand, or be composed of any matter which can be "conveniently and gracefully" used. Indeed, Bacon insists that speakers plan and anticipate their conclusions:

. . . they ought to have [them] ready prepared and arranged at hand; considering within themselves and endeavoring as much as possible to anticipate what shall be the end of their speech, and how their business may be advanced and ripened thereby. Nor is this all; for it is not only proper to study perorations and conclusions of such speeches as relate to the business itself, but also to be prepared with some discourse which may be convenient and gracefully thrown in at the close, although foreign to the matter at hand.[33]

Conclusions are not always necessary, at least in forensic speaking to which Bacon is alluding in the single sentence that closes his argument against the Earl of Somerset for poisoning:

It hath . . . formerly at arraignments been a custom after the King's counsel and the prisoner's defence hath been heard, briefly to sum up what hath been said: but in this we have been so formal in the distribution that I do not think it necessary.[34]

Finally, the form and order of a speech depend to a certain extent upon its medium of communication, upon its being oral speech rather than written language. To maintain the audience's attention and interest, variety of subject matter is essential to the speech as a whole; and where content varies, the order and sequence of ideas is of course affected to some extent:

The honourablest part of talk is to give the occasion. . . . It is good, in discourse and speech of conversation, to vary and intermingle speech of the present occasion with arguments, tales with reasons, asking of questions with telling of opinions, and jest with earnest; for it is a dull thing to tire, and, as we say now, to jade, anything too far.[35]

---

[32] *Ibid.*
[34] *Letters and Life,* V, 334.
[33] *De aug.,* VIII, 2, *Works,* V, 41.
[35] *Of Discourse, Works,* VI, 455.

If a speaker is to fit his remarks to the situation, he must not be too dependent on commonplace patterns that he cannot adapt to the occasion, for "to have common places to discourse, and to want variety, is both tedious to the hearers, and shows a shallowness of conceit: therefore it is good to vary and suit speeches with the present occasions. . . ."[36] Furthermore, the continued repetition of any one idea or formula has no more effect on an audience than the repetition of a moral precept on an individual:

> In my judgment it would be an opinion more flattering than true, to think any medicine can be so sovereign or so happy as that the simple use of it can work any great cure. It were a strange speech, which spoken once, or even spoken many times, should reclaim a man from a vice to which he is by nature subject. The thing is impossible. It is order, pursuit, sequence, and skilful interchange of application, which is mighty in nature.[37]

It may be clear that Bacon's remarks on rhetoric contain definite evidence that the disposition of a speech—its order and form—depends ultimately upon the function of rhetoric itself. Rhetoric as the Illustration of Discourse recommends reason to the imagination for the moving of men's wills, and rhetorical address, if it is to fulfill this function, must so arrange, handle, and form its arguments that its audience is won to consent or to action. Bacon would not have the speaker and the writer forget that "order is a matter of illustration. . . ."[38] The disposition of a speech, in other words, is organic with the purpose that it is to accomplish, with the audience, and with the occasion. This, it appears, represents Bacon's fundamental view on disposition, and those methods of arrangement which Bacon discusses under the "Doctrine of Method" may be regarded, from the writer's and the speaker's point of view, as schemes of disposition which apply, not merely to scientific discourse, but to more inclusive forms of public address.

---

[36] *Short Notes, Works,* VII, 109.
[37] *De aug.,* IV, 2, *Works,* IV, 389.
[38] *Adv. of L., Works,* III, 357.

CHAPTER SEVEN

STYLE

By style the modern theorist ordinarily means the *manner* in which words are used to convey meaning, and under "manner" he ordinarily comprehends such processes as the choice of words and their arrangement so as to convey meaning clearly and appropriately. He customarily holds, moreover, that such a manner of expression is dependent on the type of discourse attempted, on the temperament of the author, and on the environmental and historical influences impinging upon the creator. Bacon's works contain very little material that bears directly on style in general, and still less that pertains to oratorical style. But wherever Bacon employs the term "style," it carries its customary meaning. Bacon's chief interest in style, however, seems to center on three qualities: clearness, appropriateness, and agreeableness. There are, in Bacon's works, a number of references to the appropriateness of style as dictated by subject matter and as governed by the function of both the generic art of composition and its species. One finds, moreover, independent of the notion of appropriateness, that words ought always to be used clearly and agreeably, and that an author, irrespective of his subject, his art, and even his own nature, ought to convey his meaning with perspicuity and with pleasantness. Accordingly, Bacon recognizes, either explicitly or implicitly, that the style of public address should be clear and pleasant, and consonant with its rhetorical function. In these respects, however, Bacon's observations remain on a general level; rarely are there rules of thumb.

Rawley, in his life of Bacon, writes that Bacon would "often ask if the meaning were expressed plainly enough, as being one that accounted words to be but subservient or ministerial to matter. . . ." [1] Rawley's testimony, accordingly, constitutes indirect evidence that Bacon, if he preached what he practiced, would advise the speaker to speak plainly. Bacon's extant speeches, furthermore, bear evidence that he successfully carried out his intention to express himself clearly. Sentences are short; words are used accurately, and the few Latin quotations that appear were undoubtedly as familiar to the audience as their English equivalents. Coherence, also, is usually excellent. But the evidence which establishes clearness as the basic element in style—whether it be literary or oratorical—is Bacon's idea that Grammar, "the harbinger of the sciences," exists fundamentally to render language clear.

Bacon holds that the historical justification of grammar has been to overcome the confusion of meanings that arose with the first confusion of tongues. Grammar must not be esteemed of little dignity:

> . . . it serves for an antidote against the curse of the confusion of tongues. For man still strives to renew and reintegrate himself in those benedictions of which by his fault he has been deprived. And as he arms and defends himself against the first general curse of the barrenness of the earth, and of eating bread in the sweat of his face, by the invention of all other arts; so against this second curse of the confusion of tongues he calls in the aid of Grammar. . . . [2]

Of modern grammar, moreover, the two parts, Literary and Philosophical, have as their chief purpose the clear and precise rendering of meanings. Literary grammar refers to the practical use of languages only, "that they may be learned more quickly or spoken more correctly and purely." [3] Philosophical grammar, on the other hand, attempts a comparative study of languages in order that through them mankind may discover information "concerning the dispositions and manners of peoples and nations," [4] and may arrive at the most explicit and beautiful word for the rendering of a thought:

---

[1] *Works,* I, 11.   [2] *De aug.,* VI, 1, *Works,* IV, 440-441.

[3] *Ibid.,* 441.   [4] *Ibid.,* 441-442.

. . . the noblest species of **grammar** . . . would be this: if some one well seen in a great number of tongues, learned as well as vulgar, would handle the various properties of *languages;* showing in what points each excelled, in what it failed. For . . . so may languages be enriched by mutual exchanges, . . . the several beauties of each may be combined (as in the Venus of Apelles) into' a most beautiful image and excellent model of speech itself, for the right expressing of the meanings of the mind.[5]

It is noteworthy that the standard of beauty creeps, as it were, into the passage. But the emphasis here is what Rawley noted concerning the ministerial function of words: "the right expressing of the meanings of the mind."

That style should conform to matter, Bacon makes clear when he takes to task the writers in the Marprelate controversy, who insist on expressing religious matters in the style of the stage:

. . . it is more than time that there were an end and surseance made of this immodest and deformed manner of writing lately entertained, whereby matters of religion are handled in the style of the stage. Indeed, bitter and earnest writing may not hastily be condemned; for men cannot contend coldly and without affection about things which they hold dear and precious. A politic man may write from his brain, without touch and sense of his heart, as in a speculation that pertaineth not unto him; but a feeling Christian will express in his words a character either of zeal or love. The latter of which as I could wish rather embraced, being more fit for these times, yet is the former warranted also by great examples. But to leave all reverent and religious compassion towards evils, or indignation towards faults, and to turn religion into a comedy or satire; to search and rip up wounds with a laughing countenance; to intermix Scripture and scurrility sometime in one sentence; is a thing far from the devout reverence of a Christian, and scant beseeming the honest regard of a sober man. . . . ; *there is no greater confusion, than the confounding of jest and earnest.* The majesty of religion, and the contempt and deformity of things ridiculous, are things as distant as things may be.[6]

---

[5] *Ibid.*

[6] *An Advertisement Touching the Controversies in the Church of England, Letters and Life,* I, 76-77. Bacon's recognition, in the quotation above, that there is a style of the brain and a style of the heart is repeated in a speech against the repeal of an act designed to prevent the misapplication of hospital

The same notion that style should be consonant with subject matter appears in Bacon's suggestions and hints for the writing of a Natural History. One who would write on this subject properly selects his ideas carefully, rejects others, and then expresses his thought regardless of the pleasure of the reader; ". . . in a great work it is no less necessary that what is admitted should be written succinctly than that what is superfluous should be rejected; though no doubt this kind of chastity and brevity will give less pleasure both to the reader and the writer." [7] The historian, accordingly, will dispense with the beauties and graces of style:

> And for all that concerns ornaments of speech, similitudes, treasury of eloquence, and such like emptinesses, let it be utterly dismissed. Also let all those things which are admitted be themselves set down briefly and concisely, so that they may be nothing less than words. For no man who is collecting and storing up materials for ship-building or the like, thinks of arranging them elegantly, as in a shop, and displaying them so as to please the eye. . . .[8]

Finally, the conformity of style to content is again apparent in Bacon's own comment upon the style of his treatise, *A Discourse Concerning the Plantation of Ireland*. The style, he states at the beginning, is "a style of business, rather than curious and elaborate." [9] Indeed for the transaction of business the "simpler words are wanted." [10]

On the basis of these remarks concerning the general relation obtaining between content and manner of expression, it would appear that the style of address, in one respect at least, should conform to the subject matter with which it deals. This relationship seems to mean, also, that the quality of content that is evident in any speech is mirrored in the style. If a wise man speaks, his lan-

---

and university revenues. Townshend reports Bacon as saying: "I speak . . . out of the very strings of my heart; which doth alter my ordinary form of speech; for I speak not now out of the fervency of my brain. . . ." (*Letters and Life*, III, 38.)

[7] *Aphorisms on the Composition of the Primary History, Works*, IV, 255.

[8] *Ibid.*, 254.   [9] *Letters and Life*, IV, 114.

[10] *De aug.*, VI, 1, *Works*, IV, 442. In his dedicatory epistle to the King, Bacon refers to the style of his introductory address: " . . . let us discuss the question solidly and distinctly, in a style active and masculine, without digressing or dilating." (*De aug.*, II, *Works*, IV, 284.)

guage is precise and compact, but if a fool speaks, one notices with
Bacon that "words and discourse abound most where there is
idleness and want." [11]

Clearness and adaptation to content, however, do not suffice for
a good rhetorical style. Manner of expression also must be appropriate to the function of rhetoric and to its various species.

If rhetoric is to apply reason to imagination for the better moving of the will, a speaker must realize that what will stimulate the
imagination of one audience will not suffice for all. He must constantly adapt his language to the intellects of his hearers:

> For the proofs and demonstrations of logic are the same to all men;
> but the proofs and persuasions of rhetoric ought to differ according to
> the auditors; . . . the application and variety of speech, in perfection
> of idea, ought to extend so far, that if a man should speak of the same
> thing to several persons, he should nevertheless use different words
> to each of them. . . . [12]

The adaptation of language to the auditors, however, goes beyond
the level of mere understanding. The style of the speech must be
such as to move the imagination to the support of reason rather
than the passions. Hence, the orator will avoid using "barbarous
words, of no sense, lest they should disturb the imagination" and
move it in the wrong direction; he will try, on the contrary, to
employ "words of similitude, that may second and feed the imagination," and also "Scripture words; for that the belief that religious texts and words have power, and may strengthen the imagination." [13] By words of similitude Bacon may mean to include
figures and tropes, but he does not explicitly name them.

The style of the speech is appropriate not only as it conforms
to the function of the art of rhetoric, but also as it conforms to any
species of discourse that a speaker may undertake. The forensic
orator, particularly the judge, has a style of speech imposed on
him by his office, a circumstance to which Bacon alludes in his
speech that lays down the lines and portraitures of a good judge
for the benefit of Justice Hutton upon his admittance to the Court
of Common Pleas. Of the eleven precepts that Bacon formulates,

---

[11] *Adv. of L., Works,* III, 451. [12] *De aug.,* VI, 3, *Works,* IV, 457-458.
[13] All three quotations are from *Sylva sylvarum,* Century X, *Works,* II, 657.

one states "that your speech be with gravity, as one of the sages of the law; and not talkative, nor with impertinent flying out to shew learning." [14] The deliberative speaker or Parliamentarian also has a style of his own, as Bacon points out in a speech to the Commons: "let your speeches in the House be the speeches of counsellors, and not of orators; let your committees tend to dispatch, not to dispute. . . ." [15] The scholar or divine, furthermore, does not speak like the politician or the lawyer. In the introduction of his charge against Owen for treason, Bacon asserts that he "will not argue nor speak like a divine or scholar (I am scholar enough to know the disadvantage), but as a man bred in civil life. . . ." [16] Finally, we notice that Zebedaeus, the protagonist in Bacon's dialogue on a Holy War, declares of his manner of expression: "Your lordships will not look for a treatise from me, but a speech of consultation; and in that brevity and manner will I speak." [17] It is apparent, consequently, that Bacon thinks of each species of rhetorical discourse as having a style of its own.

Principally because of Bacon's hints for the writing of natural history, those scholars interested in the development of prose style suggest that the Lord Chancellor favors what Professor Croll calls an Attic, "essay" or "philosophical" style of expression, rather than a Ciceronian, "oratorical" manner of composition.[18] Bacon is associated with that character of style known as the *genus humile*, rather than with that of the *genus grande;* he is held

---

[14] *Letters and Life,* VI, 202.

[15] *Letters and Life,* VII, 179. Bacon's essay *Of Dispatch* gives suggestions for the expediting of Parliamentary speaking.

[16] *Letters and Life,* V, 161.

[17] *Advertisement Touching a Holy War, Works,* VII, 28.

[18] For an understanding of the broad development of prose style, the studies of Croll and of Hendrickson are indispensable. See M. W. Croll, "Attic Prose in the Seventeenth Century," *Studies in Philology,* XVIII (1921), 79-128, "Attic Prose: Lipsius, Montaigne, Bacon," *Schelling Anniversary Papers* (New York, 1923), Muret and the History of Attic Prose, *Publications of the Modern Language Association,* XXXIX (1924), 254-309; and G. L. Hendrickson, "Origin and Meaning of the Characters of Style," *American Journal of Philology,* XXVI (1905), 248-290, "The Peripatetic Mean of Style and the Three Stylistic Characters," *Ibid.,* XXV (1904), 125-146. Cf. R. F. Jones, "Science and Prose Style in the Third Quarter of the Seventeenth Century," *Publications of the Modern Language Association,* XLV (1930), 977-1009.

to be more concerned with the figures of thought—the metaphor, aphorism, antithesis, and paradox—than with the sonorous schemes that appeal more directly to the ear, such as isocolon, parison, and paromion. It must be observed, however, that Bacon, so far as one can deduce his theory of style, by no means commits himself in precept or in practice to a single "character" of language expression. Although he seems to have influenced, as will be evident later, the founders of the Royal Society in favor of simple, concise syntactical patterns and of denotative diction in their writing and speaking, he clearly sees that the natural and witty aspects of the *genus humile* when applied generally can become as distasteful, affected, and vain as the Ciceronian ornamentation against which Erasmus, Muret, and Montaigne were in rebellion. He sees, as a distemper of learning, not only the watery and flowery vein of Carr and Ascham and other Ciceronians, but also the studied and tortured conciseness of the antithesis and the paradox of those who would unintelligently copy Seneca, Tactitus, and Pliny.[19]

Bacon's own practice in writing, furthermore, cannot be neatly fitted into the style of the *genus humile*. The later Essays are far from being concise, pointed, and antithetical; copious in illustrations, they are discursive rather than compact. And although the early Essays are often brief, studiously balanced, and aphoristic, it is doubtful that Bacon thus wrote because he had become a disciple of Attic prose; rather, he thought of himself as a scientist in morals, collecting observations on conduct and affairs for the observation and criticism of others; he was handing on the lamp and used such a style, not because he was rebelling against Ciceronian elegance, but because he thought the manner appropriate to his purpose and to his subject matter. Between the two books of the *Novum organum* there is a similar difference in style, and the difference seems attributable to the same cause. In the *Advancement* and its later translation, no one fails to observe the radical difference in style, tone, and method when Bacon shifts from his addresses to the King, to his exposition of the divisions of knowledge. The speeches that were written for the revels at Gray's Inn betray

---

[19] *De aug.*, I, *Works*, I, 452.

some of the artificial, balanced periods of Lyly's *Euphues*;[20] so also do some of Bacon's letters, especially those to Elizabeth and James.[21] Indeed, both letters and speeches stand in the strongest contrast to the free-running, conversational narrative of the *New Atlantis*. In brief, if Bacon's style can be said to be that of the *genus humile*, it is only in the sense that this manner of writing represents a simplicity, directness, and clarity of diction, syntax, and disposition that Bacon seems always to aim at. Basically, his style is *functional*, for it reflects his purpose, his material, and his public. Perhaps no scholar since Spedding has seen how many-mannered Bacon is; persistently trying to win acceptance for his great scientific method of discovering nature's laws, he employs various modes of presentation, and in them all he seems never to forget his audience:

... it is in deprecating general objections; in answering, mollifying, conciliating, or contriving to pass by prejudices; in devising prefaces, apologies, modes of putting his case and selecting his audience so as to obtain a dispassionate hearing for it; that we find him, if not chiefly, yet much and anxiously employed.[22]

Although Bacon may be primarily the philosopher, he is also the rhetorician.

But beyond the notion that manner of expression is dependent upon subject matter, upon the function of communication and the species of address, Bacon suggests a further stylistic requirement for the speech. Perhaps it is best described by the term "agreeableness" or "beauty," for, as Bacon states in the essay *Of Discourse*, "to speak agreeably to him with whom we deal, is more than to speak in good words or in good order." [23] The speaker, then, has some concern with what Bacon calls the "Accidents of Grammar," the Sound, Measure, and Accent of words. These have been considered earlier, in conjunction with Bacon's general theory of language communication. It is sufficient merely to repeat here that Bacon's concern for the sound of language leads him to recognize

---

[20] Spedding believes that the authorship of these speeches is beyond question. They may be found in *Letters and Life*, I, 332-342.

[21] *E. g.*, see a short letter to James, *Letters and Life*, IV, 391.

[22] Spedding's preface to *Cogitations de scientia humana*, *Works*, III, 172.

[23] *Works*, VI, 456.

that the combination and pronunciation of sound elements result in sweetness and harshness:

Of these some are common to all nations; for there is no language that does not in some degree shun the hiatus caused by vowels coming together, and the harshnesses caused by consonants coming together. There are others again which are respective, being found pleasing to the ears of some nations and displeasing to others.[24]

Evidently Bacon attached some value to the qualities of speech sounds.

Whether Bacon would encourage a deliberately rhythmical prose is not known. His only explicit discussion of rhythmical feet is very brief, and relates only to verse.[25]

As a conclusion to Bacon's observations on the manner of writing and speaking, it is fitting to cite his comment on James I's style of speech. It contains advice to the student of speech-making who would cultivate his style:

. . . for your gift of speech, I call to mind what Cornelius Tacitus saith of Augustus Caesar; (. . . that his style of speech was flowing and princelike:) for if we note it well, speech that is uttered with labour and difficulty, or speech that savoureth of the affectation of art and precepts, or speech that is framed after the imitation of some pattern of eloquence, though never so excellent,—all this has somewhat servile, and holding of the subject. But your Majesty's manner of speech is indeed prince-like, flowing as from a fountain, and yet streaming and branching itself into nature's order, full of facility and felicity, imitating none and inimitable by any.[26]

---

[24] *De aug.*, VI, 1, *Works*, IV, 443.

[25] When writing of poesy and prosody, Bacon again recognizes the principle that form is appropriate to content. "The Measure of words has produced a vast body of art; namely Poesy, considered with reference not to the matter of it . . . but to the style and form of words: that is to say, metre or verse; wherein the art we have is a very small thing, but the examples are large and innumberable. Neither should that art (which the grammarians call Prosody) be confined to the teaching of the kinds and measures of verse. Precepts should be added as to the kinds of verse which best suit each matter or subject. The ancients used hexameter for histories and eulogies; elegiac for complaints; iambic for invectives; lyric for odes and hymns." *De aug.*, VI, 1, *Works*, IV, 443.

[26] *Adv. of L.*, *Works*, III, 262.

CHAPTER EIGHT

MEMORY

When the speaker has invented his arguments and has tested their logical validity—processes which in Bacon's system are comprehended within the arts of invention and judgment—he must, if ideas are to be communicated, retain them long enough to be delivered. The Art of Memory as the third intellectual art accordingly stands between the Art of Judgment and the Art of Transmission. By placing it thus Bacon suggests that the activities of invention and judgment are completed before the memory begins to function. This is the most important assumption that underlies the brief discussion of memory in the *Advancement of Learning* and the *De augmentis*. Memory is an intellectual phenomenon necessary to the communication of ideas, and comes into operation after the rational processes of invention and judgment have taken place.

But to conceive of the memory as serving primarily the needs of transmitting knowledge does not preclude memory from ministering to other ends. Bacon is well aware that the mental processes of inventing and of judging are impossible without the aid of the memory. Ideas once discovered must be kept in mind long enough to permit inference. The scientist who would interpret nature helps his memory by jotting down his observations in tables from which he adduces general axioms and fundamental laws concerning natural phenomena. Bacon himself follows this practice in the *Novum organum*. Memory, accordingly, is a mental operation which comes into play whenever the mind functions. It may, like the other rational processes of judgment and of invention, attain the dignity of an art; it may be strengthened and developed in conscious accordance with correct principles. As an art, however, it is useful, for it serves to facilitate the invention, the judgment, and the delivery of knowledge.

One who would deliver speeches, like one who would convey ideas in any medium, must give some consideration to the Art of Memory. He must, in other words, study and make use of those expedients which will facilitate the recall of ideas at the moment of utterance.

An important means of aiding recall consists in what Bacon calls "cutting off of infinity of search." [1] A speaker, at the moment of delivery, Bacon explains, must have some "prenotion" of what he is going to say:

. . . when a man desires to recall anything into his memory, if he have no prenotion or perception of that he seeks, he seeks and strives and beats about hither and thither as if in infinite space. But if he have some certain prenotion, this infinity is at once cut off, and the memory ranges in a narrower compass; like the hunting of a deer within an enclosure.[2]

The problem, therefore, is to restrict the mind's wandering. This may be solved in part by order and by "places." Order, the *De Augmentis* states, "manifestly assists the memory." [3] It restricts the mind to a pattern and sequence of ideas. The prenotion, however, is only clear and certain when the idea suits the order, a balance that is nearest perfection in verse. This is why poetry is "more easily learned by heart than prose; for if we stick at any word, we have a prenotion that it must be such a word as fits the verse." [4] Infinity of search, moreover, is cut off by "topics or 'places' in artificial memory." [5] Bacon's explanation of this aid to memory is vague. He suggests that places may "either be *places* in the proper sense of the word, as a door, angle, window, and the like; or familiar and known persons; or any other things at pleasure (provided they be placed in a certain order), as animals, vegetables; words too, letters, characters, historical persons, and the like; although some of these are more suitable and convenient than others." [6] Apparently Bacon here refers to the traditional

---

[1] *De aug.*, V, 5, *Works*, IV, 436.   [2] *Ibid.*
[3] *Ibid.* Cf. *Nov. org.*, *Works*, IV, 162.   [4] *De aug.*, V, 5, *Works*, IV, 436.
[5] *Nov. org.*, *Works*, IV, 162.   [6] *Ibid.*

scheme of rhetoricians, that allows a speaker to select arbitrarily
a visual whole with which the main points or parts of his speech
are associated. The orator may, for example, associate the introduction of his address with the front door of a house, transitions
with halls and passageways, the chief parts of the discussion with
certain rooms, the conclusion with the back door. Thus the order
and sequence of ideas are readily remembered when associated with
the parts of a house. Such a visual aid to memory the speaker may
adopt for his continued use; the "places" to which he relates the
parts of his speech become habitual and fixed, only the ideas or
images which fill the "places" changing from speech to speech, from
occasion to occasion. It is the *habit* of employing a fixed, visual
whole, that suggests in a measure the connection between ideas—
though varying as does the occasion—and the physical order and
place to which they are tied. Accordingly Bacon writes:

. . . prenotion is the principal part of artificial memory. For in artificial memory we have the *places* digested and prepared beforehand; the
images we make extempore according to the occasion. But then we have
a prenotion that the image must be one which has some conformity with
the place; and this reminds the memory, and in some measure paves
the way to the thing we seek.[7]

The aid to memory gained by the use of places is intimately
connected with another help to recall, that of "emblem." Here
Bacon points out that subject-matter relating to concrete objects
of real life is more readily recalled than mere concepts:

Emblem . . . reduces intellectual conceptions to sensible images; for
an object of sense always strikes the memory more forcibly and is more
easily impressed upon it than an object of the intellect; insomuch that
even brutes have their memory excited by sensible impressions; never
by intellectual ones. And therefore you will more easily remember the
image of a hunter pursuing a hare, of an apothecary arranging his
boxes, of a pedant making a speech, of a boy repeating verses from
memory, of a player acting on the stage, than the mere notions of invention, disposition, elocution, memory, and action.[8]

In other words, concepts that have no objective existence can

[7] *De aug.*, V, 5, *Works*, IV, 436-437. Cf. *Adv. of L.*, *Works*, III, 399.
[8] *De aug.*, V, 5, *Works*, IV, 437.

best be remembered by relating them to objects which can be perceived by the senses. Imagery, figures of speech, and "whatever brings the intellectual conception into contact with the sense (which is indeed the method most used in mnemonics) assists the memory." [9]

Another aid to memory consists in a digest of good Commonplaces. ". . . there can hardly be anything more useful even for the old and popular sciences, than a sound help for the memory: that is a good and learned Digest of Common-Places." [10] In spite of contemporary criticism against the practice of making commonplace books, Bacon maintains that, properly used, they strengthen the memory, rather than retard it:

I am aware indeed that the transferring of the things we read and learn into common-place books is thought by some to be detrimental to learning, as retarding the course of the reader and inviting the memory to take holiday. Nevertheless, as it is but a counterfeit thing in knowledge to be forward and pregnant, except a man be also deep and full, I hold diligence and labour in the entry of common places to be a matter of great use and support in studying; as that which supplies matter to invention, and contracts the sight of the judgment to a point. But yet it is true that of the methods and frame-works of common places which I have hitherto seen, there is none of any worth; all of them carrying in their titles merely the face of a school and not of a world; and using vulgar and pedantical divisions, not such as pierce to the pith and heart of things.[11]

Such are the helps to memory, to which Bacon concedes more than a mere mention. Other methods and aids occur in Bacon's works, particularly the *Novum organum*. They are named, but not discussed. Writing, it is observed, strengthens the faculty of recall. In conjunction with writing, the arrangement of a speech into points and focal ideas also helps memory: "a multitude of circumstances or points to take hold of aids the memory; as writing with breaks and divisions, reading or reciting aloud." [12] So also do those ideas which have a strong emotional coloring, those "things which make their impression by way of a strong affection, as by inspiring fear, admiration, shame, delight, assist the mem-

---

[9] *Nov. org., Works*, IV, 163.
[11] *Ibid.*
[10] *De aug.*, V, 5, *Works*, IV, 435.
[12] *Nov. Org., Works*, IV, 163.

ory." [13] Furthermore, "things which are chiefly imprinted when the mind is clear and not occupied with anything else either before or after, as what is learnt in childhood, or what we think of before going to sleep, also things that happen for the first time, dwell longest in the memory." [14] Lastly, the speaker in the actual practice of his speech before delivery should appreciate that the effort to recall ideas, carried on persistently, gradually develops the ease and facility of recall; ". . . things which are waited for and raise the attention dwell longer in the memory than what flies quickly by. Thus, if you read anything over twenty times, you will not learn it by heart so easily as if you were to read it only ten, trying to repeat it between whiles, and when memory failed looking at the book." [15]

In Bacon's works, the only other direct comment on memory as it relates to the communication of knowledge is the recommendation that the type of speaking best suited to develop the student's memory is one in which matter is partly memorized and partly extemporaneous. The contemporary practice of requiring young speakers in the schools and universities to deliver either set declamations or to speak entirely extempore separates too widely the intellectual processes of invention and memory. Such exercises are not practical:

> . . . they make too great a divorce between invention and memory; for their speeches are either premeditate *in verbis conceptis,* where nothing is left to invention, or merely *extemporal,* where little is left to memory: whereas in life and action there is least use of either of these, but rather of intermixtures of premeditation and invention, notes and memory; so as the exercise fitteth not the practice, nor the image the life; and it is ever a true rule in exercises, that they be framed as near as may be to the life of practice; for otherwise they do pervert the motions and faculties of the mind, and prepare them.[16]

In one respect Bacon agrees with the critics of the prevalent system that the art of memorization, especially the practice of repeating mere names, words and mnemonic verses, "may be raised

---

[13] *Ibid.*   [14] *Ibid.*   [15] *Ibid.*

[16] *Adv. of L., Works,* III, 326-327. The translator of *De Augmentis* renders *"in verbis conceptis,"* "delivered in pre-conceived words." See preface "To the King," which precedes Book II, *Works,* IV, 289.

to points of Ostentation prodigious." [17] On the other hand, however, it is not so dangerous to the development of memory as it is barren of intellectual fruit; it is not "dexterous to be applied to the serious use of business and occasions":

And therefore I make no more estimation of repeating a great number of names or words upon once hearing, or the pouring forth of a number of verses or rhymes *ex tempore,* or the making of a satirical simile of every thing, or the turning of every thing to a jest, or the falsifying or contradicting of every thing by cavil . . . than I do of the tricks of tumblers, funambuloes, baladines; the one being the same in the mind that the other is in the body; matters of strangeness without worthiness.[18]

---

[17] *Adv. of L., Works,* III, 398.
[18] *Ibid.*

CHAPTER NINE

DELIVERY

In no instance in Bacon's works is the word "delivery" applied to the oral utterance of ideas, whether in private or in public situations. By delivery Bacon means transmission, and he applies the term to the entire process of communicating thought, regardless of a special medium or a particular form of communication. The writer, whether he be an essayist, a scientist, an historian, or a logician, and the speaker, whether he be publicly addressing an assemblage or discussing privately, both "deliver over" knowledge. Nor, in Bacon's works, is there any instance of the word *pronuntiatio* being employed to denote the utterance of thought. The delivery of a speech as we understand it today or *pronuntiatio* as the ancients employed it is a phase of speech-making to which Bacon does not give explicit and extended discussion. But despite this, one discovers evidence that *pronuntiatio* would merit some attention if Bacon were to construct a rhetorical theory as such. One finds hints for an entire art of declamation, suggestions concerning the most practical type of delivery, and observations on action or gesture.

The *Promus* often contains a few consecutive entries that are related in content, and may perchance constitute the "skeins or bottoms of thread" for an essay which Bacon later intended to develop at length. From Ovid's *Ars amandi*, for example, the following extracts stand together and contain the seeds of a treatise on the art of declamation and delivery:

Keep your strength back, and display no eloquence in your face.

Let your speech be credible, and your words well weighed (but gentle),
that you may seem to speak as one who was present.
He was wont often to relate or repeat the same thing in different man-
ner.
And do not spoil your words by your looks.
Nor let the frenzied poet recite his own works.
Let art simulate chance.
What when a letter defrauded of its lawful sound, and the forced tongue
begins to lisp the sound commanded (desired).[1]

These entries indicate that Bacon did not overlook the art of delivery. He suggests that the reader or orator should not expend
his voice at the beginning of a speech, but conserve his energy for
the places that demand emphasis, that the speaker should try to
impart a sincerity and reality to his utterance so as he "may seem
to speak as one who was present." There is the hint that uncontrolled emotion often defeats effective utterance, a circumstance
that Bacon may have had in mind when he alludes, in a private
memorandum drawn up in mid-life, to a fault in his own delivery.
He must learn, so he writes, "to suppress at once my speaking
wth panting and labor of breath and voyce." [2] The entries hint,
too, that the art of reading or of declamation should produce the
illusion of extempore address.[3] There is then the suggestion that
articulation must not be slovenly nor forced, and that gesture of
countenance and body should suit content.

In addition to the art of delivery which the *Promus* suggests,
the *Short Notes for Civil Conversation* offers advice that is applicable, not merely to conversation, but to all public address, and
reveals Bacon's perception of how the rate of utterance influences
the working of the mind during the delivery:

In all kinds of speech, either pleasant, grave, severe, or ordinary, it
is convenient to speak leisurely, and rather drawlingly, than hastily;

---

[1] This translation is taken from Bacon's *Promus of Formularies and Elegancies*, ed. by Mrs. Henry Pott, 334-336.

[2] *Transportata, Letters and Life*, IV, 93.

[3] Of declamation as it appears in stage-playing, Bacon writes that it is "an
art which strengthens the memory, regulates the tone and effect of the voice
and pronunciation, teaches a decent carriage of the countenance and gesture,
gives not a little assurance, and accustoms young men to bear being looked at."
De aug., VI, 4, *Works*, IV, 496.

because hasty speech confounds the memory, and often-times, besides unseemliness, drives a man either to a non-plus or unseemly stammering, harping upon that which should follow; whereas a slow speech confirmeth the memory, addeth a conceit of wisdom to the hearers, besides a seemliness of speech and countenance.[4]

Bacon criticizes the contemporary practice in the schools of requiring students either to declaim their speeches or to speak impromptu, on the spur of the moment. "The exercises in the universities and schools are of memory and invention; either to speak by heart that which is set down *verbatim*, or to speak *ex tempore;* whereas there is little use in action of either or both. . . ."[5] In real life, "most things which we utter are neither verbally premediate, nor merely extemporal."[6] Hence Bacon recommends what he regards as a mixture of the two practices. The student should be allowed a little time in which to organize his ideas, and should then proceed to the actual delivery in which he would express and amplify them on the spur of the moment: ". . . exercise would be framed to take a little breathing; and to consider of heads; and then to form and fit the speech *ex tempore*."[7] In this practice the student may speak either with notes or without. The exercise "would be done in two manners, both with writing and tables, and without; for in most actions it is permitted and passable to use the note; whereunto if a man be not accustomed, it will put him out."[8] On the ground of inutility Bacon also condemns the school exercises that are narrative in character: "There is no use of a Narrative Memory in academies, viz. with circumstances of times, persons, and places, and with names; and it is one art to discourse, and another to relate and describe; and herein use and action is most conversant."[9] From this criticism of sixteenth century pedagogy, therefore, we may legitimately infer that for most purposes Bacon prefers what we today describe as the extemporaneous speech. In fact, in describing his procedure in the prosecution of Oliver H. John, he records his preference for the extempore presentation, at least in the law-court. "I spoke," he writes to King James, "out of a few heads which I had gathered (for I seldom do

---

[4] *Works*, VII, 109.
[5] *Helps for the Intellectual Powers*, *Works*, VII, 103.
[6] *Ibid.*   [7] *Ibid.*   [8] *Ibid.*   [9] *Ibid.*

more). . . ." [10] Such a preference, however, does not prevent him from perceiving the utility, in his own case at least, of written composition as preliminary to oral expression. To Burghley he writes: "And for myself, I thought it would better manifest what I desire to express, if I did write out of a deep and settled consideration of mine own duty, rather than upon the spur of a particular occasion." [11]

Bacon recognizes that a speaker's physical appearance and movement are of considerable importance. The force of one's words and one's deeds may be completely destroyed by weak and inappropriate expression of countenance and of gesture:

The poet saith . . . a man may destroy the force of his words with his countenance: so may he of his deeds, saith Cicero; recommending to his brother affability and easy access . . . it is nothing to admit men with an open door, and to receive them with a shut and reserved countenance. So we see Atticus, before the first interview between Caesar and Cicero, the war depending, did seriously advise Cicero touching the composing and ordering of his countenance and gesture. And if the government of the countenance be of such effect,[12] much more is that of the speech and other carriage appertaining to conversation. . . .[13]

Gesture is important, moreover, because action and movement on the part of the orator attracts the foolish and uncritical side of man's nature. Bacon seems to express this opinion in the essay *Of Boldness*:

Question was asked of Demosthenes, *what was the chief part of an orator?* he answered, *action:* what next? *action:* what next again?

---

[10] Letter to the King, *Letters and Life*, V, 135. The quotation might well be extended, not only as showing Bacon's habit of delivery but also as hinting at the trustworthiness of what has been printed as the texts of Bacon's speeches: ". . . having spoken out of a few heads which I had gathered (I seldom do more), I set down as soon as I came home cursorily a frame of that I said; though I persuade myself I spake it with more life."

[11] *Letters and Life*, II, 52.

[12] Here Bacon's meaning is made clear if one reads: ". . . if the government of the countenance be of such effect *in regard to deeds,* much more is that of speech. . . ." Though not expressed in the text, the comparison is clearly implied.

[13] *Adv. of L., Works*, III, 445-446. Cf. *De aug.*, VIII, 1, *Works*, V, 33.

action. He said it that knew it best, and had by nature himself no advantage in that he commended. A strange thing, that that part of an orator which is but superficial, and rather the virtue of a player, should be placed so high, above those other noble parts of invention, elocution, and the rest; nay almost alone, as if it were all in all. But the reason is plain. There is in human nature generally more of the fool than of the wise; and therefore those faculties by which the foolish part of men's minds is taken are most potent.[14]

Thus gesture is regarded as an effective help to persuasion. We observe, consequently, that Bacon, like Atticus advising Cicero, admonishes Essex to suit his countenance to his compliments if he would regain Elizabeth's favor:

> . . . when at any time your Lordship upon occasion happen in speeches to do her Majesty right (for there is no such matter as flattery amongst you all), I fear you handle it *magis in speciem adornatis verbis, quam ut sentire videaris;* so that a man may read formality in your countenance; whereas your Lordship should do it familiarly *et oratione fida.*[15]

Gesture and countenance, after all, are mirrors of the mind, and an art of gesture, if set up, would prove as useful as Aristotle's analysis of the body's structure:

> Aristotle has very ingeniously and diligently handled the structure of the body when at rest, but the structure of the body when in motion (that is the gestures of the body) he has omitted; which nevertheless are equally within the observations of art, and of greater use and advantage. For the lineaments of the body disclose the dispositions and inclinations of the mind in general; but the motions and gestures of the countenance and parts do not only so, but disclose likewise the seasons of access, and the present humour and state of the mind and will. For as your Majesty says most aptly and elegantly, 'As the tongue speaketh to the ear so the gesture speaketh to the eye.' . . . Nor let any one imagine that a sagacity of this kind may be of use with respect to particular persons, but cannot fall under a general rule; for we all laugh and weep and frown and blush nearly in the same fashion; and so it is (for the most part) in the more subtle motions.[16]

Though gesture is of practical persuasive value and though

---

[14] *Works,* VI, 401-402.   [15] Letter to Essex, *Letters and Life,* II, 42.
[16] *De aug.,* IV, 1, *Works,* IV, 376. Cf. *Adv. of L., Works,* III, 368.

Bacon thinks it important enough to consider its possibility as an art, the speaker should ever keep gesture within the bounds of good taste. ". . . if behaviour and outward carriage be intended too much, it may pass into a deformed and spurious affectation." [17] Nothing, Bacon insists, can be more uncomely than to bring "the manners of the stage into the business of life." Also, even though the speaker does not become an actor, "yet too much time is consumed in these frivolous matters, and the mind is employed more than is right in the care of them." [18] In general, in so far as the orator does concern himself with action, with gesture and movement, he must ever remember that "behaviour is as the garment of the mind, and ought to have the conditions of a garment." [19] Behaviour, in the first place, "ought to be made in fashion"; it should conform to contemporary style. Gestures, in the second place, "should not be too curious or costly"; [20] the attention of either the speaker or the audience must not be attracted to them as such. In the third place, they "ought to be so framed, as to best set forth any virtue of the mind, and supply and hide any deformity." [21] Finally, gestures ought to be such as to demand a minimum of conscious attention on the part of the orator; they "ought not be too strait, so as to confine the mind and interfere with its freedom in business and action." [22] In brief, the true model of countenance and gesture, states Bacon, "seemeth to me well expressed by Livy . . . the sum of behaviour is to retain a man's own dignity, without intruding upon the liberty of others," [23] and without violating the canons of good taste. The important matters in speech-making are invention, disposition, and style, not gesture.

---

[17] *De aug.*, VIII, 1, *Works*, V, 33.
[18] *Ibid.*
[19] *Ibid.*, 34.
[20] *Ibid.*
[21] *Ibid.*
[22] *Ibid.*
[23] *Adv. of L., Works*, III, 446.

CHAPTER TEN

BACON

AND THE

CLASSICAL RHETORICIANS

The study of a rhetorical theory is only partly completed with the exposition of its characteristics. It is important, in addition, to perceive how the theory under observation relates to other theories of the same species. In such an undertaking, the method of the rhetorical historian does not differ essentially from the method of the literary historian as set forth briefly by Edwin Greenlaw. Commenting on the significance of H. J. C. Grierson's *Cross Currents in English Literature of the Seventeenth Century,* Greenlaw writes:

Such a history takes into account literature as reflecting not the externals of contemporary manners alone but the spiritual conflicts of an age; an epoch is rarely to be explained in terms of simple propositions, since its life is very complex and is filled with cross currents; and, finally, the "life" of an age or of a representative major intellect of that age is not a matter of household economy, daily experience, party warfare, but includes the intellectual sources, the influence of a past time, transformed or translated into terms of the age or of the writer's genius.[1]

There should now be made in the present study an attempt to sur-

---

[1] *Province of Literary History* (Baltimore and London, 1931), 84.

vey briefly those chief intellectual sources, past and contemporary, that constitute Bacon's rhetorical heritage.

We know from such studies as Foster Watson's *The English Grammar Schools to 1660*,[2] J. B. Mullinger's history of Cambridge University,[3] and W. Fraser Mitchell's *English Pulpit Oratory from Andrewes to Tillotson*,[4] that the curricula of English schools and colleges of the late sixteenth and early seventeenth centuries found a prominent place for rhetorical instruction.[5] Chief among the Greek theorists studied were Plato, Aristotle, Hermogenes, and Aphthonius; among the Roman, Cicero, Tacitus, Quintilian, Seneca the Elder, and the author of the *Rhetorica ad Herennium*. Through rhetorical study and practice in the schools, a sixteenth-century student became well-acquainted with the principles of classical rhetoric, and Bacon, who had spent three years at Trinity College, Cambridge, was no exception. On the other hand, we possess little direct evidence concerning Bacon's reading. Without citing his authority, W. A. Wright says in his edition of the *Advancement* that Whitgift, Master of Trinity College, at one time supplied Bacon with the following "books": Livy, Cicero, Caesar, Aristotle, Sallust, Demosthenes's *Olynthiacs*, Homer's

---

[2] Cambridge, 1908.

[3] *The University of Cambridge from the Royal Injunctions of 1535 to the Accession of Charles*, Cambridge, 1884.

[4] London, 1932.

[5] Foster Watson writes: "The teaching of rhetoric is emphasized in the Statutes for Ipswich School, founded in 1528. The Elizabethan schools included it, if not specifically as a separate subject, at least in the manner and spirit of reading classical authors as well as in the exercises for the theme and oration. Indeed, if there is one school subject which seems to have pre-eminently influenced the writers, statesmen, and gentlemen of the 16th and 17th centuries, in their intellectual outfit in after life, probably the claim for this leading position may justly be made for Rhetoric and the Oration." *Op. cit.*, 440. One of Watson's chief sources is John Brinsley's *Ludus literarius*, first published in 1612. Mitchell seeks to sum up the Elizabethan interest in rhetoric: "Rhetoric held its place partly as survival from the Middle Ages, partly owing to revival of interest in classical studies which came with the Renaissance, partly . . . because university education continued to be dominated by the disputation, partly . . . because the diplomatic address of the ambassador and the polite welcome accorded to distinguished visitors on most official occasions remained the Latin oration." *Op. cit.*, 68.

Iliad, Plato, Xenophon, and Hermogenes.[6] For his model in collecting the *Colours,* Bacon himself acknowledges his indebtedness to Aristotle in such a manner that one infers a careful reading of the *Rhetoric* or the *Topics.* But beyond this, explicit and trustworthy evidence that Bacon read a particular book or author is lacking. It is of course true that, as he writes, Bacon frequently attributes an idea by quotation or paraphrase to a definite author, but most of his editors and interpreters testify to the chronic inaccuracy of his quoting. This habit, then, together with the intensive study and practice of rhetoric in the schools and the customary use of common-place books as sources of material for speakers and writers, prevents us from determining what Bacon really read at first hand. It is certain, however, that he shared the rhetorical background of his generation if we may trust the testimony of Paule, one of Whitgift's biographers. Paule asserts that the Archbishop, while Master of Trinity, had many famous pupils, among them Francis Bacon, and that they together with other scholars "he held to their publick Disputations, and Exercises. . . ."[7] Accordingly, it is against certain elements of contemporary rhetorical background that one must endeavor to set Bacon's theory of rhetoric. In so doing, we shall point out special correspondence wherever possible.

In view of the classical bias of rhetorical education in Elizabethan England, of the high authority in which Aristotle was held, and of Bacon's first-hand acquaintance with Plato as well as with Aristotle, it is particularly interesting to compare and contrast the Baconian rhetoric with that of the ancient Greeks.

In the *Phaedrus,* Plato defines rhetoric as "the art of enchanting the soul."[8] By this he suggests that the proper function of oral discourse is the instruction and persuasion of men that they may be led to believe or to act in accordance with ideal truth. In formulating such a definition, Plato does not echo the rhetorical

---

[6] Oxford, 1880, vi. Theodore Goulston's edition of Aristotle's *Rhetoric* appeared in 1619. According to the Catalogue of the British Museum, there was a presentation copy from Goulston to Bacon.

[7] George Paule, *The Life of John Whitgift, Archbishop of Canterbury* (London, 1699), 23.

[8] *Phaedrus,* 271. In *The Dialogues of Plato,* tr. by B. Jowett, with an introduction by Ralph Demos (New York, 1937).

theories held by the sophists and orators of contemporary Athens. What he formulates is an ideal rhetoric that might function in an ideal State. On contemporary oratory, Plato looked with contempt. He held that rhetoric was as apt to further bad causes as good. He maintained that the rhetoricians taught nothing of justice and injustice, an essential part of rhetoric. In brief, as rhetoric was practiced in democratic Athens, it was only "the art of persuading an ignorant multitude about the justice or injustice of a matter, without imparting any real instruction." The depraved state of contemporary oratory leads Plato to suggest the broad outlines of a true art of rhetoric whose persuasions would lead men to just and righteous action. The *Phaedrus*, then, presents a rhetoric that is ethically idealistic.

Aristotle, however, looked at rhetoric in no such idealistic manner. As a scientist content with observing and recording Greek theories of rhetoric, he arrived at a realistic view: "Rhetoric is the faculty of finding in any given case the available means of persuasion," [9] a definition which neither explicitly requires nor necessarily implies a moral purpose on the part of the practical rhetorician. Aristotle as a scientific observer accepted reality and human life as he found them, and he assigned to public speaking an honorable role in political and social life of Athens in the fourth century, B.C.

Bacon's rhetorical theory seems to be partly Aristotelian, partly Platonic. Like Aristotle, Bacon observed, analyzed, and classified all knowledge; he marked its deficiencies and in some instances set out to remove them by a method of investigation which, scientific in nature, he held applicable to all sciences. It is partly in this scientific spirit that Bacon, within his great cyclopedia, notes the deficiencies of rhetorical theory, and then proceeds to recommend expedients for the invention of ideas and to some extent for their manner of expression. Like Aristotle, moreover, Bacon sees rhetoric as a practical art which is useful in controlling men's wills and thereby their actions. But although Bacon looks at rhetorical address analytically as a practical art having a validity quite its own, nevertheless he gives to rhetoric a moral purpose, and in this respect his theory becomes Platonic. Indeed in imputing to rhetoric

---

[9] *De rhetorica,* 1355 b 26; by W. Rhys-Roberts in the Oxford translation of Aristotle's works, XI.

a moral end, Bacon explicitly acknowledges Plato's lead, stating that "Plato said elegantly . . . 'that virtue, if she could be seen, would move great love and affection,' and it is the business of rhetoric to make pictures of virtue and goodness, so that they may be seen." [10] Yet Bacon does not admit Plato's implication of the *Gorgias*,[11] that rhetoric, like cookery, is as facile in making a bad product appear good as in making a good product seem attractive. Instead, he employs Aristotle's argument,[12] and declares that the good naturally prevails and that skill enhances its chance of success geometrically while increasing only arithmetically the chances of the bad cause. "No man," says Bacon, "can speak fair of causes sordid and base; while it is easy to do it of causes just and honorable." [13] To this argument he adds that there is "no man but speaks more honestly than he thinks or acts." [14] It is perceived, consequently, that although Bacon asserts an inherent superiority of good over evil, he entertains enough doubt on the subject to state specifically that rhetoric must make pictures of the good. Concerning the morality of rhetoric, then, he is not content to rely solely on the rhetorical ethics of the *Phaedrus* or on Aristotle's argument; he must use both.

The manner in which Bacon, Plato, and Aristotle look at rhetoric is determined in part by the province that each assigns to the art. Plato's thoroughgoing idealism admitted no truth other than ideal form. What Aristotle recognized as probable truth and the province of contingent reasoning, was to Plato no truth at all. To deal with probabilities was to traffic with ignorance. Hence the ideal orator must know the absolute or ideal truth, and since in Platonic philosophy ideal form could only be contemplated by a philosopher, this was tantamount to requiring that the speaker be also a philosopher. But the scientific outlook of Aristotle permitted different degrees of truth: the universally true and the probably true. Aristotle saw that science and logic, as he understood them, yielded knowledge of universal validity, and that rhetoric together

---

[10] *De aug.*, VI, 3, *Works*, IV, 456. Cf. *Phaedrus*, 250.

[11] *Gorgias*, 462-465. Cf. *Phaedrus*, 263, in which Socrates gets Phaedrus to admit that it is about differences of opinion that rhetoric has the most power, rather than about the things on which we agree.

[12] *Rhet.*, 1355 a 38.   [13] *De aug.*, VI, 3, *Works*, IV, 456.

[14] *Ibid.*

with its complement, dialectic, properly dealt with probable truth. In short, rhetoric claimed a legitimate place in the Aristotelean scheme of arts and sciences; public speaking in company with dialectic dealt with any judgments in the field of the contingent. Now Bacon, a realist as scientific as Aristotle, also perceives that inference exhibits degrees of validity. Scientific inferences yield universal truth, and for his own scientific method of interpreting nature Bacon unhesitatingly claims universal validity. Occasionally he hints that divine revelation constitutes a source of knowledge more certain than scientific observation and inference, but, in the main, the conclusions obtained by all other subject-matter are probable. And hence the discourses of rhetoric and the disputations of lawyers properly have only a contingent validity.

Thus to define the province of rhetoric is to recognize that the speaker should be acquainted with the stock of current opinions and beliefs involved in political and social discussion. Aristotle believes that knowledge of these makes it possible for the speaker to mould his persuasions accordingly, to fit his arguments to his audience. Similarly, Bacon suggests that the beliefs, prejudices, and attitudes represented by the idols and by the Colours of Good and Evil must claim the speaker's attention if he is successfully to circumvent or to employ these in making his point. Plato likewise seems to imply that his ideal orator besides knowing absolute truth, shall also be acquainted with opinions and resemblances.[15]

When we turn to examine the theory of Plato, Aristotle, and Bacon with respect to the ways and means by which each desired the speaker to effect his persuasions, we notice, in the main, a closer kinship between Bacon and Plato than between Bacon and Aristotle. Perhaps the fundamental point lies in the similarity between Plato's phrase, "enchanting of the soul," and Bacon's state-

---

[15] He who is master of the art of rhetoric "must understand the real nature of everything; or he will never know either how to make the gradual departure from truth into the opposite of truth which is effected by the help of resemblances, or how to avoid it." (*Phaedrus*, 264.) The rhetorician, furthermore, will require knowledge of classes of things about which men agree, like "iron and silver," and information about classes of things on which men disagree, like "justice and goodness." Moreover, "the rhetorician ought to make a regular division, and acquire a distinct notion of both classes, as well as of that in which the many err, as of that in which they do not err." (*Ibid.*, 263.)

ment that rhetoric "recommends reason to imagination." By such a description he undoubtedly signifies that, whatever the logical, pathetic, and ethical proof employed, at least the means of proof must be vividly adapted to the audience; the mind of the auditor is to be filled with images. A similar attitude toward the means of persuasion in general seems to be imputed to Plato by Jowett's use of the word "enchanting," [16] and by Plato's own suggestion to Cratylus that language itself may be a kind of "image" of the real and the true.[17] It seems probable, accordingly, that from Plato Bacon may have derived his functional statement of rhetoric's peculiar way of attaining its end, although he expressed it in the terms of a mature faculty-psychology of which his precursor had only a primitive notion.

In Bacon's attitude toward the logical means of persuasion there is considerable similarity to Plato and Aristotle, but in the last analysis his interest in the rational side of persuasion and his classification of rhetoric as a logical art brings his theory closer to Aristotle's than to Plato's. When Plato gives to speaking a moral purpose, he sees clearly that the first duty of the philosopher-orator is to know the truth, even though his persuasions to a popular audience must deal with debatable matters and "resemblances" that will promote temperance and justice.[18] What is called the "resemblance of truth" Plato seems to think of as having a high degree of probability, for resemblances are close to ideal truth without attaining to the certainty of true knowledge. He of course objects to the rhetorician's uncritical use of probabilities, for only when the rhetorician knows truth can he "always know best how to discover the resemblances of the truth." [19] To perceive the truth and to guard against confusing the ideal truth with resemblances, the speaker will be skilled in distinguishing particulars from universals, false reasoning from true inference; he will be, in short, a keen dialectician. It is clear, then, that Plato lays great stress on universal truth and on logic in the speaker's preparation. But in the speech as presented, the orator will choose his main

---

[16] *Phaedrus*, 271.   [17] *Cratylus*, 432.

[18] In the *Gorgias*, Plato shows that the social purpose of rhetoric consists in implanting in men the virtues of temperance and justice. (*Gorgias*, 504,.527.)

[19] *Phaedrus*, 273.

types of proof—whether logical, pathetic, or ethical—in accordance with the audience addressed. Plato does not admonish him to prefer one type of proof over another; in fact, when he insists that the speaker, once having discovered the truth of a matter, must turn all his attention to "discover the different modes of discourse which are adapted to different natures," [20] he seems to suggest that the audience determines the type of proof to be employed. Aristotle, however, pointedly evaluates the types of proof. He selects logical argument and the enthymeme as the "substance of persuasion;" [21] it is with some reluctance that he yields to practical necessity and discusses emotional proof. Now it will be remembered that Bacon also assumes that logical inference will be the basis of any speech. First, rhetoric as a practical art is classified as one of the arts that employ reason in fulfilling their function. Its rationality, to Bacon, determines its place in his cyclopedia; otherwise, it might just as well have been put in the train of ethics where Plato in effect places it. Public speaking, since it is to "recommend reason" to imagination, must in the last analysis always present reasons and arguments. Second, Bacon sees the human being primarily as a rational and good creature, and therefore following the dictates of right reason if not perverted by emotional appeal. Hence, the use of reason in speaking is the natural and direct way of influencing conduct. Finally, Bacon's theory of public address assumes a rational bias by virtue of the prominence given to the invention of arguments. It is apparent, consequently, that the place, the definition, and the treatment of rhetoric as Bacon understands it take on a rational character for which one looks to Aristotle, rather than to Plato, for a parallel.

As a corollary to logical proof both Aristotle and Bacon view fallacious reasoning as a necessary part of rhetorical inference. Each holds that the speaker should be acquainted with certain fallacious arguments that customarily are accepted as sound by the uncritical. Upon an understanding of these fallacies, the orator may properly test both his own inferences and those of his opponent. Thus Bacon's compilation of the Colours or sophisms of rhetoric and his fallacies of interpretation find their precedents in Aristotle's Sophistical Refutations forming the ninth book of

---

[20] *Ibid.*, 277.   [21] *Rhet.*, 1354 a 15.

the *Topics* and in the spurious lines of argument that appear in the *Rhetoric*.[22] It is to Aristotle's observations on popular notions of the good that Bacon specifically acknowledges his indebtedness for his *Colours*. As he introduces his doctrine of fallacies in the *De augmentis*, moreover, he pays tribute to Plato in a way that suggests an intimate acquaintance with the *Dialogues*:

> This part concerning the detection of sophistical fallacies is excellently handled by Aristotle in the way of precepts, but still more excellently by Plato in the way of examples; and that not only in the persons of the ancient sophists (Gorgias, Hippias, Protagoras, Euthydemus, and the rest), but even in Socrates himself, who professing to affirm nothing, but to infirm that which was affirmed by another, has most wittily expressed all the forms of fallacy, objection, and redargution.[23]

Because Aristotle and Bacon hold that logical proof is more appropriate to rhetoric than emotional proof, both develop a more specific and detailed method of invention than does Plato. To the speaker who must discover arguments for any given occasion, the *Dialogues* afford only general advice: become expert in definition and in analysis, because the orator thus trained will never be at loss for appropriate arguments. In contrast with this general suggestion, Aristotle and Bacon present specific aids to invention, although the later theorist sets up a more definite and methodical system than the earlier. Both men explicitly recommend the use of topics, but whereas Aristotle cites only four in his *Rhetoric*,[24] Bacon allows the utility of the ten topics of traditional logic. Both men see the practicability of commonplace arguments, especially those concerning good and evil, and of pros and cons gathered from the most common subjects of popular discourse. Bacon, however, extends his theory of invention to include that aspect of prose discourse that Aristotle would restrict to style. The formularies and elegancies, those transitional and interstitial passages that make for grace of coherence, those striking phrases and analogies

---

[22] *Rhet.*, II, c. 24.   [23] *Works*, IV, 430.

[24] The four definitely named in the *Rhetoric* as being common to all types of discourse are the Possible and Impossible, Fact Past, Fact Future, and Magnitude (II, c. 19). Although called a "line of argument," perhaps the topic of Degree should be admitted as a fifth topic. (1358 a 10-15.)

that appeal so strongly to the imagination, all in part depend for their effectiveness upon manner of expression.

Although Bacon and Aristotle make much of the necessity of logical proof in rhetoric, they do not neglect pathetic and ethical proof any more than does Plato. But the position that Bacon takes on this aspect of rhetoric, like his stand on the morality of oratory, represents an attempt to combine the views of Plato and Aristotle. Bacon is Aristotelian in that he belittles emotional proof to the enhancement of reasoning. He resembles Aristotle, moreover, in that he sometimes speaks of the audience as composed of types, rather than of individuals. Previously it has been pointed out that the Essays serve, in the Baconian rhetoric, as do the chapters on character in the Aristotelian.

Both men see human nature as types, Aristotle writing of such characters as old men, rich men, and youth, Bacon writing on such topics as "Of Adversity," Of Nobility," and "Of Good Fortune." The two philosophers, it is true, have a slightly different point of attack: whereas Aristotle speaks of typical men Bacon talks of typical qualities. But at bottom both theorists generalize about human nature, and Bacon, in urging a more thorough study of men's characters, calls attention to the work of his great predecessor: "These observations and the like I deny not but are touched a little by Aristotle in his Rhetoric. . . ." [25]

Although Bacon, in recommending that the speaker should know the qualities and characteristics of men in general, does not explicitly mention Plato, it is worth observing that the general suggestion offered by the *Phaedrus* anticipates the detailed analysis of Aristotle and of Bacon. The rhetorician, Plato says, will arrange "men and speeches, and their kinds and affections" in different classes, and as part of the analysis "he will tell the reasons of his arrangement and show why one soul is persuaded by a particular form of argument and another not." [26] But to say that Bacon on the subject of emotional proof is both Platonic and Aristotelian is not to deny him individuality. Actually he goes beyond the Greeks, suggesting that the perfect rhetorician will extend his knowledge of human character to the study of specific per-

---

[25] *De aug.*, VII, 3, *Works*, V, 22.   [26] *Phaedrus*, 271.

sons as well as types, when he says that ". . . the proofs and persuasions of Rhetoric ought to differ according to the auditors . . .
which application, in perfection of pleas, ought to extend so far,
that if a man should speak of the same thing to several persons,
he would speak to them all respectively and several ways. . . ." [27]

When we come to consider the form or the order and arrangement of a speech, Bacon cannot be described as either Platonic or
Aristotelian. He seems here to have a distinct contribution of his
own. The *Rhetoric*, we remember, declares that the essential disposition of a speech may be resolved into two parts: state the case,
and then prove it. Such a resolution argues a conception of speech
form as a logical unity. Plato, however, had suggested an organic
and aesthetic unity of the speech, and this Aristotle saw fit to
apply to tragic poetry. The *Phaedrus* declares that "Every discourse ought to be a living creature, having its own body and head
and feet; there ought to be a middle, beginning, and end, which
are in a manner agreeable to one another and to the whole." [28]
But Bacon, as he amplifies his notion of disposition under the
caption "Wisdom of Transmission," hints that a speaker or writer
always exercises a certain discernment in the arrangement and
expression of his ideas, in accordance not merely with the end
aimed at, but with the persons addressed. And this implies, accordingly, that he thought of speech form as being organic with the
audience. Change the character of those addressed and immediately
the form of presentation also changes. To be sure, this does not
constitute Bacon's entire conception of the order and structure of
a speech. His attention to the formularies and elegancies of public
utterance, to the interstitial or transitional passages of a speech,
to deft introductions and conclusions, and in general to the need of
weaving utterance into a well-articulated whole, all point to a notion of form that is essentially aesthetic in character. One may
say, accordingly, that Bacon's notion of speech form is determined

---

[27] *Adv. of L., Works,* III, 411. It may be that the phrase "several persons"
refers to listeners not as individuals but as types. Yet Bacon goes on immediately to criticize the "greatest orators" for their inability to adapt their
thoughts in their *"private speech,"* and thus suggests that he may be advising
the orator on all occasions to acquire a more exact knowledge of his audience
than would be possible through an analysis of types.

[28] *Phaedrus,* 264.

fundamentally by the practical necessity of communicating ideas to an audience and secondarily by some perception of what constitutes an aesthetic whole.

Bacon's view of delivery has little in common with Greek rhetoric. Plato has nothing directly to say on voice and gesture; Aristotle admits an art that he calls "the right management of the voice to express the various emotions—of speaking loudly, softly, or between the two; of high, low, or intermediate pitch; of the various rhythms that suit various subjects." [29] He suggests, too, that vocal expression is capable of systematic treatment. Although he presents his own system of *pronuntiatio*, he appears to offer it somewhat grudgingly; "delivery is necessary but "unworthy"; it is not "an elevated subject of inquiry." [30] On the other hand, Bacon neither indicates his attitude toward delivery, nor calls for its systematic treatment. The extracts concerning voice that appear consecutively in the *Promus* show only that he was aware of the principal elements of *pronuntiatio*.

Perhaps it is apparent, at this juncture, that Bacon may have inherited some of his ideas on rhetoric from Plato and Aristotle. That he also inherited from Cicero seems probable if one may judge by the comparatively frequent references to the Latin author. The allusions to Cicero are almost always brief and isolated, and we have, therefore, no certain knowledge whether Bacon cited directly from his own reading or merely jotted down from memory Ciceronian precepts and sayings that were current in the education and conversation of Elizabethan England. We have, of course, Wright's testimony that Bacon possessed the books of Cicero. We observe, furthermore, that wherever Bacon characterizes Cicero's rhetorical thought his description is accurate; he thus suggests more than a superficial acquaintance. In the essay *Of Building*, for example, is a statement which compares the scope and purpose of the essay with Cicero's *De oratore* and *Orator:* "To pass from the seat to the house itself; we will do as Cicero doth in the orator's art; who writes books *De Oratore*, and a book he entitles *Orator;* whereof the former delivers the precepts of the art, and latter the perfection." [31] Again, when Bacon wishes to clarify his point of

---

[29] *Rhet.*, 1403 b 28-31.   [30] *Ibid.*, 1404 a 1.
[31] *Works*, VI, 482.

view in describing the politic man, he compares his production to Cicero's *Orator:*

. . . Cicero, in his portrait of a perfect orator, does not mean that every pleader should be or can be such; and again, as in the description of a prince or courtier by such as have handled those subjects, the model is always framed according to the perfection of the art, and not according to common practice; so likewise have I done in the description of a politic man. . . .[32]

In brief, the most direct evidence that can be culled from Bacon's works points to a familiarity with the two chief rhetorical treatises of Cicero. Hence for a proper appreciation of the Baconian rhetoric, it is necessary to examine briefly its precepts in relation to those of the *De oratore.*

Cicero's *De oratore* is concerned in the main with the content of the speech and to a lesser degree with the treatment of its material. Cicero, consequently, has much to say about the province and training of the orator, his subject matter, where to look for arguments and how to analyze a question. To a lesser extent, the *De oratore* deals with pathetic and ethical proof, with the arrangement of material, with wit and humor, and with aspects of style and delivery. In short, of the five parts of a speech—invention, disposition, elocution, memory, and delivery—Cicero gives the chief place to invention and discovery of ideas. Bacon, like Cicero, is also most interested in invention. Both men, influenced perhaps by their work as lawyers, see that the most fundamental phase of speaking lies in the discovery and selection of apt ideas. But although both recognize the importance of invention, their development of the subject differs. Cicero is content with setting forth a scheme of general topics drawn in the main from Aristotle's *Topics* and the *Analytics,* that are most useful in forensic rhetoric, and the form assumed by his topics is largely that of a series of questions designed to suggest pertinent ideas. It is true, of course, that Bacon also acknowledges the application of the logical categories of invention to rhetoric and therefore envisages a general system of topics. But because he felt that Cicero and other theorists had admirably discoursed on topics in general, he accepts their general

---

[32] *De aug.,* VIII, 2, *Works,* V, 75.

outline of invention and concerns himself with working out in detail what he believes to be of most practical utility to the speaker, namely, the doctrine of common-places. Consequently, Bacon attempts to improve on Aristotle's arguments concerning good and evil; further, he appropriates Cicero's suggestion concerning the compilation of pros and cons on persistent questions:

> . . . Cicero himself, taught by long experience, directly asserts that a diligent orator may have by him premeditated and carefully handled beforehand everything which he shall have occasion to speak of; so that in the pleading of any particular cause, he shall not have to introduce anything new or on the sudden, except names and some special circumstances. [33]

It is to be observed, in addition, that the Baconian aids to invention are in the form of ideas completely phrased, so that the speaker has at one stroke solved both the problem of discovery and of composition. Bacon's contribution to invention, then, is not topics, but true common-places.

Besides sharing Cicero's judgment on the importance of invention, Bacon also agrees with the Roman lawyer in maintaining the basic relation between wide knowledge and good speaking. The Elizabethan seems to hold that all the canons of invention and the precepts of rhetoric are of little avail unless the speaker has gathered knowledge by study, observation, and conversation. And when Bacon inveighs against contemporary preachers who substitute stylistic gymnastics for content he demonstrates his sympathy with Cicero by using him as an authority: ". . . we see Cicero the orator complaining of Socrates and his school, that he was the first who separated philosophy and rhetoric; whereupon rhetoric became an empty and verbal art." [34] Again, in the *Interpretation of Nature*, there is a similar but more explicit statement of Cicero's position:

> Cicero, the orator, willing to magnify his own profession, and thereupon spending many words to maintain that eloquence was not a shop of good words and elegancies but a treasury and receipt of all knowledges, so far forth as may appertain to the handling and moving of the

---

[33] *De aug.*, V, 3, *Works*, IV, 422-423.
[34] *De aug.*, IV, 2, *Works*, IV, 373. Cf. *De oratore*, III, 16.

minds and affections of men by speech, maketh great complaint of the school of Socrates. . . .[35]

Bacon's theory of rhetorical address, accordingly, is Ciceronian in so far as it views content and invention as important rhetorical problems.

Bacon's treatment of disposition and memory, however, stands in marked contrast to that of Cicero. To Bacon, both memory and disposition are subjects of investigation independent of rhetoric, whereas to Cicero both appear as part of a rhetorical system. The Roman is interested only in practical suggestions that enable the orator to remember his speech; and he cites, therefore, as aids to retention only the order and sequence of ideas as they appear in a written outline. Bacon, on the contrary, attempts in the *Novum organum* and *De augmentis* to understand the nature of the retentive faculty and to suggest the aids that improve the memory in general, regardless of the specific activity with which the mind may be engaged. Because he is primarily interested in the theory of the Art of Memory as distinguished from other arts, he leaves the rhetorician to make his own application to the needs of speaking. It is noteworthy, however, that Bacon's principal helps to the retentive faculty, though discussed under the art of memory in general, are those which are treated specifically in Cicero's rhetoric. Similarly, whereas Cicero approaches the question of disposition or arrangement from the point of view peculiar to rhetoric Bacon looks at disposition apart from rhetoric and as constituting an art of its own. But beyond this divergence in attack—and perhaps because of it—Bacon and Cicero differ significantly in their conception of speech form. Cicero is interested primarily in the traditional order and arrangement of a speech, in which the parts are the exordium, narration, proof, refutation, summary, and peroration. He barely recognizes a second form of arrangement, which is dictated by the orator's own judgment in view of a given occasion and circumstances. Bacon, on the contrary, has little to say of the traditional parts of the oration. That he is well aware of them is amply indicated by an occasional use of the terms, "exordium,"

---

[35] *Works,* III, 228.

"narration," and "conclusion." He is chiefly concerned however with the form of communication that is determined by the character of the persons addressed and the end or effect that one aims to achieve.

In his attitude towards style, Bacon perhaps differs most from Cicero. Where the Roman has much to say concerning the manner of expressing ideas in words and essentially makes style a matter of fine art, the Englishman, if not relegating it entirely to Grammar, sees it as a relatively insignificant part of rhetoric. Beyond the general advice to speak clearly, appropriately, and agreeably—advice which is found, for the most part, in the *Essays*—Bacon does not go. Perhaps his abhorrence of the emphasis given to style in contemporary rhetoric led him not to mention it explicitly in connection with public address, and to include the process of embellishing and heightening language as an essential part of discovering what to say. The striking analogy, the vivid phrase, and the apothegm, we recall, are regarded as aids to invention. In short, those ways of expressing ideas that engage the imaginative faculty and therefore are necessary to the proper function of rhetoric, Bacon regards as determined by the audience which is being urged to act. Effective presentation of content is in no way considered as mere ornamentation of language. Where eloquence to Cicero means the heightening of language, eloquence to Bacon means the expression that derives from the speaker's perception of a great occasion. Bacon, perhaps more than any other rhetorical theorist up to his time, realized that *all* rhetorical precepts have their origin and sanction in the audience.

If Bacon was aware of the principles of one of the classical Roman rhetoricians, can one say with any validity that he knew the *Institutes* of Quintilian? Professors were supposed to discuss Quintilian at Cambridge during Bacon's time, but there is no direct evidence that Bacon used the *Institutes*. His allusions to Cicero establish his knowledge of *De oratore* and the *Orator*, but he never mentions Quintilian. It is indeed probable that the *Institutes* were less widely published in England than Cicero's treatises. Although Mullinger in his history of Cambridge declares that the Statutes of Edward VI required the professor of dialectics and rhetoric to use "the *Elenchi* of Aristotle, the *Topica* of Cicero, Quintilian, and Hermogenes" ;[36] although Sir Thomas Elyot recommends that the young student of rhetoric should of all rhetoricians first study Hermogenes and Quintilian, and although Roger Ascham in his *Scholemaster* mentions Quintilian, nevertheless the *Institutes* seems not to have been much in vogue as a text-book until the seventeenth century. The famous Elizabethan schoolmasters, Richard Mulcaster and John Brinsley, for example, take no notice of Quintilian, though they mention many other classical and contemporary authors who wrote on rhetoric or compiled grammars and phrasebooks. Quintilian's rhetorical system, then, may not have been well known to Bacon; that system was essentially Ciceronian, and it is not probable that a reading of Quintilian would have modified Bacon's theory. Quintilian's detailed treatment of the education of the orator, however, might well have drawn Bacon to a formal discussion of this topic.

---

[36] *Op. cit.*, II, 403.

CHAPTER ELEVEN

BACON

AND CONTEMPORARY

RHETORICAL THEORY

When one turns to examine Bacon's rhetoric in relation to the theories prevalent in the sixteenth and early seventeenth centuries, one must again focus on the general character of the rhetorical tradition which Tudor England inherited. In the first place, there is apparent the classical tradition, represented by the chief logical and rhetorical works of Aristotle and Cicero and by the *Dialogues* of Plato. Bacon's theory as it relates to classical rhetoric we have already examined. In the second place, sixteenth-century rhetoric was deeply indebted to medieval theories of grammar, rhetoric, and dialectic that had found application in the disputations of continental schools and monasteries and in preaching. Of course medieval rhetoric itself is chiefly classical in bias, but in its development and application to meet the conditions of the times two main trends appear. There is, first of all, a marked tendency to emphasize the stylistic aspect of rhetoric, particularly in the early school declamations and in letter-writing. Secondly, prominence is given to the inventive aspect of rhetoric, especially in the disputations of the schoolmen. In the former movement rhetoric seems to be confused with or subordinate to grammar and poetic; in the latter, to be combined with logic and dialectic.[1]

---

[1] For a survey of medieval rhetoric, see C. S. Baldwin, *Medieval Rhetoric and Poetic* (New York, 1928). For a brief account of medieval preaching, see W.

The English Renaissance, in spite of its great interest in the study of classical literature and the arts, contained much that was essentially medieval in character. English education reflected the medieval interest in logic, rhetoric, and grammar. The grammar schools found it convenient to teach Latin grammar and rhetoric by means of prepared declamations and exercises that reflected the taste of the time. The niceties of the Elizabethan court discourse, the vogue of the epistolary art, the admiration of Italian drama and poetry, and the entertainment of royal personages, all demanded that much attention be given to style or manner of expression in language. We observe, therefore, that in the schools the elementary rhetorical manuals of Hermogenes and Aphthonius rival the popularity which they enjoyed in the early schools of Gaul. The stylistic tradition, given impetus by the Renaissance, deluged the English schools with rhetorical exercises that aimed to give facility and grace of expression. Symptomatic of this interest in style, partly as cause and partly as result, Englishmen published a number of rhetorics in which the niceties of expression were analyzed in detail.

The stylistic tradition was by no means the only concern of rhetorical theorists in the sixteenth century, particularly in the last three decades of Elizabeth's reign. The English system of courts, the movement of jurists to codify English common law, the growing importance of Parliamentary debate and diplomatic discussions, the impetus that the Reformation gave to preaching, and the Anglican-Puritan pulpit debate concerning the efficacy of preaching as opposed to high-church homilies produced a tremendous interest in both the extemporaneous and the memorized speech. Schools and universities were quick to see the utility of logic and reasoning, and medieval dialectic took on new energy, not merely as an agent for the study and analysis of any subject, but also as a practical art whose mastery might assure advancement and position in Elizabethan life. Consequently, disputations and debates formed part of the school and university curricula, and

Fraser Mitchell, *English Pulpit Oratory* (London, 1932), Part I; J. M. Neale, *Medieval Preachers and Medieval Preaching* (London, 1856); Harry Caplan, *A Medieval Tractate on Preaching,* in *Studies in Honor of James A. Winans* (New York, 1925), and "Classical Rhetoric and the Medieval Theory of Preaching," *Classical Philology,* XXVIII (April, 1933), 73-96.

English text-books of logic and rhetoric began to complement the works of Aristotle, Cicero, and the pseudo-Ciceronian *Rhetorica ad Herennium*. The English writers on logic began to regard their subject as "an arte which teacheth to dispute well";[2] those writers on rhetoric who were not solely occupied with style and delivery looked at their subject broadly, and adapted to their purpose the apparatus of topics and the rules of logical proof that the art of logic treated exhaustively and scientifically. As precedent and authority for their action, they pointed to the classical rhetoricians.

It appears, then, that the English theorists on prose discourse move in two directions: the stylistic and the classical.[3] In fact, an examination of the writers who deal systematically with rhetoric and public address from the accession of Henry VIII (1509) to the death of James I (1625), finds them falling into two such groups.

First are those who see rhetoric as a complete, independent art of speaking and writing prose. Following in the classical tradition of rhetorical theory, they hold that the composition and delivery of discourse embraces five main operations: inventing or discovering ideas and arguments appropriate to the audience and occasion; organizing and arranging ideas into an articulate whole; managing language and diction with a view to clarity, impressiveness, and distinction of style; retaining or memorizing what must be uttered; and finally, pronouncing or delivering the speech. Accordingly, each theorist in this group, after his own emphasis, discusses all five of these processes. The chief treatises on rhetoric written by Englishmen who view their subject as a full-bodied, independent art include Leonard Cox's *Arte or Crafte of Rhetoryke* (1524), Thomas Wilson's *Arte of Rhetorique* (1553), Thomas Vicars' *Manuductio ad artem rhetoricam* (1619), Thomas Farnaby's *Index rhetoricus* (1625), and Charles Butler's *Oratoriae libri duo* (1629).

---

[2] *The Logike of P. Ramus*, 17.

[3] Such a classification emerges in part from W. P. Sandford's English Theories of Public Address, 1530-1828 (Mimeographed dissertation, Columbus, O., 1931), in part from W. S. Howell's "Nathaniel Carpenter's Place in the Controversy between Rhetoric and Dialectic," *Speech Monographs*, I (September, 1934), 20-41.

In discussing the five processes of rhetorical address, these works aim to furnish principles and procedures that will promote judgment and skill in writing and speaking. Their authors are practical-minded teachers who for the most part do not discuss the academic philosophy of rhetoric. Anxious to give directions that will take the student through the complete act of composition and presentation, they remain unperturbed over the strict relation of rhetoric to logic and ethics, and consequently wisely refrain from trying to make logic, rhetoric, and ethics mutually exclusive arts. Hence, each writer in this group applies some of the subject-matter of logic and ethics to his own ends. From logic is adapted the apparatus of *topics* and the formal laws of arranging inferences, whose use is to aid the speaker in finding arguments and testing their validity. From ethics are presented generalizations on men's passions and character, which are to help the speaker stir his hearers emotionally. As teachers of rhetoric, then, these men intend to give practical advice for composing and delivering an address.

To perceive more explicitly the position of this group, one must look briefly at Thomas Wilson. His *Arte of Rhetorique* offers the best-developed and best-proportioned discussion written by those who see rhetoric as a complete art of public address. In content and emphasis, his theory shows something of the proportion and balance of Quintilian's *Institutes of Oratory;* in fact, he is the first English theorist to present an adequate picture of the five classical rhetorical processes, and not until Farnaby's *Index rhetoricus* (1625) and not until Butler published his *Oratoriae libri duo* (1629) as complement to the third edition of his *Rhetoricae libri duo* (1619), does an English rhetorician exhibit comparable perspective and balance. Towards the beginning of our period, for example, Cox pays relatively little heed to style and delivery, despite his characterization of rhetoric as an art of disputation which makes the simple, terse language of logic "gay and delectable." [4] At the end of the period, Farnaby, in contrast to both Vicars and Butler[5] as well as to Wilson, omits all reference to the problems of memorizing the speech.

---

[4] For knowledge of Cox, I have made use of the edition by F. I. Carpenter (Chicago, 1898) which is based on the second edition (1532).

[5] Charles Butler, *Rhetoricae libri duo* (London, 1619); Thomas Vicars, *Man-*

Wilson defines rhetoric as "an art to set forth by utterance of words, matter at large . . . that may through reason largely be discussed." [6] Wilson declares that its subject matter embraces all questions, except those in the physical sciences, "which by law and man's ordinance are enacted and appointed for use and profit of man, such as are fit for the tongue to set forward." [7] The ends of rhetoric, he suggests, are to teach, to delight, and to persuade. By thus indicating the scope and content of rhetoric, Wilson sets up at the outset of his treatise a broad art of address. He then divides his art into invention, disposition, elocution, memory, and pronunciation or delivery. In explaining how to find what is to be said—a most fundamental matter to Wilson—he presents a full treatment of the topics or suggestive heads that may lead the speaker to discover and select appropriate ideas. One set of topics is applied to the deliberative address, one set to law-court speeches, and a third group to the demonstrative or occasional discourse and to letters. After explicit directions for the ordering of a composition, with particular reference to the selection of ideas, Wilson discusses amplification. Here at some length he treats of the affections, and reveals a keen understanding of the motives of men and the psychology of moods. Having thus devoted more than half of his treatise to the means of finding speech-content and of adapting it to one's hearers, Wilson next takes up the manner of presenting discourse. Most concerned here with style, he offers a long section on elocution, where, leaning heavily on Cicero, Quintilian, Erasmus, and the *Auctor ad Herennium*[8] he sets out most of the venerated tropes and schemes, complete with definitions and illustrations. Less attention is accorded other aspects of presentation; there is but a short chapter on memorization, and a still shorter one on utterance.

uductio ad artem rhetoricam (London, 1628); Thomas Farnaby, *Index rhetoricus* (London, 1633). For these works in the editions as indicated, I am indebted to the Folger Memorial Library.

[6] Edition by G. H. Mair (Oxford, 1909), i. A more accurate edition of Wilson is that by R. H. Wagner (Cornell University doctoral dissertation, 1929). Consult Professor Wagner's "The Text and Editions of Wilson's *Arte of Rhetorique*," *Modern Language Notes*, XLIV (November, 1929), 421-428.

[7] *Rhetorique*, i.

[8] R. H. Wagner, "Wilson and His Sources," *Quarterly Journal of Speech*, XV (November, 1929), 525-537.

Although in content and emphasis, Wilson's theory is fairly representative of his group, he differs significantly in one respect that sets him off sharply from his class and, as will be evident later, from Bacon. He assigns an unimportant position to the deliberative address, *i.e.*, the controversial discourse which weighs future policy, and writes as if its chief use were in letter-writing. Such an attitude towards deliberative discourse may seem strange unless it is perceived that Wilson here, as in other kinds of address, reflects the place held by the principal prose forms in English life.

All the rhetoricians speak of three kinds of address: the deliberative, the forensic, and the demonstrative or occasional address of display. Like his predecessor Cox, Wilson pays most attention to the forensic and demonstrative speech; thus he reflects, on the one hand, the interest in legal activity during the Tudor era, and on the other, the great value that the Renaissance man attached to fame and position. Henry VII and Henry VIII had, through the Court of Star Chamber, brought the mighty baron to acknowledge Law; through this agency they showed the English that the common man and the baron were to be treated equitably in the courts. As a result, the common law courts enjoyed great activity, and skillful legal speakers were in demand.[9] On the other side, the Tudor monarchs consistently held out attractive positions in Court life, in diplomatic negotiations, and in the conduct of Crown business in local government. Accordingly, the middle class gentleman who could demonstrate his ability in the occasional address—the welcome, the presentation, the response, the character eulogy, the narrative and expository tale—often was able, like Morton, Dudley, Walsingham, the Cecils, and Bacon, to secure fame and position in political affairs.

But in his attitude towards the deliberative address, Wilson could not follow Cox. Whereas Cox perceives that his cursory remarks on this species of address may be useful to preachers, to "framers" of epistles, and to those engaged in "civil" matters,

---

[9] For historical background of the period, I am depending chiefly on G. M. Trevelyan's *History of England* (New York, 1929) and *England under the Stuarts* (London, 1925); A. D. Innes, *England under the Tudors* (London, 1905); H. A. L. Fisher, *Political History of England, 1547-1603* (New York, 1906).

Wilson associates the political composition almost solely with letter-writing and affairs of *personal*, private colloquy. In this light he defines the deliberative address as that "whereby we do persuade, or dissuade, entreate, or rebuke, exhort, or dehort, comment, or comfort any man." [10] To promote these functions, he sets out the topics or "places" that may suggest relevant arguments, and largely from letters illustrates how to develop them into connected discourse. Thus, Wilson's attitude towards deliberatives is symptomatic of the sixteenth century vogue for letter-writing and limits the political discourse to private questions, rather than public. It is probable, moreover, that Wilson's emphasis on the epistolary art mirrors the dearth of a widespread, sustained interest in political speaking. Neither in Parliament nor on the hustings was there yet any real occasion for vigorous discussion. Indeed, not until Bacon's time, forty years after Wilson, does the speech dealing with public policy first come into its own, stimulated by pamphlet debate over the vices of poetry and Anglican-Puritan religious differences on the one side, and on the other by Parliamentary oratory over the Elizabethan-Jacobean religious settlement and the Commons' privilege of personal immunity and liberty of discussion.

The second group interested professionally in rhetorical theory consists of those who, by and large, restrict rhetoric to style and delivery. The writers of this group believe that the processes of public address cannot be adequately or properly brought within the term "rhetoric." They appreciate, of course, that the prose artist must discover his arguments and bind them together as a unit, but believe that to acquire these skills he should go to logic and dialectic. Since these arts deal with the traditional *topica* of finding arguments and with the methodology of judging inferences and arranging ideas both in the smaller parts of a composition, like the sentence, and in the entire address, the rhetorical theorist does well to restrict his exposition to the arts of style and pronunciation, with emphasis upon the intricacies of tropes and schemes. Similarly, since ethics, in its search for the good, probes into character and the springs of conduct, the rhetorician properly leaves any mention of the passions to ethics. The Elizabethan

[10] *Rhetorique*, 29.

elocutionists and pronouncers, then, appear as "scientists" and strict constructionists. So interested are these men in dissection and analysis, and in preserving the proper subject matter of each art, that neither they nor the logicians, moralists, or grammarians, can see a place for a *single*, well-rounded art that would meet the practical needs of composition. Nor do they perceive that such an art, although drawing upon allied arts, would derive its principles and procedures from the topics and language of everyday discussion. The typical figures of this group are men who in some cases have labelled their works with titles that suggest the rhetoric of Ciceronian elegance: Talaeus' *Rhetoric* (Eng. ed. 1577), Richard Sherry's *A Treatise of Schemes and Tropes* (1550) and *Treatise of the Figures of Grammar and Rhetorike* (1555), Henry Peacham's *Garden of Eloquence* (1577), Dudley Fenner's *The Artes of Logike and Rethoricke* (1584), Abraham Fraunce's *The Arcadian Rhetoricke* (1588), George Puttenham's *The Arte of English Poesie* (1589), Charles Butler's *Rhetoricae libri duo* (1597), and John Hoskins' *Directions for Speech and Style* (1599).

Among those theorists who confine writing and speaking largely to stylistics alone, or to style and delivery taken together, Henry Peacham and his *Garden of Eloquence* (1577) are typical. This Elizabethan restricts his discussion to the sweet harmonies of speech and the mysterious powers of persuasion that work "after a most wonderfull manner." [11] For use in both public and private speech, he offers the entire apparatus of rhetorical figures:

> The principal instruments of mans help in this wonderfull effect, are those figures and formes of speech conteined in this book, which are the fruitful brances of eloqqution, and the mightie streames of eloquence: whose utilitie, power, and vertue, I cannot sufficiently commĕd, but speaking by similitude, I say they are as stars to give light, as cordials to confort, as harmony to delight, as pitiful spectacles to move sorrowfull passions, and as orient colours to beautific reason.[12]

Peacham defines a figure as "a forme of words, oration, or sentence, made new by art, differing from the vulgar maner and custome of writing or speaking." [13] He then proceeds for two hundred pages

---

[11] (London, 1593), dedicatory epistle.   [12] *Ibid.*   [13] *Ibid.*, 1.

to divide, subdivide, and illustrate some one hundred and forty figures. The broadest classification, of course, is into tropes and schemes, the former class breaking down into tropes of words and tropes of sentences, the second group consisting of the "Schemates Rhetorical," with its subdivision into three great orders, each with its own families and numerous species. Throughout a long, manual-like book, Peacham, like other stylists, is preoccupied with the novel, the distinctive and glittering turn and expression. Indicative of his attitude are his definitions of a trope and a scheme:

"A Trope is an artificiall alteration of a word, or a sentence, from the proper and natural signification to another not proper yet nigh and likely." [14]

Schemates Rhetorical be those figures or forms of speaking, which do take away the wearisomness of our common speach, and do fashion a pleasant, sharpe, and evident kind of expressing of our meaning; which by the artificiall forme doth give unto matters great strength, perspicuitie and grace. . . .[15]

Except in detail and comprehensiveness of treatment, Talaeus and Sherry, at mid-century, share Peacham's point of view and method. Talaeus' *Rhetoric* (1577), popular in English schools for a century, is restricted to style and delivery, avowedly including "everything written in the art of Aristotle, Isocrates, Cicero, and Quintilian sufficiently and closely expounded . . . and illustrated by examples taken from poets and orators." [16] The point of view, the content, and the method of the section on style are similar to those of Richard Sherry's *Treatise of Schemes and Tropes* (1550) and his later *Figures*. Of all the parts of rhetoric, elocution is to Sherry "the goodliest," and "the profitablest." [17] More important than simply adding fullness and variety to matter, "it setteth out and garnisheth with certaine lights and endighting the thinges that be spoke of." [18] To find arguments and to arrange the

---

[14] *Ibid.*, dedicatory epistle.   [15] *Ibid.*, 40.
[16] Watson, *English Grammar Schools,* 441. For information concerning Talaeus, I am drawing principally on Watson, on Sandford's *English Theories,* 51-52, and on Charles Waddington, *Ramus (Pierre de la Ramee) sa vie, ses écrits et ses opinions* (Paris, 1855), 98, 352.
[17] *Figures of Grammar and Rhetorike* (1555), fol. iii.
[18] *Ibid.*

parts of discourse, after all, are merely "the partes of a witty and prudent man, but eloquence of an orator." [19] In keeping with this point of view, Sherry devotes the greater part of his books to the definition and illustration of some forty figures.

If, in the years of Edward VI and Mary, Wilson's well-conceived *Rhetorique* serves to keep alive the classical tradition in the face of Talaeus, no successor to Peacham in Elizabeth's time cares to identify the theory of his subject with anything but the wonders of presentation. Fully half of Puttenham's *Arte of English Poesie* (1589) discusses language ornamentation and its application to both poetry and oratory. Asserting that it is "an imperfection in mens utterance, to haue none use of figure at all, specially in our writing and speeches public," [20] he sets out the figures like one who holds the speaker to be an ingenious painter of language. Yet Puttenham is not as extreme as Peacham. He warns against foolish and indiscreet figures; he never explicitly limits the business of public discourse to style merely; and he understands that style as "a constant & continuall phrase or tenour of speaking and writing," is influenced by the audience, the genre of discourse, and the author's temperament and education.[21] Not so judicious are Abraham Fraunce and Charles Butler. Fraunce not only ignores the psychological and functional aspects of style, but he rigidly binds rhetoric to "Eloqution and Pronuntiation." Elocution, concerned with "the ordering and triming of speach," consists of "Congruitie and Braverie," the former dealing briefly with purity and coherence, the latter handling figures at length.[22] Butler's *Rhetoricae Libri Duo* (1597) likewise confines rhetoric to elocution and delivery. Even John Hoskins, in his *Directions for Speech and Style* (1599), views skill in speech and writing as comprising skill in figurative language. His treatise is limited to the conventional figures, despite his perception that the Elizabethan's interest in style had led to fine fashions in special figures,[23] and notwithstanding his knowledge of classical doctrine, derived at first hand from Sidney's translation of Aristotle's *Rhetoric*.

---

[19] *Ibid.*

[20] Ed. by Gladys D. Willcock and Alice Walker (London, 1936), 138.

[21] *Ibid.*   [22] *The Arcadian Rhetoricke* (London, 1588), 2-3.

[23] Ed. by H. H. Hudson (Princeton, 1935), 38-39.

Because they view rhetoric chiefly as elocution and delivery the Peacham stylists have no traffic with the processes of finding ideas and arguments, and of their selection, arrangement, and adaptation to the reader or hearer. The broader aspects of composition they deliberately neglect. Impelled by a spirit of intense English nationalism during the last half of the sixteenth century, they are disposed to analyze and experiment with the English language as such, with a view of determining whether it had the capacity of Latin and Greek for expressing the subtler turns of thought. Furthermore, narrowing the scope of rhetoric reflects the habit of the Elizabethan scholar of specializing in the arts of discourse. The great interest in learning, the popularity of the dialectical disputation in educational circles, and the steady growth in legal activities served to sharpen investigation and analysis into ways of discovering arguments and of formal ways of arranging them for purposes of proof and criticism. As a result, classical works on *topica* and dialectic, notably Aristotle's and Cicero's, received intensive study and application, and anything pertaining to invention and disposition became associated with logic. At the same time, an interest in fine preaching together with enthusiasm for demonstrative eloquence called forth by entertainments at court and on the Queen's progresses led to a study of the niceties of presentation. As a result, the stylistic beauties and elegancies of the Italian poets, the church fathers, and the Roman orators claimed close analysis and imitation, and elocution became associated with rhetoric. Thus, through specialization, logic and rhetoric divided discourse between them.

Not only was there a sharp division between logic and rhetoric taking place, but both parties to the specialization were conscious of it. Among the rhetoricians in Peacham's group, Dudley Fenner illustrates the scholar's penchant for specialization and the division of the art of composition into logic, a rational science, and rhetoric, a figurative and imaginative art. In his *Artes of Logike* and *Rethorike* (1584), everything pertaining to invention and disposition goes to logic; to rhetoric, as "an Arte of speaking finely," goes "the garnishing of speech, called Eloquution, and garnishing of the maner of utterance, called Pronunciation." [24] Typical of

---

[24] From a transcript of the first edition in the British Museum.

the logician's desire to mark out the strict boundaries of the arts is Rollo MacIlmaine's translation (1574) of Peter Ramus' *Dialecticae institutiones* (1543):

> . . . In this booke there is thre documents or rules kept, whiche indeede ought to be observed in all artes and sciences. The first is, that in setting forthe of an arte we gather only togeather that which dothe appertayne to the Arte which we intreate of, leauing to all other Artes that which is proper to them, this rule . . . thou shalt see here well obserued. For here is all which dothe appartayne to logike, and nothing neither of Grammar, Rhethoricke, Phisicke, nor any other arte. . . . Is he not worthie to be mocked of all men, that purposethe to wryte of Grammar, and in euery other chapiter mynglethe something of Logike, and some thing of Rhethoricke: and contrarie when he purposethe to wryte of Logike dothe speake of Grammar and of Rhethoricke?[25]

As perhaps the most significant result of dividing discourse into strict logical and rhetorical compartments, the Elizabethan scholar gradually became aware of two mental operations in composition which, to him seemed entirely different. There is, first, a *literal* or rational operation and movement of the intellect, embracing the processes of discovery, arrangement, and judgment or criticism. Then there is an *imaginative* operation which, although definitely felt, is only hinted at in terms of "dress," "ornament," "heightening," and "garnishing." Not until Bacon late in Elizabeth's reign formulates the function of rhetoric is the imaginative operation stated in more analytical terms and given broader scope.

The rhetorical theorists, it is apparent, see public address in terms of discovering and selecting content and arguments, of arranging the composition and adorning its language, of memorizing the speech and pronouncing it. As theorists, they either associate all these operations with the art of rhetoric, or, as happens with Bacon's contemporaries, divide them neatly between rhetoric and logic. In the division, rhetoric and style became inseparable. If one now considers briefly what ideas of public address the young Englishman probably derived from his training and study in the grammar school and university, we can come perhaps even closer to an appreciation of the climate of rhetorical theory to which

---

[25] *The Logike of P. Ramus*, 8-9.

Bacon as a product of his age must have been exposed, whether directly or indirectly. What were the chief school exercises which made for knowledge and skill in oral composition? What notions of public discourse would the Tudor boy derive from the university lecturer? To what books on rhetoric might he have access? It may be said that Tudor pedagogy fully appreciates that public address involves the five classical operations of invention, disposition, elocution, memory, and delivery. It is clear, furthermore, that except in a few significant cases, teachers and textbooks seem to be more concerned with the processes of invention and disposition, than with style per se.[26]

The general interest in storing the mind, in finding ideas for discourse, and in arranging prose in simple patterns is well demonstrated by those exercises which aim to equip the student with a stock of ideas together with their pattern of arrangement and expression. During the sixteenth and seventeenth centuries, the English grammar schools devoted much time to instruction in rhetoric, partly as a means of learning Latin and Greek, partly as a way of indirectly teaching morals, and partly as a means of improvement in writing and speaking. By reading selections from classical authors, by employing the double translation, by compiling commonplace books of sententious and witty sayings, by writing themes and declamations according to various formulas and speak-

---

[26] If one wishes to determine what the men of a period knew about a subject, one must obviously investigate not merely the books that mature men read, but also the books and ideas that boys and young men may have read or heard in the schools and universities. Knowledge of educational practice during the period may be gained from the following sources: Foster Watson, *Grammar Schools;* Erasmus, *De ratione studii* (1511), in W. H. Woodward's *Desiderius Erasmus Concerning the Aim and Method of Education* (Cambridge, 1904); J. L. Vives, *De tradendis disciplinis* (1531), translated in Foster Watson's *Vives: On Education* (Cambridge, 1913); Roger Ascham, *The Scholemaster* (London, 1570); Richard Mulcaster's *Positions* (London, 1581) and *The Elementarie* (London, 1582); John Brinsley, *Ludus literarius* (London, 1612); J. B. Mullinger's *The University of Cambridge from the Earliest Times to the Royal Injunctions of 1535* (Cambridge, 1873), and *The University of Cambridge from the Royal Injunctions of 1535 to the Accession of Charles I* (Cambridge, 1884); C. E. Mallet, *A History of University of Oxford* (Oxford, 1924); and H. Rackham, *Early Statutes of Christ's College, Cambridge* (Cambridge, 1927). For the chief sources of educational statutes bearing on the teaching of rhetoric, see K. R. Wallace's "Rhetorical Exercises in Tudor Education," *Quarterly Journal of Speech,* XXII (February, 1936), 28-51.

ing them, the young student was not only gaining experience in delivery and acquiring a stock of knowledge, but he was at the same time more or less consciously memorizing its form of expression. Thus he was assimilating ideas that could be useful later in university disputations, in literary endeavors, in letter-writing, and in all social and political discussion. The statutes that Henry VIII set up for his new Cathedral Schools in 1541 are indicative of school exercises for a century afterwards. The schoolmasters, so the regulations stipulate "shall endeavor to teach their pupils to speak openly, finely and distinctly, keeping due decorum both with their body and their mouth." [27] Scholars in the higher forms "shall commit to memory the Figures of Latin Oratory and the rules for making verses; and . . . shall be practiced in making verses and polishing themes. . . ." [28] They shall be instructed, moreover, in the "formulae of 'Copiousness of Words and Things' written by Erasmus; and learn to make varyings of speech in every mood, so that they may acquire the faculty of speaking Latin. . . ." [29] They must, furthermore, "compete with one another in declamations so that they may leave well learned in the school of argument." [30] It is noteworthy that such exercises are intended to be more than pure training in voice production and oral expression; they entail laborious compilation of fine sayings, either taken directly from classical sources or from compendia like Erasmus's *Adages, Apothegmes,* and *De copia de rerum verborum.* By application of the rules laid down by Hermogenes, Aphthonius, and Richard Rainolde, the exercises entail, also, considerable experience in the forms and patterns of such elements of discourse as the illustrative narrative, the comparison, and the sententious passage. Richard Rainolde's *Foundations of Rhetorike* (1563),[31] for example, is accurately indicative of such exercises. Clearly in the vein of Aphthonius' *Progymnasmata*[32] and Hermogenes'

---

[27] C. P. Cubberly, *Readings in the History of Education* (New York, 1920), 266.

[28] *Ibid.*   [29] *Ibid.*   [30] *Ibid.*

[31] I have employed a photostat copy of the first edition.

[32] The *Progymnasmata,* written in Greek, was first printed by Aldus in 1508, and translated into Latin, 1515. A London edition appeared in 1583. In Foster Watson's *The English Grammar Schools to 1660* (Cambridge, 1908), 429-434, is a careful epitome of Aphthonius' book.

Progymnasmata,[33] elementary textbooks whose popularity endured for over a century in English grammar schools, it offers the boy directions and illustrations for practice in all the *elements* or parts of a discourse: the fable, the narration, the chria, the sentence, the confutation, the confirmation, the commonplace, the praise, the dispraise, the comparison, the description, the ethopoeia, the thesis, and the legislation. Though these are but school-boy tasks, and though their persistent practice in the schools may have contributed to the "rhetorical" and formalistic patterns often manifest in Elizabethan prose and verse, the exercises were believed to promote readiness of invention in matter and words, and facility in amplification and dilation.

In the exercises they use, then, the pedagogues of the time recognize the importance of matter and arrangement in prose composition. In their testimony, too, they emphasize the broader aspects of composition at the expense of stylistics. In setting forth a plan of instruction in rhetoric for the fourteen-year-old boy, Thomas Elyot in 1531 inveighs against the emptiness and artificiality of conventionally-taught rhetoric, and insists that eloquence lies not in the words and colors of thought, but in sound invention.[34] In his work on pedagogy, Vives, while praising rhetoric as one of the great subjects of study, constantly warns both the university scholar and the grammar school master against the pitfalls of emphasizing style:

> The aim of Rhetoric is not directed to any empty use of words; that they be accounted beautiful and splendid kinds of speech; that they may be elegant and connected by a pleasant style of composition; but that we should not speak impurely and inaccurately and, to put the whole matter shortly, we should speak so that it may be made clear that this most powerful of arts is a part of wisdom.[35]

Brinsley's *Ludus literarius,* a dialogue on education that probably

---

[33] The rhetorical works of Hermogenes, including the *Progymnasmata,* were first printed in Venice, 1508-9. Paris editions followed during the century, some under the aegis of John Sturm. For part of the text of the *Progymnasmata,* see C. S. Baldwin, *Medieval Rhetoric and Poetic* (New York, 1928), 23-38. A comparison of Baldwin's translation with Rainolde's text shows close correspondences.

[34] Thomas Elyot, *The Book Called the Gouvenour* (London, 1531).

[35] Watson, *Vives,* 181.

reflects the best Elizabethan pedagogy, is likewise principally interested in the content side of rhetoric; his chapter entitled "Of making Theames full of good matter, in pure stile, and with judgment," suggests that good oratorical composition is a product of good matter.[36] Finally, Bartholomew Keckermann's *Ecclesiastical Rhetoric* (1612), held by Bass Mullinger to rival the stylistic rhetoric of Ramus and Talaeus in early seventeenth-century schools, discusses elocution most sanely.[37] For Keckermann, a good manner of expression lies, not in using figures merely, but in securing simplicity and clarity, wealth of language, and effective arrangement.

If most teachers thus appear to be primarily concerned with methods that make the student find matter for future discourse and exercise him in the broad patterns of arranging discourse and their parts, there are some pedagogues, however, who were interested chiefly in the figures and niceties of style. For the most part it is the university teacher and scholar who conceives of style narrowly, as a traffic in fine phrases and unusual, melodious arrangement. One thinks at once of Ascham's plaint that "ye know not what hurt ye do learning that care not for words, but for matter. . . ."[38] One need only recall that John Rainolds, despite an intimate knowledge of the Stagirite's *Rhetoric*, was proudly aware of developing a new manner of expression, a style that is now thought to be the direct source of Euphuism.[39] Gabriel Harvey, too, seems never to have repented whole-heartedly of his inordinate love for Ciceronian elegance of expression, and largely in imitation of him and his classical manner, many Presbyterian preachers affected the rhetoric of display to the point that Bacon could brand their style as that of the stage player.[40] To promote the formation of a fine manner of oral expression, stylists favored the declamatory exercise. Illustrative of their favoritism is Silvayn's

---

[36] Ed. by E. T. Campagnac (London, 1917), 172-190.

[37] W. F. Mitchell, *English Pulpit Oratory from Andrewes to Tillotson* (New York, 1932), 98, affords a good resumé of Keckermann.

[38] *The English Works of Roger Ascham*, ed. by W. A. Wright (Cambridge, 1904), 265.

[39] William Ringler, "The Immediate Sources of Euphuism," *Publications of the Modern Language Association*, LIII (September, 1938), 678-686.

[40] *Letters and Life* I, 76-77.

Orator, a collection of one hundred declamations after the model of Seneca. For both youth and adult, they constitute examples of "the fruits and flowers of Eloquence," [41] with perhaps the implication that upon occasion their purple passages might be conveniently employed in toto. As more than an exercise in style, the declamation also was intended to encourage fertility and readiness of thought. But although it may have in some degree developed readiness of thought, at best it constituted doubtful training, as Bacon himself recognized.[42]

To have been conscious of current rhetorical practice, the Tudor student would not have been limited merely to indoctrination through school and university exercises. He could have derived his notions of composition and rhetoric from his learned university lecturer. From him he could have become aware of the classical tradition of public address, in which rhetoric emerged as an independent, self-contained art with emphasis upon the inventive and formal aspects of composition. If the young man were at Oxford during the first half of the sixteenth century, his teacher would have read or discussed the *De oratore* and the *Partitiones oratoriae* of Cicero, and the *Institutes* of Quintilian.[43] Later in the century he might have heard Jewel's discourse on the *Partitiones oratoriae*,[44] or have listened to Rainolds elucidate upon Aristotle's *Rhetoric*.[45] Had he been at Cambridge during the earlier decades, he might have been exposed to *De ratione concionandi*, for John Fisher's purpose in founding the Lady Margaret readership (1503) was, through the use of Erasmus' treatise on preaching, to change the character of the pulpit oratory then in currency

---

[41] From Anthony Munday's Epistle to the Reader. The Chapin Library, Williams College, kindly allowed me to use a copy of the first edition.

[42] To Bacon, the declamation is impractical. He suggests that the parlimentarian, lawyer, tradesman, and ordinary converser find little occasion for the memorized speech. Worse still, the declamation, by encouraging undue attention to tropes and figures, breeds uncritical imitation and vain ostentation in the use of words, thus marking discourse with "copie rather than weight." (*Adv. of L., Works*, III, 326-327.)

[43] *The Statutes for Corpus Christi College, All Souls College, and Magdalen College, Oxford*, tr. by G. R. M. Ward (London, 1843), 99-104.

[44] H. H. Hudson, "Jewel's Oration Against Rhetoric: A Translation," *Quarterly Journal of Speech*, XIV (June, 1928), 376.

[45] Anthony à Wood, *Athenae Oxonienses* (London, 1721), I, 339.

and "to abolish the customary cavillings about words and parade of sophistry, and to have those who were designed for preachers exercised in sound learning and sober disputations. . . ." [46] Thus, even in the earliest days there was an attempt to emphasize invention rather than elocution. By mid-century at Cambridge a student would have heard the professor of dialectics and rhetoric lecture on "the *Elenchi* of Aristotle, the *Topica* of Cicero, Quintillian, and Hermogenes." [47] About the same time, so Ascham writes to Cranmer, students of divinity read Plato and Aristotle for a knowledge of oratory. [48] Still later at Cambridge, the young scholar might have been enticed by Harvey's famous lectures on rhetoric, and have witnessed the lecturer's shift from an emphasis on Ciceronian style as the hallmark of eloquence, to a stand that showed a deeper perception of the roots of rhetoric. [49]

In many cases the student did not have to depend solely on the lecturer for a knowledge of classical rhetoric. Having both money and desire, he could possess many rhetorics in which an exposition of the invention of arguments appropriate to deliberative, judicial, and demonstrative discourse at least held its own with style and delivery. He had access to the masters themselves. He could have procured at any time during the sixteenth century Cicero's *De oratore, Brutus, Topica, De partitiones oratoriae,* and *De inventione.* [50] Probably only the late Elizabethan or early Jacobean scholar could obtain Aristotle's *Rhetoric* [51] or Quintilian's *Insti-*

---

[46] Mullinger, *op. cit.,* I, 440.   [47] Mullinger, *op. cit.,* II, 110-111.

[48] *Strype's Memorials to Archbishop Cranmer* (Oxford, 1854), II, 73.

[49] *The Works of Gabriel Harvey,* ed. by A. B. Grosart (London, 1884), II, xv-xxii.

[50] Beginning with the *editio princeps* (Rome, 1467), Cicero's works received frequent publication. If, in inspecting Watt's *Bibliotheca brittannica,* we eliminate the unrevelatory entries, it appears that the chief rhetorical works, either separately or as parts of general editions, must have had wide distribution during the continental and the English Renaissance. *De inventione* had at least fourteen editions, to 1546; the *Topica,* six editions; the *Partitiones Oratoriae,* seven editions; *De oratore,* eleven editions to 1569. These are continental issues; yet English presses in the sixteenth century did not ignore Cicero as they did Aristotle's *Rhetoric* and Quintilian's *Institutes.* There were two editions of *Opera Ciceronis* (Perth, 1566-77; London, 1585), and three appearances of *De oratore* (London, 1573, 1575; Cambridge, 1589).

[51] The first English edition of this work is *Aristotelis de rhetorica,* edited by T. Goulston, 1619. There are, of course, numerous allusions in the literature of

tutes of Oratory in a complete text.[52] But despite limited circulation of Aristotle and Quintilian in England, Cicero's works enjoyed wide currency, and if many Tudor writers and speakers, in fond pursuit of an elaborate and novel style of expression, chose to overlook the central position that Tully assigns to invention and lines of argument, the fault cannot be entirely the Roman's. If, again, the student were denied direct contact with the original classical sources, he had recourse to works that transmitted much of the classic point of view to English readers. He could have read the *Rhetorica ad Herennium*,[53] a work that is devoted almost entirely to invention and so closely resembles the doctrine of Cicero's *Topics* and *De inventione* that its authorship was for a long time attributed to Tully. He could have studied Thomas Wilson, whose *Arte of Rhetorique*, as we have already suggested, exhibits something of the balance and proportion of Quintilian's *Institutes*, and whose work passes on to Tudor England much of the *Ad Herennium*, Cicero's *De oratore*, and Erasmus' *De ratione concionandi*. If he were interested in theology or the ministry, he could have turned to *De ratione concionandi* or to Melanchthon's *Rhetoric* and in those works discover a broad view of composition.

Such, then, is the knowledge of rhetoric and public address of which a Tudor figure was more or less aware, and with which

the sixteenth century to the *Rhetoric*, but whether they are derived directly from the text or from university lectures, epitome books, and collections of commonplaces, is problematical. Rainolde indubitably knew the work; Sidney, so Hoskins asserts (*op. cit.*, 41), translated Books I and II; John Astely and Roger Ascham read it together [*Works of Roger Ascham*, ed. by W. A. Wright (Cambridge, 1904), 123]; and Erasmus helped Sturm with an edition. Cf. M. T. Herrick, "The Early History of Aristotle's *Rhetoric* in England," *Philological Quarterly*, V (July, 1926), 242-257. As Herrick suggests and as Watt reveals, continental presses rarely produced a reliable text of the *Rhetoric*, although Aristotle's other works, especially the logical treatises, had wide circulation. Harvey may have known the *Rhetoric;* Bacon probably did.

[52] If we may accept Watt's authority, the *Institutes* went through forty-seven editions from 1470 to 1561. The numerous continental printings may have rendered English editions needless, for not until 1641 does one appear. Because of its mention in educational statutes, sixteenth century students through their teachers probably were better acquainted with Quintilian than with Aristotle. Erasmus, Thomas Elyot, Ascham, Vives, Wilson, and Harvey knew it at first hand.

[53] This work was almost invariably published with Cicero's works. By conservative count, there were twelve appearances from 1470-1569.

Bacon was probably conversant. The processes of oral and written composition, fully recognized, were either admitted under rhetoric as a complete art of composition, or were carefully divided among logic, rhetoric, and ethics. Early in the period, systematic rhetoricians allow rhetoric to treat of all the operations of speech-making; in the last half of the period, rhetoric is vouchsafed pronunciation and the machinery of figures only; in the Jacobean period, the scholars become less preoccupied with analysis and experimentation in style, and view rhetoric again as a broad art of address. The grammar school teachers, if we may judge by their procedures, steadily view discourse largely as a compound of matter and broad patterns; the university pedagogues see oral composition in terms of the five classical processes, though the strict analysts and innovators among them put great stress upon fine elocution with which they associate rhetoric.

CHAPTER TWELVE

BACON'S CONTRIBUTION

If we now compare Bacon's conception of public address with that of his predecessors and contemporaries, it is evident that the Lord Chancellor as a cyclopedist has done more than accept the conventional notions on public discourse and work them, unmodified, into his chart of knowledge. By centering his attention almost exclusively upon the invention of ideas and arguments, he has, in the first place, emphasized the importance of content and rational argument in literary and oratorical composition. His classical forbears, Aristotle, Cicero, and Quintilian, devote considerable time to the *Topica* of invention and to the means of logical proof, but in their rhetorical theories—especially Quintilian's—style and delivery are developed quite as fully as invention. Cox and Wilson, Vicars and Farnaby, Rainolde and Harvey likewise discuss presentation at length, and at times talk so copiously of the gay and delectable function of rhetoric that their real emphasis is uncertain. Bacon's chief concern, on the other hand, is never in doubt. Almost alone among the Tudor and early Stuart theorists, he refuses to discuss style systematically and disdains to treat formally of delivery; rather, he prefers to direct his energy to the "true and solid" part of rhetoric, and stir "the earth a little about the roots of this subject." When most Elizabethan scholars thought of rhetoric and style almost interchangeably, it is remarkable that Bacon should value content and logical argument so highly.

As aids to the finding of content and sound argument, *The Colours of Good and Evil*, the *Antitheta*, the *Formulae*, and the *Apothegms* must be weighed for their originality. In them, Bacon thought he was making significant additions to the theory of public address. But whether the *Colours* can be considered a contribution to the history of rhetorical theory is doubtful. Inspired by Aristotle's *Rhetoric* and his *De sophisticis elenchis*,[1] Bacon intended to improve upon the Stagirite by concentrating on the logical weaknesses and refutation of current sophisms on good and evil. He shows that they, as the expressed or implied premises of deliberative discourse, bear the appearance of universal truth without the reality, and he conducts the refutation admirably. But the content and method of the *Colours* are definitely drawn from Aristotle's *Rhetoric*. Bacon's service, therefore, lies chiefly in the shrewdness of his refutation, rather than in any substantive contribution. Yet, despite his failure to make a substantive addition, Bacon gives his *Colours* an application that is new to Tudor theorists. Since he is interested in having rhetoric second reason rather than oppress it, he intends that the sophisms should help the speaker guard against bad reasoning, whether his own or others. Bacon desires, above all else, to prevent the miscarriage of reason. The *Colours*, as a result, are to rhetorical inference what the Idols and formal fallacies are to the inferences of logic and science. Unique, then, among the rhetoricians of his time, is the emphasis Bacon puts upon the detection of popular errors in thinking.

In supplying an extended illustration of *antitheta*, or pro and con arguments on everyday traits of character, Bacon makes a noteworthy contribution to the methodology of finding ideas for discourse. Although he took the scheme from Cicero and Seneca,[2] his application is extensive. Whereas Cicero had offered but a general suggestion for *antitheta*, Bacon supplies the specific amplification, and whereas Cicero had limited their utility to forensic situations, Bacon emphasizes their applicability to the deliberative and the demonstrative speech as well. Bacon's *antitheta*, furthermore, are shrewdly calculated to promote originality of thought. Seneca's *suasoriae* had offered, in semi-narrative treatment, possible lines of argument on common subjects, set out in an easy sequence and with much of their amplification suggested.[3] But

---

[1] Letter to Lord Mountjoy, *Works*, VII, 70.

[2] So Bacon acknowledges; *Works*, IV, 472.

[3] See the *Suasoriae of Seneca the Elder*, tr. by W. A. Edward (Cambridge, 1928).

Bacon seems to have perceived that such *suasoriae* might breed rigidity and superficiality of thought and application. His *antitheta*, consequently, are isolated, general statements, bound together only by a general head. In fact, he intentionally makes some of them farfetched—"exaggerated both ways with the utmost force of the wit" [4]—in order to stimulate thinking, and thus to encourage originality and freshness of invention. He is here clearly trying to remedy the stiffness and conventionality of thought that a narrow application of commonplace books, epitomes, general *topica*, and rhetorical patterns of arrangement had brought to much of English discourse.

The *formulae* and the *apothegms* need little discussion. The suggestion that a speaker should collect stock phrases of introduction, transition, and repartee appears to have come out of Bacon's experience as a lawyer, and to apply particularly to the forensic situation where skill in using signposts, transitions, and other devices to keep clear the line of proof and refutation are especially valuable. They constitute practical expedients that are new to rhetorical theory, but unimportant. The apothegms, if somewhat more important than *formulae*, find considerable precedent in the literature of rhetorical theory. Cicero mentioned them, and suggested a classification. Erasmus' great collection received an English edition in 1542, in which the nature of the apothegm and its rhetorical application is clearly indicated.[5] Bacon's offering, accordingly, is little more than restatement and illustration.

Of the four aids to invention, then, the *formulae* and *antitheta* appear to be novelties in the history of public address; the popular sophisms represent departures from Tudor practice only. Another departure from contemporaneous opinion on public discourse is the dominant position which Bacon gives to the political or deliberative address. Strikingly unlike any other theorist, whether Cox, Wilson, Vicars, or Farnaby, he rarely does more than allude to the forensic speech and the demonstrative address as such. In fact, the bulk of those additions which he supplies to meet the "deficiencies" of rhetoric is directed primarily to deliber-

---

[4] *De aug.*, VI, 3; *Works*, IV, 472.

[5] *The Apophthegms of Erasmus, translated into English by Nicolas Udall*, ed. by Robert Roberts (Boston, 1877), xvii-xxii.

atives. Furthermore, Bacon sees the deliberative speech not as letter-writing, but as a virile form of address in public affairs. Perhaps his years as a respected member of the House of Commons led him to think of rhetorical discourse largely in terms of political speaking. It is probable, too, that his concern over the political speech reflects the growth of earnest and widespread political discussion during the reigns of Elizabeth and James. The debates over the religious policies of both monarchs, and the sharp controversy over the Common's privileges, particularly freedom of speech and control of the purse, produced the first great political speeches of our language. Some evidence of increased interest in the deliberative address, both on Bacon's part and in English thought generally, is the difference in treatment accorded *antitheta* in the *Advancement* (1605) and the *De augmentis* (1623). The later work of course expands at some length all of the topics, as well as the *antitheta,* that are discussed in the early work. Yet the care that Bacon took with the *antitheta* in the intervening years is strikingly apparent, for in the *Advancement* those aids to deliberative discourse are represented by only one short example; in the *De augmentis* they are spun out to forty-seven tables, each with a considerable list of pros and cons. It appears that Bacon cannot have held the deliberative address lightly.

Whether we compare Bacon with those theorists who, viewing rhetoric as a complete art of address, deal with invention as well as with elocution, or with those who restrict rhetoric to style and delivery, it is clear that no Tudor or early Stuart rhetorician pays as little respect to the figurative dress and ornamentation of language as he. Herein he differs markedly from his period. He of course values style; indeed, "it is a thing not hastily to be condemned, to clothe and adorn the obscurity even of philosophy itself with sensible and plausible elocution." [6] At times in his works when rhetoric is caught up in a phrase, Bacon even speaks of it as the art of graceful utterance, and associates it with ornament. But in paying tribute to style, he has little sympathy with its vogue in English discourse. He would repudiate Rainolde's premise that "the most noble and excellent thing in life is to dilate copiously any matter or sentence, by pleasantness and ingeniousness of

---

[6] *Adv. of L., Works,* III, 284.

witte and by skill of oracion, to move multitudes of people to one's ends." [7] Similarly, Bacon would scorn Roger Ascham:

Ye know not what hurt ye do learning that care not for words, but for matter, and so make a divorce betwixt tongue and heart. For mark all ages; look upon the whole course of both the Greek and Latin tongue, and ye shall surely find that when apt and good words began to be neglected . . . then also began ill deeds to spring, strange manners to oppress good order, new and fond opinions to strive with old and true doctrine, first in philosophy and after in religion. . . .[8]

Indeed, Bacon saw that the result of Ascham's over-weening interest in words had brought forth "a delicate and polished kind of learning," and that Ascham, in company with Carr, Sturm, and Hermogenes, had turned much of Renaissance writing "rather towards copie than weight." [9] Bacon perceives, furthermore, that in the years of Elizabeth and James, men took up Seneca and cultivated a style in which words were pointed, the sentences concise, and the whole composition twisted into shape rather than being allowed to flow, a trick that seemed to make a thing more ingenious than it really is.[10] In short, though vain matter is worse than vain words, "substance of matter is better than beauty of words." [11]

If, by subordinating style to invention, Bacon has not made a substantive contribution to rhetoric, at least he has done yeoman service in the cause of good writing and speaking in times that were over-weeningly fond of stylistics. Beyond this, he offers a profound suggestion for a theory of style. The rhetorician, he asserts, ought to look deeply into allied arts and sciences, not only to understand the workings of his tropes and figures, his word-arrangements and harmonies, but also to discover new principles:

. . . a man should be thought to dally, if he did not note how the figures of rhetoric and music are many of them the same. The repetitions and traductions in speech and the reports and hauntings of sounds in music are the very same things. . . . The figure that Cicero and the rest commend as one of the best points of elegancy which is the fine checking of expectation, is no less well known to the musicians when

---

[7] *Foundations of Rhetorike,* Epistle to the Reader.
[8] Quoted by Mitchell, *op. cit.,* 71.   [9] *Adv. of L., Works,* III, 283-284.
[10] *Works,* I, 452.   [11] *Adv. of L., Works,* III, 285.

they have a special grace in flying the close or cadence. And these are no allusions but direct communities, the same delights of the mind being to be found not only in music, rhetoric, but in moral philosophy, policy, and other knowledges, and that obscure in the one, which is the more apparent in the other, yea and that discovered in the one which is not found at all in the other, and so one science greatly aiding to the invention and augmentation of another.[12]

Bacon suggests, also, that a knowledge of style—and indeed all aspects of the arts of speech—would be vastly improved by a study of the comparative grammar and philology.[13] Though similar suggestions for the theory and study of style may be implied by Aristotle, Cicero, and Quintilian, Francis Bacon seems to have been the first English Renaissance figure to understand elocution broadly.

Bacon speaks of style incidentally, partly because it is a phase of rhetoric that has been "excellently well-laboured," and partly because he sees rhetoric as a complete art of composition in which elocution is but one problem of many. That rhetoric is a full-bodied, independent art is, in fact, another significant aspect of the Baconian rhetoric, and although recognized by both theorist and pedagogue is so opposed to the main current of Elizabethan literary theory that Bacon deserves some credit for maintaining it. In his cyclopedia, as we have seen, rhetoric has its own province, and is set off from the allied arts by its peculiar function of "recommending reason to the imagination for the better moving of the will." Consequently, any operation that a speaker may go through in performing his proper function is the legitimate concern of rhetoric. When thus regarded as a distinct activity, rhetoric for its own ends may quite properly deal with invention and disposition as well as with style. Similarly, logic is to Bacon a distinct activity. His "new logic," as explained in the *Novum organum*, is a methodology of science. It is designed to discover new facts or laws that are characterized by both universality and necessity. His ordinary or "common logic" is a methodology of the popular arts. It aims, on the one hand, to invent knowledge and

---

[12] *Of the Interpretation of Nature, Works,* III, 230.
[13] *Ibid.*

proofs that are distinguished by probability, rather than necessity; on the other, it aims to test judgments and proofs in order to
establish their truth and validity. Furthermore, whatever techniques and procedures logic may want in realizing its objects, it
is free to examine and use, even though they may include the art
of composition. It is highly significant, in fact, that in Bacon's eyes
a scientist is to employ a peculiar kind of composition whenever
he conveys scientific information to another scientist. He is to write
aphoristically in precise, denotative language, and as a scientist,
not as a rhetorician or a logician, he should study this method
and become skilled in it. Clearly, then, Bacon sees the arts and
sciences as separate activities which in pursuing their own ends
use any methodology they may need. To him, accordingly, rhetoric
legitimately has its own problems of invention and disposition.
Hence, he is willing to commend Aristotle for showing that rhetoric
stands between logic and ethics, "as participating of both."

The view that rhetoric is a full-bodied art of composition was,
as has been heretofore explained, not new to Tudor and Stuart
minds. Aristotle's works demonstrate that science, dialectic (or
logic), and rhetoric are separate arts, distinguished chiefly by their
ends. Science aims to set up universal and necessary truths by
means of the syllogism and induction; dialectic aims, through discussion, at discovering truths and testing inferences in the realm
of the probable, and it, like science, uses the syllogism and induction; rhetoric aims at persuasion in the realm of the probable,
everyday affairs, and employs in continuous discourse, rather than
by question and answer, the enthymeme (rhetorical syllogism) and
the example as its principal means of inference. Using the same
inferential methods, each art adapts them to its own purposes.
Such is the Aristotelian position, and Tudor scholars doubtless
understood it. When compared to that of Aristotle, then, Bacon's
position is not unusual. When set against that of Elizabethan and
Jacobean rhetoricians, however, Bacon's stand is both novel and
surprising. From Thomas Wilson's *Arte* (1553) to Vicar's *Manuductio* (1619), no English treatise on rhetoric or logic views
speech-making as a fully-rounded art. As we have noticed already,
the rhetors, like Talaeus, Sherry, Peacham, Fraunce, Fenner, and

15

Butler, rigidly restrict their art either to stylistics alone, or to style and delivery. The logicians, especially Ramus, Lever, Fenner, and Fraunce, aid and abet them.[14] Against the stylists and the logicians Bacon has taken issue; contrary to the preponderant thought and practice of his times, he refrains from emasculating rhetoric, or, for that matter, any art. He believes that each art and science should pursue its own course after its own way. Yet simultaneously each is to maintain a close connection with related subjects and with the First Philosophy, not for the sake of borrowing bodily the results of another art, as would rhetoric were it to depend solely on ethics for a knowledge of man's affections, but rather for allowing each art to gain that "light and information which the particulars and instances of one science do discover and present for the framing or correcting of the axioms of another science. . . ."[15]

It has been hitherto suggested that Bacon considered the order and arrangement of all discourse, both scientific and rhetorical, as determined chiefly by the audience, purpose, and occasion. In thus perceiving that the structure of discourse should be functional, he takes an unequivocal stand that is unrepresentative of his age. Although they permit some elasticity, the chief theorists prefer that prose structure should conform to the classical order, with its exordium, narration, proof, and peroration.[16] Cox in 1524

---

[14]Ralph Lever may be an exception. In his *Arte of Reason* (1573), he proposes to teach how "to reason wittily of doubtfull matters and to speake forcibly on all," thus suggesting that his logic may be readily applied to public discourse. Indeed, he is fully aware that speaking has fallen upon stylistic ways: "As for Ciceronians and sugar tongued fellowes, which labour more for fineness of speach, than for knowledge of good matter, and shaking forth a number of choice words, and picked sentences, they hinder good learning, wyth their fond chatter." (From the preface, or "Forespeache.") Lever's book, however, is limited strictly to the Aristotelian Categories, and to invention and judgment.

Nathaniel Carpenter seems to have maintained seriously that all rhetorical amplification, including even tropes and figures, should fall within the scope of dialectic. Consult W. S. Howell, "Nathaniel Carpenter's Place in the Controversy Between Dialectic and Rhetoric," *Speech Monographs,* I (September, 1934), 23-24.

[15] *Of the Interpretation of Nature, Works,* III, 229.

[16] R. L. Irwin has pointed out that the classical speech divisions may be described as four. Consult his "The Classical Speech Divisions," *Quarterly Journal of Speech,* XXV (April, 1939), 212-213.

and Wilson in 1553 both treat the classical divisions as if their content and order must be closely respected. Both men are far more concerned with topics appropriate to each speech-division than with adapting the form and plan of the entire speech to the rhetorical purpose and occasion. Wilson's long discussion of disposition gives him special opportunity for suggesting ways in which the speaker or writer might adapt the classical arrangement to his needs, but beyond admitting that the introduction and the narration may be left out occasionally, Wilson hardly goes. We derive the impression, accordingly, that if an author employs the traditional sequence, the frame of his composition is substantially fixed. Vicars in 1619 and Farnaby in 1625 appear somewhat less exacting; they allow the omission of one or more of the conventional divisions, and advise their transposition when the occasion warrants.[17] In truth, it is mainly the sacred rhetoricians, rather than the secular, who seem eager to modify the classical order in favor of greater functional utility.[18] Among them all, it is Bacon who barely recognizes the classical divisions; to him they are purely incidental.

Although it is clear that the classical form of discourse is undergoing some modification in Bacon's time, it is not equally clear that the theorists are aware of the principle of functional arrangement. The earlier writers seem but dimly aware of an order that is governed by the circumstances of communication. Cox perhaps recognizes it;[19] and Wilson, as if he were rebelling against

---

[17] So both Vicars and Farnaby assert early in their chapters on Disposition.

[18] See D. Erasmus, *Ecclesiastes* (Basle, 1535); Niels Hemmingsen, *The Preacher, or Methode of Preaching,* trans. by John Horsfall (London, 1574); Andreas Hyperius, *The Practise of Preaching, otherwise called the Pathway to the Pulpit* (first English edition, 1577); William Perkins, *The Arte of Phophecying* (London, 1587). These men see much adaptation of the classical parts of the sermon; they reduce their number, permit numerous digressions to facilitate emotional appeal, and suggest alternative arrangements that fit both content and occasion. Consult Ruth Bozell, *English Preachers of the Seventeenth Century on the Art of Preaching* (Cornell University doctoral dissertation), Ithaca, 1939; and K. R. Wallace, "Early English Rhetoricians on the Structure of Rhetorical Prose," *Papers in Rhetoric,* edited by D. C. Bryant (Saint Louis, 1940), 18-26.

[19] On the one hand, Cox seems to stand for considerable elasticity in the selection of the various types of proof and in their amplification; and so far as the adaptation of argument will alter the broad outlines of discourse, Cox accord-

the classical order on which he lavishes his time, offers counsel
which would allow great plasticity of structure: ". . . a wise man
. . . will not be bound by any precise rules, nor keepe any one order,
but such onely as by reason he shall thinke best to use, being master
ouer him. . . ." [20] Much later, Farnaby hints at an order determined
by Wisdom and Expediency, but he does not amplify or apply his
hint in any way. Vicars, although not wanting to abandon the
classical order, points out that every division of rhetorical discourse, from the Exordium through to the Conclusion, offers possibilities of "suitable" argument and of working in appropriate
emotional appeal. In Vicars' mind, then, the content and the in-
ternal amplification of each speech-division look directly to the
audience. But although Wilson and Vicars exhibit some realization
that prose structure may be functional, it is Bacon who fully appreciates the relation between form and function. In treating Disposition, not as an adjunct of rhetoric or of logic, but as a separate
art of order and method, he sees that the structure of all prose
discourse is governed by subject, purpose, and audience. In both
scientific discourse and rhetorical address, form is a necessary expression of the essential circumstances that call a composition into
being. This was a great lesson for the times of Elizabeth and James,
and to Bacon should go some of the credit.

With respect to memory, Bacon's advice to the speaker does not
improve upon Wilson or Cicero. Like Wilson, he recommends that
the orator should adopt some arbitrary visual structure or unit
with which ideas, their order and their sequence, are readily associated. His point of attack, however, differs from that of Wilson,
because in both the *De augmentis* and the *Novum organum* he
makes memory an independent art which he investigates in the
spirit of a psychologist; the art of memory ceases to subserve
rhetoric. But in thus treating memory, Bacon does not banish it
from rhetorical theory entirely, as do both Cox and Farnaby.

---

ingly may be conscious of the connection between structure and the rhetorical
situation. On the other hand, Cox discusses the three species of address—political, forensic, and demonstrative—by formally treating each of them in terms of
the traditional divisions, and thus implies that the pattern of discourse has been
adequately fixed by tradition.

[20] *Arte of Rhetorique*, 159.

When Bacon's handling of memory is set beside that of Butler's,[21] the Lord Chancellor neither gains nor loses stature. Where Butler is more detailed, more practical, and more thorough in suggesting helps for the "artificial" memory, Bacon is somewhat more provocative and penetrating. Not constrained, as is Butler, to present his remarks after the one and only Ramean method, and not bound to aim at the school-boy, he is free to ruminate over the nature of memory and to make only those practical suggestions that seemed to him to require emphasis. In the advice given to the speaker for the strengthening of memory, it is particularly interesting that both men emphasize the value of the extemporaneous speech rather than the exercise that is memorized verbatim; both believe that in extempore utterance the effort or desire to recall develops the memory far better than repetition by rote.

Of delivery, Bacon has taken a broader view than Cox or Wilson. If we may judge by the art of declamation suggested in the *Promus*, Bacon sees delivery as an art that has rules and technique, and is not merely a matter of God-given "eloquence" as Cox implies. But though he looks at *pronuntiatio* more comprehensively than Wilson, his discussion of the topic goes little beyond him. Both men venerate Demosthenes' judgment as to the importance of action and utterance in oratory, and both, consequently, are explicit on the subject of gesture, although Wilson is somewhat more concerned with correctness of articulation. In treating of delivery, then, Bacon has been suggestive, provocative, and at times practical. He is neither as systematic nor as comprehensive as his contemporaries, whether he is set beside Wilson, early in the period, or beside Vicars, Farnaby, and Butler, late in the period. Beyond hinting at an art of delivery and dropping a few rule-of-thumb injunctions on deportment and movement, he does not go.

One comes, finally, to the most distinctive aspect of Bacon's thoughts on public discourse, the association of rhetoric with the imagination. The duty and office of rhetoric, as has been noted,

---

[21] For Butler, see Lee S. Hultzén's "Charles Butler on Memory," *Speech Monographs*, VI (1939), 43-65. Professor Hultzén includes a translation of the chapter on Memory in Butler's *Oratoriae Libri Duo* (London, 1629), and asserts that the chapter "may be taken as typical of the best that was being done at the time in English scholarship in the field of rhetoric."

is to apply the dictates of reason to the imagination for the better moving of the will. At the outset of the *Advancement* Bacon assigns to poetry the province of the imagination, to history, the realm of memory, and to philosophy, the realm of reason. Distrustful of the free and uncontrolled play of the imagination in poesy," [22] he decides later in the *Advancement* to make imagination subservient to reason, and assigns it to rhetoric as one of the rational arts. Simultaneously, he decrees that logic and ethics shall have their psychological provinces; man's understanding is assigned to logic, man's will and affections to ethics. To Bacon, however, neither the understanding nor the will can operate successfully unless the imagination which performs "the office of an agent or messenger or proctor in both provinces" comes into play; "for sense sends all kinds of images over to imagination for reason to judge of; and reason again when it has made its judgment and selection, sends them over to imagination before the decree be put into execution." [23] Similarly, in practical affairs neither logic nor ethics can lead mankind to right reason and to right action unless rhetoric steps in and by valid inferences and vivid expression holds up pictures of the true and good. "For the end of logic is to teach a form of argument to secure reason, and not to entrap it; the end likewise of moral philosophy is to procure the affections to fight on the side of reason, and not to invade it; the end of rhetoric is to fill the imagination with observations and images, to second reason, and not to oppress it." [24] Rhetoric thus appears to Bacon as the art of "insinuative reason"; it teaches the art of selecting, ordering, and illuminating whatever may turn the will, on a given occasion, toward the good course of action.

It is to be observed, however, that the imagination of rhetoric is licensed. Were it free, it would rise up and overpower reason, as it does when the unscrupulous but eloquent orator inflames men's minds and passions until they lose sight of reason.[25] Furthermore, if the imagination were free, it might, during those moments when we recall and recreate former impressions, recombine the stuff of

[22] *De aug.*, V, I; *Works;* IV, 406. See Murray W. Bundy, "Bacon's True Opinion of Poetry," *Studies in Philology*, XXVII (1930) 260.

[23] *De aug.*, V, 1; *Works*, IV, 405-406.

[24] *De aug.*, VI, 3; *Works*, IV, 455-456.   [25] *De aug.*, V, 1; *Works*, IV, 406.

memory capriciously. For when the mind divides and combines impressions "according to the pleasure of the mind, and . . . parts are arbitrarily transposed into the likeness of some individual, it is the work of the imagination; which, not being bound by any law and necessity of nature or matter, may join things which in nature are never found apart. . . ." [26] On the other hand, when composition and division proceed "according to the evidence of things, and as they really show themselves in nature, or at least appear to show themselves, this is the office of reason; and all business of this kind is assigned to reason." Palpably, then, unrestricted imaginative activity is irrational. Hence, in viewing rhetoric, like logic or ethics, as a rational art, and in assigning the serious work of the imagination to rhetoric rather than to poetry, Bacon apparently intends the rhetorical imagination to be that which sticks to the "evidence of things." Consequently, in the invention of both his basic arguments and their style of presentation, the prose artist must not allow his imagination to range too far afield. To Bacon, of course, the imagination that operates in rhetorical prose may be no different in essence from the imagination that functions in poetry. But whereas in poetry both the inventor and the listener may be concerned with *ideal* representation and presentation, in rhetorical composition both the inventor and the listener are devoted to practical questions whose reference to probable fact and reality are direct and unmistakable. It is in this sense that the imagination in rhetoric is less licensed than in poetry. It would appear, indeed, that the prose artist, once he has mapped out his basic lines of argument, is free to use any means whatsoever in addressing the imagination, providing his amplification and illumination are not far-fetched and fantastic.

Bacon's view that rhetoric, along with logic and ethics, is to subserve right reason and good conduct is traditional; almost every theorist, whether ancient, medieval, Tudor or Stuart, claimed that his art promoted reason and virtue, and the logician, grammarian, and rhetorician was no exception. But the idea that rhetoric makes peculiar use of serious imaginative activity is perhaps the most novel of Bacon's thoughts on public address.

---

[26] *Descriptio globi intellectualis, Works*, V, 504. Cf. Phillip Sidney, *An Apologie for Poetrie*, ed. by E. Arber (London, 1868), 25, 26.

Only Plato's opinion that rhetoric enchants the soul can be considered comparable. Yet Plato makes no attempt to suggest the specific peculiarities of the enchantment, nor to show that imaginative activity may be bound to the needs of practical reason as well as serve the ends of poetic creation. Other rhetoricians define their art in terms of general ends: to persuade, to instruct, to delight, to speak well. Most of them speak of the conventional processes of composition; inventing proofs, arranging the arguments and the parts of the discourse, forming the style, memorizing the speech, and delivering the finished product. But none perceives that in achieving either the general ends or in going through the conventional operations, all may be described pyschologically as a certain stimulation of the listener's mind to imaginative activity. Like Sherry and Peacham, the exponents of a strictly stylistic rhetoric understood that tropes and figures delighted the mind and addressed the imagination, but none tried to point out that the action of the imagination in poetry and in rhetoric may differ in range and degree, if not in kind. The honor of making that distinction is Bacon's.

In final judgment, it may be said that Francis Bacon, viewing rhetoric in its relation to all learning, saw public address with greater perspective than his English kin. Yet his perspective did not keep him from offering new and practical suggestions that would help both speaker and writer to discover content and to estimate the soundness of his inferences, particularly in the deliberative address. His aggrandizement of content and sound argument at the expense of style and his view of rhetoric as a complete art of composition in its own right, while not new to the early Tudor theorists and their classical progenitors, were certainly not in the tradition of Elizabethan and early Jacobean rhetoric. Bacon's contemporaries paid tribute to the manner of expression; Bacon himself levied tribute from elocution. Most important of all, he was the first to work out the central function of rhetoric on psychological grounds.

CHAPTER THIRTEEN

BACON

AND POST-ELIZABETHAN

RHETORICAL THEORY

In taking the last steps of this study, it would be a pleasure to record that Bacon's views on communication and public address had clearly and directly left a large imprint on rhetorical theorists. But only in a few instances is the mark distinct. Among the older historians of rhetorical theory, Gibert, in his *Jugemens des Savans sur les Auteurs qui ont traité de la Rhétorique*, quotes rather extensively from the *Advancement of Learning*,[1] and R. C. Jebb, in his article on Rhetoric in the eleventh edition of the *Encyclopedia Britannica*, thinks that Bacon's *antitheta* constitute a significant addition to the method of analyzing a case and to the discovery of arguments. Among the later historians, Sandford, in his *English Theories of Public Address*, 1530-1828, has made way for him, and Howell makes reference to him in treating of Nathaniel Carpenter's place in the controversy between dialectic and rhetoric.[2] No twentieth-century analyst and teacher who constructs a system of rhetoric takes notice of Bacon. Yet in the three centuries following the publication of the *Advancement*, a few teachers, in one respect or another, have drawn directly upon the Lord Chancellor.

Thomas Blount is the seventeenth-century rhetorician who ac-

---

[1] (Paris, 1713-1719), II, 420-428.
[2] For Sandford, see *English Theories* (Columbus, Ohio, 1929), 94-98; for Howell, see *Speech Monographs*, I (September, 1934), 20-41.

knowledges specific indebtedness to Bacon. The full title of his
Academy of Eloquence (1654) directs special attention to "Common Places and Formula's digested into an Easie and Methodical
Way to speak and write fluently. . . ." Among the four medallions
on the frontispiece, in company with Demosthenes, Cicero, and
Sidney, is an engraving of Bacon! After thus paying his respects
to "my Lord," Blount fills half his volume with examples and collections of commonplaces and formulae. He declares that Bacon
gave him the hint for these, and quotes almost verbatim the *Advancement* and the *De augmentis*. In the second part of his treatise,
so his preface asserts, "you have Formulae majores, or Common-
places, upon the most usual subjects for stile and speech: The use
and advantage whereof is asserted by my Lord Bacon, who (in his
Advancement of Learning) says thus: I hold the diligence and pain
in collecting *Commonplaces,* to be of great use and certainty in
studying, as that which aids the memory, sub-ministers copy to the
invention, and contracts the sight of Judgement to a strength." [3]
In the third part of his volume, he tells the reader that he shall find
"Formulae minores (as my Lord calls them), lesser forms, which
he then reckoned among the defects in our Language, and says
they are as it were, the Portals and Postern-doors of Stile and
Speech, and of no small use." [4] Blount, then, bows to Bacon. Yet,
despite such first-hand acquaintance, he appears not to have ap-
preciated that Bacon's emphasis, both in his system as a whole and
in the doctrine and use of commonplaces, was on invention and matter. When viewed in its entirety, the *Academy* seems to be a legacy
of the stylists rather than the classicists; starting off with a
comprehensive survey of tropes and figures, it suggests that Blount
developed the *formulae* principally because they facilitated ease
and grace of utterance. If he had been interested in the common-
place as a means of strengthening the speaker's powers of analysis,
judgment, and memory, he would, like Bacon, have urged the student to make his own collection, rather than offering him a sixty-
eight page compendium.

Almost a century after Blount, John Lawson published his

---

[3] Cf. Bacon's *Works,* III, 398; IV, 435.
[4] Cf. *Works,* IV, 492. These quotations appear in at least two editions of the
Academy of Eloquence, 1656, 1670.

Lectures Concerning Oratory (1752). Although the theory they reveal is essentially classical and was probably derived mainly from close acquaintance with the classical rhetoricians, he gives weight to two of the more important aspects of his system by citing Bacon as authority. First, he insists that the social utility of rhetoric lies in the service of truth:

> Eloquence, saith Lord *Bacon,* is inferior to Wisdom in Excellence, yet superior in common use . . . signifying, that Profoundness of Wisdom will help a man to Name, or Admiration; but that it is Eloquence which prevaileth in active life.

> Let us then consider Eloquence in this Light, in her genuine state, as the Handmaid of Truth.[5]

Lawson observes in the second place, that a speaker's ability to select readily the material proper to an occasion can be improved by collecting and classifying commonplace arguments:

> *Sagacity* may be improved by experience, and the mind helped, if it be not blind: Art can supply Helps to it's Faculty of seeing, can strengthen it where weak. . . .

> With respect to this question it is that the same Lord *Bacon* observes Rhetorick to be defective; that one Branch is almost wholly wanting, namely, the *Topical Part:* By which is meant, a Number of Observations on all common Heads, digested into convenient order; which shall be ever at Hand, that the Orator may have Recourse to them;

---

[5] (Ed. 1760, 126-127). Cf. the *Advancement, Works,* III, 409: ". . . although in true value it [Rhetoric] is inferior to wisdom as it is said by God to Moses, when he disabled himself for want of this faculty, *Aaron shall be thy speaker, and thou shalt be to him as God;* yet with the people it is more mighty: for so Soloman saith, *Sapiens corde appellabitur prudens, sed dulcis eloquio majora reperiet,* signifying that profoundness of wisdom will help a man to a name or admiration, but that it is eloquence that prevaileth in an active life." The principal points of the next two pages of the *Advancement* are contained in these two passages: " . . . the end of Logic is to teach a form of argument to secure reason, and not to entrap it; the end of Morality is to procure the affections to obey reason, and not to invade it; the end of Rhetoric is to fill the imagination to second reason, and not to oppress it. . . ." " . . . Logic handleth reason exact and in truth, and Rhetoric handleth it as it is planted in popular opinions and manners." Lawson's second sentence in the quotation above thus appears to be his own way of combining the gist of the passages just cited with the 'handmaid' image that Bacon uses to describe his additions to rhetorical theory.

and draw from them, as from a general Store, Materials on all Occasions.[6]

The passage continues as a close paraphrase of Bacon, even to the point of citing Bacon's own authorities, Cicero and Demosthenes.[7] It would seem, accordingly, that Lawson knew at first hand those parts of the *Advancement* in which rhetoric is formally discussed, and that, in contrast to Blount, he recognized some of the emphatic aspects of the Elizabethan's theory.[8]

To some extent George Campbell's *Philosophy of Rhetoric* (1776) is indebted to Bacon. Campbell calls Bacon "perhaps the most comprehensive genius in philosophy that has appeared in modern times," [9] and to the study of this genius he may owe some of the good sense and sharpness of perception revealed in his theory. He specifically draws upon Bacon in stating the peculiar purpose and function of rhetoric. In explaining that the art of speaking makes use of all the faculties and powers of the mind whereas logic and ethics employ single faculties, he relies on Bacon's position that "logic, whose end is the discovery of truth, is founded on the doctrine of the understanding; and ethics (under which may be comprehended economics, politics, and jurisprudence) are founded in that of the will." [10] After thus stating the ends of logic and ethics, Campbell turns immediately to talk of rhetoric, or eloquence, in a paragraph[11] that parallels in content, though not in phraseology, the view of rhetoric that Bacon sketches in the early part of the *De augmentis scientiarum*, Book VI, Chapter I. Rhetoric requires the aid of the imagination and thereby holds attention and rouses the passions; rhetoric is useful; though it is inferior to wisdom, it is "absolutely necessary for dif-

---

[6] *Lectures Concerning Oratory* (Dublin, 1760), 127-128.

[7] Cf. the *Advancement, Works,* III, 390-391.

[8] Lawson makes only one other direct reference to Bacon. In advising the speaker to rest his case on a few strong arguments rather than to use many arguments indifferently, he brings forth Bacon as witness: "Lord *Bacon* justly observes, that one idle Reason weakeneth all the good which went before." (*Lectures Concerning Oratory,* 387.)

[9] *Philosophy of Rhetoric* (Boston, 1823), 17.

[10] *Philosophy of Rhetoric* (Boston, 1823), 17. Campbell's footnote cites in Latin the *De augmentis scientiarum, Works,* I, 614-615.

[11] *Philosophy of Rhetoric,* 17-18. See the paragraph, "But there is no art . . . right rules of action upon others."

fusing valuable knowledge, and enforcing right rules of action upon others." Those are Campbell's points, and save for slight adaptation they are Bacon's points, even to the use of Bacon's quotation from the Psalms. Indeed, the sequence of thought is Bacon's also. In this paragraph, in fact, the only omission is Bacon's refutation of Plato's position that rhetoric makes the worse appear the better reason. The omission, however, is repaired later in the *Philosophy of Rhetoric* when Campbell treats of the adaptation of logical argument to the audience;[12] he asserts that rhetoric is not "the art of deception," for in translating reason into images for the better influencing of the passions, the imagination, as a handmaid to argument, is not indifferent to good and evil; in reality, "imagination and passion are by nature . . . more friendly to truth than to falsehood, and more easily retained in the cause of virtue than in that of vice." This is Bacon's argument precisely, and Campbell acknowledges it in a footnote that quotes the relevant passage from the *De augmentis*. It would appear, therefore, that Campbell in associating rhetoric with the imagination and in giving eloquence an ethical mission is leaning upon the Lord Chancellor.

Whether Joseph Priestley's *Lectures on Oratory and Criticism* (1777) draws directly upon Bacon is problematical. The work makes no definite reference to the Elizabethan, yet in introducing his remarks on the recollection and invention of ideas Priestley's diction and phrase would arrest anyone who knows the *Advancement*. Besides order, style, and delivery, so Priestley declares, the art of oratory must deal with recollection:

. . . it must assist the speaker in the habit of *recollection,* or to direct him which way to turn his thoughts, in order to find the arguments and illustrations with which his mind is already furnished; and likewise, when a general topic, or head of discourse, is found, in what manner to confirm or illustrate it. . . . In this manner oratory may assist the *invention;* but it is not in finding things with which the mind was wholly unacquainted, but in readily recollecting, and judiciously selecting, what is proper for his purpose, out of the materials with which the mind was previously furnished.[13]

Although the general doctrine here is Ciceronian, the view that

---

[12] *Philosophy of Rhetoric,* 100-101.   [13] (London, 1777), 5.

oratorical invention consists in bringing dormant information to the speaker's consciousness reminds one of Bacon's position that rhetorical invention is but a remembrance. Reminiscent of the *Advancement*, too, are the terms "general topic," "head of discourse," "recollection," and "to direct him which way to turn his thoughts." One cannot, of course, demonstrate any direct indebtedness by such means, but the similarity to the corresponding part of the *Advancement* may not be due entirely to chance.

The last rhetorical treatise to make extensive use of Bacon is Richard Whately's *Elements of Rhetoric* (1828). In his brief history of rhetoric at the outset of his work, Bishop Whately does Bacon the honor of admitting him to the company of the great; for the principal contributors, the seminal inventors, to the art of public discourse, in the Bishop's view, are Aristotle, Cicero, Quintilian, Bacon and Campbell.[14] The Bishop draws upon the Lord Chancellor in two principal respects. First, he puts considerable emphasis, as does Bacon, upon the colors, the sophisms, and artifices of rhetoric, in order that both parties to communication, the speaker and the listener, may detect and guard against them. "With respect to what are commonly called Rhetorical Artifices," he writes, "what I have endeavoured to do, is, *clearly to set forth* . . . (as Bacon does in his Essay on Cunning,) these sophistical tricks of the Art, and as far as I may have succeeded in this, I shall have been providing the only effectual check to the employment of them." [15] Second, Whately makes full use of Bacon's *antitheta*, or popular arguments pro and con. He reprints thirty of the original forty-seven, altering them only by infrequent omissions such as serve to balance them against each other and sharpen their antithetical character.[16] Though at first he praises them as "a wonderful specimen of acuteness of thought and pointed conciseness of expression," [17] he later indicates that they stimulate the invention and selection of arguments in the realm of probable or contingent truth. The realm of necessary or universal truth, Whately suggests, is reserved for science where, in any line of investigation, there is but *one* truth—that which is demonstrated.

---

[14] (New York, 1846), 25.   [15] *Elements of Rhetoric*, 8.
[16] The *antitheta* appear in a separate appendix in the *Elements*, 449-458.
[17] *Elements of Rhetoric*, 25.

But in the pros and cons on any point of dispute in everyday affairs there are many truths, and the antagonist will have arguments that are as "real and solid" as the protagonist. Hence, the purpose of public discussion is always to establish "a *preponderance* of probability." To accomplish this, Whately rightly points out, a speaker or a writer must look to both sides, or to all sides, of a controversy; and to set up tables of antitheses will help a man discover where, for him, the preponderance of probability lies. Hence, it is as an aid to analysis as well as an aid to ready and concise expression that Whately incorporates Bacon's *antitheta*.

Bacon's witnesses among the modern rhetoricians, then, are few. Nevertheless, with the exception of Blount, they are men who have kept alive the classical view of rhetoric as a broad, full-statured art of composition and discussion. Accordingly, it may not be over-statement to suggest that Bacon through his impact upon others, has helped to maintain the dignity and solidity of rhetoric. If, from John Bulwer's *Chirologia ...Chironomia* (1644) to the present, teachers of speech have in the main specialized on the beauties and qualities of gesture and voice, in the hope of sharing the glamour and prestige of aestheticians and scientists; and if, from Sherry's *Figures* (1555) and Robinson's *Art of Pronunciation* (1614) to the nineteen hundreds, teachers of English composition and of English language have largely specialized on the behavior of language elements, the rules of grammar, and the niceties of style, they have acted without the approbation of Francis Bacon and the classicists.

If Bacon enjoyed no extensive influence upon rhetorical theorists, his mark upon the users of our language has been large. As a model of compact, balanced sentences and a master example of exact diction, his *Essays* have been studied by nearly all English and American schoolboys. This, of course, is familiar to everyone. Not so well known, perhaps, is Bacon's probable influence both as a theorist and a practitioner, upon the style of scientific prose. If we may accept the authority of Sprat, Weld, and Wheatley,[18]

---

[18]Thomas Sprat, *The History of the Royal Society for the Improving of Natural Knowledge* (London, 1722), 35-36; Charles R. Weld, *A History of the Royal Society* . . . (London, 1848), I, 57-64; Henry B. Wheatley, *The Early*

the precursors and founders of the Royal Society held Bacon in great respect. Many of the founders seem to have considered him as the father of the society. Accordingly, it is probable—though direct evidence is lacking—that the members knew intimately the *Novum organum* and the *Advancement of Learning.* They were, then, doubtless aware of Bacon's position that knowledge had lagged, not only because of an incorrect method of observation and investigation, but because learned men in communicating with one another wrote and talked like orators rather than like scientists; they exhibited the attitudes, the purposes, and the language of dialecticians and stage-players; they aimed to convince rather than to report. The founders, also, may have been keenly aware of Bacon's suggestion for the improvement of scientific reports, of his *Handing-on-of-the-Lamp* method of discourse in which the scientist aims to make himself perfectly clear to another scientist by the use of accurate, denotative language in the manner of aphorisms. The Baconian criticism of scientific prose and the suggestions for its improvement may have led the early English scientists to eliminate the colors and flowers of rhetoric and to banish argument and opinion from their scientific discussions. Sprat reports, for instance, that since the Society aimed "to make faithful *Records* of all the Works of *Nature,* or *Art,*" they endeavored to separate "the Knowledge of *Nature,* from the Colours of *Rhetorick,* the Devices of *Fancy,* or the delightful deceit of Fables." [19] In fact, the group was "most solicitous" of their manner of discourse, and if Sprat's attitude is representative they waged sharp warfare against Eloquence and her figures. They held that "Eloquence ought to be banish'd out of all *civil Societies,*" and although backing down from this categorical position to admit that "eloquence does have use outside of science," they railed at the current "vicious abundance of *Phrase,* this Trick of *Metaphors,* this Volu-

---

History of the Royal Society (Hertford, 1905), 2-4. In the discussion that follows, I have had the benefit of R. F. Jones's article, "Science and English Prose Style in the 3rd Quarter of the 17th Century," *Publications of the Modern Language Association,* XXXXV (December, 1930), 977-1009. See also Professor Jones's *Ancients and Moderns. A Study of the Background of the Battle of the Books,* Washington University Studies, New Series, No. 6, Saint Louis, 1936, especially Chapter III.

[19] Sprat, *op. cit.,* 62.

bility of Tongue, which makes so great a noise in the *World*." [20]
The ultimate result of such an attitude towards rhetoric was formally expressed in the official statutes of the Society, enacted in
1663:

> In all Reports of Experiments to be brought into the Society, the
> matter of fact shall be barely stated, without any prefaces, apologies,
> or rhetorical flourishes. . . . And if any Fellow shall think fit to sug-
> gest any conjectures, concerning the causes of the phaenomena in such
> Experiments, the same shall be done apart.[21]

It is not unlikely, therefore, that from Bacon comes the scientists'
preference for a prose style that is concise, denotative, and repor-
torial. If the modern scientist does not care to admit that Bacon
taught him to *observe* phenomena and to undertake *systematic* experimentation, he may acknowledge that a Lord Chancellor taught
him to write and speak in a style appropriate to his business. Bacon may not have written the dramas of Shakespeare, but he may
have dictated to Science her proper symbol and mode of communication.

---

[20] Sprat, *op. cit.*, 112.
[21] Quoted by Weld, *op. cit.*, II, 527.

BIBLIOGRAPHY

The titles that appear below fall into three main classes. (1) There appears first the best edition of Bacon's collected works, together with such editions of his separate works as relate most directly to public address. (2) Included next is a list of books that deal with rhetorical theory from 1500-1700, printed in England and on the continent. In compiling the list my aim has been to cite the *first* printing of a work during the period, rather than to include all editions. Thus I hope to suggest what books were available to a student of rhetoric during the sixteenth and seventeenth centuries. Excluded from the list are works on logic, grammar, poetics, and preaching unless their point of view in whole or in part is that of prose composition in general, rather than that of a special profession and discipline. In accord with this principle I have cited such books as Ascham's *The Scholemaster,* Fraunce's *The Lawiers Logike,* Day's *The English Secretorie,* Puttenham's *The Arte of English Poesie,* and Peacham's *The Compleat Gentleman;* such volumes either contain sections on the theory of rhetoric or reveal that the author, in describing his special branch of discourse, is clearly aware of the general principles that pervade all discourse. (3) There are then cited other books and articles that have aided me in understanding and estimating Bacon's theory of public address and its place in the history of rhetoric.

In compiling the list of English and continental rhetorics I have had generous aid. In the case of the English publications, I hope that the bibliography is somewhat more accurate and exact than that of Professor McGrew's (*Quarterly Journal of Speech,* XV (June, 1929), 381-412). McGrew's list, of course, has been invaluable. Very helpful, too, in the assembling of both the English and continental lists, have been the contributions and comments of Professor Lee Hultzén of the University of Missouri, Professor Harold F. Harding of George Washington University, Professor William Ringler of Princeton University, and the Consultant Service of the Congressional Library. For all errors and omissions, however, I alone am responsible.

The collection of continental rhetorics is but a beginning. Nevertheless, it appears to be unique; for it brings together titles from such cyclopedists as Draud, Gibert, Goiyet, Spachius, along with titles culled from catalogues and other miscellaneous sources. For the most part the collection includes only what seem to be original works; small attempt has been made to cite the impressive array of commentaries and epitomes. If the list serves only to call the scholar's attention to the important rhetorical productions of the Renaissance and to the great need of translation and critical editions, the labor of compilation will have been well spent.

I. Bacon's Works

A. COLLECTED WORKS

The Letters and Life of Francis Bacon Including All His Occasional Works. . . . Collected by James Spedding. 7 vols. London, 1861-1874.

The Works of Francis Bacon. Ed. by James Spedding, R. L. Ellis, and D. D. Heath. 7 vols. London, 1879.

B. SEPARATE WORKS

An Advertisement Touching the Controversies of the Church of England. London, 1640.

Apophthegmes New and Old. London, 1625.

De dignitate et augmentis scientiarum libros ix. Ed. by W. Rawley, London, 1623.

De sapientia veterum liber. London, 1609.

Descriptio globi intellectualis et thema coeli. First printed in *Scripta in naturali et universali philosophia.* Ed. by I. Gruter. Amsterdam, 1653.

The Essaies of Sir Francis Bacon Knight the Kings Solliciter Generall. London, 1612.

The Essayes or Counsels, Civill and Morall, of Francis Lord Verulam, Viscount St. Alban, Newly Written. London, 1625.

Essayes. Religious Meditations. Places of Perswasion and Disswasion. London, 1597.

Filum labyrinthi. First printed in *Letters and Remains of the Lord Chancellor Bacon.* Collected by R. Stephens. London, 1734.

Letter and Discourse to Sir Henry Savill, Touching Helps for the In-tellectual Powers. First printed in *Resuscitatio, or Bringing into Publick Light Severall Pieces of the Works . . . of Francis Bacon. . . . With his Lordships Life.* By W. Rawley. 2 pt. London, 1657.

Novum organum sive indica de interpretatione naturae. London, 1620.

Of the Coulers of Good and Euill. London, 1597.

The Promus of Formularies and Elegancies . . . Illustrated and Eluci-dated by Passages from Shakespeare . . . by Mrs. Henry Pott. Lon-don, 1883.

Sylva sylvarum; or A Natural Historie. London, 1627.

The Twoo Bookes of Francis Bacon, Of the Proficience and Advance-ment of Learning, Divine and Humane. London, 1605.

Valerius Terminus of the Interpretation of Nature. First printed in Stephens' *Letters.* London, 1734.

II. Books on Rhetorical Theory, 1500-1700.

A. WORKS ON RHETORIC PRINTED IN ENGLAND

Anonymous. *An Homelye of Basilius Howe Younge Mene Oughte to Reade Poetes and Oratours.* London, 1557.

Aphthonius of Antioch. *Praeexercitamenta interprete viro doctissimo.* [Ed. by G. Hervet], London [1520?]

———— *Progymnasmata latinitati donati.* London, 1572.

Aristotle's Rhetoric, or the True Grounds and Principles of Oratory: Shewing the Right Art of Pleading and Speaking in Full Assemblies and Courts of Judicature. Made English by the translators of the Art of Thinking. In four books (i. e., with ad Alexandrum). London, 1686.

Aristotle. *ΑΡΙΣΤΟΤΕΛΟΥΣ/ ΤΕΧΝΗΣ/ PH TOPIKHΣ/ βιβλία τρία/ Aristotelis / de rhetorica seu arte dicendi / libri tres.* Graeco-lat. . . . Ed. by T. Goulston. London, 1619.

Ascham, Roger. *The Scholemaster. Or Plaine and Perfite Way of Teachyng Children, to Understand, Write and Speake, the Latin Tong. . . .* London, 1570.

Bacon, Francis. *Apophthegmes New and Old.* London, 1625.

———— *De dignitate et augmentis scientiarum libros ix.* Ed. by W. Rawley. London, 1623.

———— *Of the Coulers of Good and Euill.* London, 1597. (These are the "places of perswasion and disswasion" in the *Essays* of 1597.)

———— *The Twoo Bookes of Francis Bacon. Of the Proficience and Ad-vancement of Learning, Divine and Humane.* London, 1605.

Barton, John. *The Art of Rhetorick Concisely and Compleatly Handled, Exemplified out of Holy Writ, and with a Compendious and Conspicious Comment.* London, 1634.

Basse, William. *A Helpe to Memorie and Discourse, the Two Syrens of the Ear.* Second impression. London, 1621.

Blount, Thomas. *The Acadamie of Eloquence, Containing a Compleate English Rhetorique, Exemplified with Common-places, and Formes.* ... London, 1654. [1653?]

Brandolinus, Aurelius. *De ratione scribendi.* London, 1573.

Brinsley, John. *Ludus literarius: or The Grammar Schoole.* ... London, 1612.

Brunus, Robert. *Rudimentorum rhetoricorum.* Aberdeen, 1666.

Bulwer, John. *Chirologia: or The Naturall Language of the Hand.* ... *Whereunto is Added Chironomia, or The Art of Manuall Rhetoricke.* ... 2 vols. London, 1644.

Burton, Nicholas. *Figurae grammaticae et rhetoricae Latino carmine donatae.* ... London, 1702.

Butler, Charles. *Oratoriae libri duo.* London, 1629.

—————— *Rameae rhetoricae libri duo, in usum scholarum.* Oxford, 1597.

—————— *Rhetoricae libri duo, quorum prior de tropis et figuris, posterior de voce et gestu, praecipie in usum scholarum accuratius editi.* Oxford, 1597.

Carew, Richard. *The Excellencie of the English Tongue.* London, [1595-96?].

Cecil, William Lord Burghley. *Certaine Precepts, or Directions for the Well Ordering and Carriage of a Mans Life.* ... London, 1617.

Cicero, M. T. *De inventione.* In *Ciceronis opera omnia quae exstant.* ... 9 vols. London, 1585.

—————— *De oratore ... libris tres.* Cambridge, 1589.

—————— *De oratore libri tres, a P. Melanchthone scholiis ac notulis quibusdam illustrati.* London, 1534.

—————— *De partitiones oratoriae.* In *Ciceronis opera omnia quae exstant.* ... 9 vols. London, 1585.

—————— *Orator.* In *Ciceronis opera omnia quae exstant.* ... London, 1585.

—————— *Topica ... a P. Melanchthonis ... scholis.* London, 1546.

Clarke, John. *Dux grammaticus.* ... *Cui suas etiam auxiliares succenturiavit dux oratorius.* ... 5 pt. London, 1633.

—————— *Formulae oratoriae in usum scholarum concinnatae una cum multis orationibus, declamationibus.* ... *Manuductio ad artem carminificam seu dux poeticus.* London, 1632.

Clarke, John (*B.D.*). *Transitionum rhetoricarum formulae.* . . . 2nd ed. London, 1628.

Comenius, J. A. *Ars ornatoriae, sive grammatica elegans, et eruditiones scholasticae atrium; rerum et linguarum ornamenta exhibens.* . . . 4 pt. London, 1664.

Coote, Edward. *The English School-Master.* . . . London, 1596.

Copland, Robert. *The Art of Memorye, that is otherwise called, The Phoenix; a Boke Uery Behouefell and Profytable to All Professors of Scyences, Grammaryens, Rethoryciens, Legystes.* . . . Translated out of French into English by R. C. London, n. d.

Cox, Leonard. *The Arte or Crafte of Rhethoryke.* London, 1524.

d'Assigny, Marius. *Rhetorica anglorum, vel exercitationes oratoriae in rhetoricam sacram et communem. Quibus adjiciuntur quaedam regulae ad imbecilles memorias corroborandas.* London, 1699.

Day, Angel. *The English Secretorie; or Plaine and Direct Method of Enditing of All Manner of Epistles or Letters.* . . . Corrected, refined, and amended . . . also tropes, figures, as usually or for ornaments sake are in this method required. London, 1586.

Demetrius, Phalereus. *De elocutione.* In *Rhetores selecti.* Oxford, 1676.

Doddridge, John. *The English Lawyer.* . . . London, 1631. [Discusses the principles of memory.]

Dugard, William. *Rhetorices elementa, quaestionibus et responsionibus explicata.* London, 1640.

Farnaby, Thomas. *Index rhetoricus.* London, 1625.

―――― *Index rhetoricus.* . . . *Cui adjiciuntur formulae oratoriae.* 2 pt. London, 1633.

―――― *Phrases oratoriae et poeticae.* London, 1631.

Fenner, Dudley. *The Artes of Logike and Rethoricke.* London, 1584.

Fleming, Abraham. *A Panoplie of Epistles . . . Containing a Perfecte Plattforme of Inditing Letters of All Sorts . . . Used of the Best and Eloquentest Rhetoricians that Have Lived in All Ages.* . . . London, 1576.

Fraunce, Abraham. *The Arcadian Rhetoricke: or, The Praecepts of Rhetorike Made Plaine.* . . . London, 1588.

―――― *The Lawyiers Logike: Exemplifying the Praecepts of Logike by the Practice of the Common Law.* London, 1588. [Offers a general treatment of the arrangement of discourse.]

Fulwood, William. *The Castel of Memorie: Wherein is Conteyned the Restoryng, Augmentyng, and Conservyng of the Memorye, and Remembraunce.* . . . Englished by W. Fulwood. London, 1563.

———— *The Enimie of Idlenesse: Teaching the Maner and Stile How to Endite, Compose and Write All Sorts of Epistles and Letters.* . . . London, 1568.

Gale, Thomas (ed.). *Rhetores selecti, Greek and Latin,* viz., Demetrius Phalereus de Electione, Tiberius Rhetor de schematibus Demosthenis, anonymus sophista de rhetorica, Severi Alexandrini ethopoeiae. Demetrium emendavit, reliquos è MSS edidit et Latini vertit, omnes notis illustravit Tho. Gale. Oxford, 1676.

Gardiner, Richard. *Specimen oratorium, et declamationibus ibidem art: Bac: necon additamentis studentium heterogeniis adoratum. Editio teria multo auctior.* . . . Oxford, 1662. [1st ed. London, 1653.]

Gerbier, Sir Balthazar. *The Art of Well Speaking, being a Lecture Read Publiquely at Sir B. Gerbier's Academy.* London, 1650.

Gibson, Edmund. *M. Fabii Quinctiliani de institutione oratoria libri duodecim.* . . . Ex tribus codicibus MSS et ecto impressis emendavit, atque lectionis variantes adjecit E. Gibson. . . . Oxford, 1693.

Granger, Thomas. *Syntagma logicum, or the Divine Logike.* London, 1620. [Contains an excellent treatment of dispositio.]

Haddon, Walter. *De laudibus eloquentiae oratio.* In *G. Haddoni legum doctoris.* . . . Lucubrationes passim collectae et editae studio et labore T. Hatcheri. London, 1567.

Hall, John (tr.). *Περι Υψους,* or D. Longinus of the height of eloquence, rendered out of the originall by J. H., 1652.

Harvey, Gabriel. *Ciceronianus, vel oratio post reditum habita Cantabrigiae ad suos auditores.* London, 1577.

———— *Rhetor, sive duorum dierum oratio, de natura, arte et exercitatione rhetorica.* London, 1577.

Hawes, Stephen. *The Pastime of Pleasure.* London, 1509. [Fragment.]

———— *The Historie of Graunde Amoure and La Bell Pucle, Called the Pastime of Plesure, Containing the Knowledge of the Seuen Sciences & the Course of Man's Life in This World.* . . . Newly perused. . . . London, 1554.

Hellowes, Edward (tr.). *Epistles familiares, Wherein Are Contained . . . Excellent Discourses . . . Expositions of Certain Figures.* . . . London, 1574.

Hemmingsen, Niels. *The Preacher, or Methode of Preachinge.* . . . Tr. by John Horsfall. London, 1574.

Hewes, John. *A Perfect Survey of the English Tongue.* . . . London, 1624.

Hobbes, Thomas. *A Briefe of the Art of Rhetorique.* London, [1635? 1637?]

—— *The Art of Rhetorick Plainly set Forth; with Pertinent Examples, for the More Basic Understanding and Practice of the Same.* London, 1681.

—— *The Art of Rhetoric, with a Discourse of the Laws of England.* 2 pt. London, 1681.

Holyday, Barten. *Oratio habita cum Aristotelis rhetoricorum librum secundum auspicarer.* In *Philosophiae polito-barbarae specimen.* . . . Oxford, 1633.

Hoole, Charles. *A New Discovery of the Old Art of Teaching Schoole.* . . . London, 1660.

Horace (Quintus Horatius Flaccus). Horace, His Art of Poetry. Made English by Ben Jonson and printed in his works. London, 1616.

Hyperius, Andreas. *The Practise of Preaching, otherwise called the Pathway to the Pulpit.* . . . Englished by J. Ludham. London, 1577.

Johnson, Ralph. *The Scholars Guide from the Accidence to the University; or Short, Plain and Easie Rules for Performing All Manner of Exercise in the Grammar School.* London, 1662. [Contains rhetorical exercises.]

Jones, Bassett. *Hermaeologium: or, An Essay at the Rationality of the Art of Speaking.* As a supplement to Lillie's Grammar. London, 1659.

Jonson, Ben. *Timber: or Discoveries Made upon Men and Matter.* London, 1641.

Kempe, William. *The Education of Children in Learning: Declared by the Dignitie, Utilitie and Method Thereof.* London, 1588. [Discusses some principles of logic and rhetoric.]

Kerhuel, John. *Idea eloquentiae seu rhetoricae.* London, 1673.

Kirk, P. *Logomachia, or The Conquest of Eloquence.* London, 1690.

Lamy, Bernard. *The Art of Speaking:* Written in French by Messieurs du Port Royal: In Pursuance of a Former Treatise, Intituled, *The Art of Thinking.* Rendered into English. London, 1676.

Lever, Ralphe. *The Arte of Reason Rightly Termed Witcraft, Teaching a Perfect Way to Argue and Dispute,* London. 1573.

Longinus, Dionysius. *Dionysii Longini . . . liber de grandi loquentia sive sublimi dicendi genere.* Latin redditus [ed. by G. Langbaine]. Oxford, 1636.

Mackenzie, Sir George. *Idea eloquentiae forensis hodierna: una cum actione forensi ex unaquaque juris parte.* Edinburgh, 1681.

Macropedius, George. *Methodus de conscribendis epistolis, et epitome praeceptionum de paranda copia verborum et rerum, item ix. speciebus argumentationum rhetoricarum.* London, 1580.

Melanchthon, Philip. *Formulae de arte concionandi; et discendi theologiae ratio.* London, 1570.

Newton, John. *An Introduction to the Art of Rhetorick.* London, 1671.

———— *The English Academy: or A Brief Introduction to the Seven Liberal Arts.* London, 1677.

Olivier, Peter. *Dissertationes academicae, de oratoria, historia, et poetica.* Cambridge, 1674.

Peacham, Henry (the Younger). *The Compleat Gentleman, Fashioning Him Absolute in the Most Necessary & Commendable Qualities Concerning Minde or Bodie.* . . . London, 1622.

Peacham, Henry (the Elder). *The Garden of Eloquence, Conteyning the Figures of Grammer and Rhetorick.* . . . London, 1577.

Pemble, William. *Enchiridion oratorium.* Oxford, 1633.

Phillips, Edward. *The Mysteries of Love and Eloquence.* . . . 2 pt. London, 1658.

Prideaux, John. *Hypomnemata / logica / rhetorica / . . . ethica / politica.* . . . Oxford, 1650.

———— *Sacred eloquence, or The Art of Rhetorick, as It Is Layd Down in Scripture.* London, 1657.

Puttenham, George. *The Arte of English Poesie.* London, 1584. [Includes a section on the figures of rhetoric.]

Quintilian, M. F. In *M. F. Quintilian institutionum librum decimum . . . annotationes* . . . P. Melanchthonis. . . . London, 1570.

————*M. Fabii Quintiliani institutionum oratoriarum libri duodecim. . . . Novae huic editioni adiecit Fabianarum notarum spicilegium subcisivum D. Pareus. Accesserunt etiam Quintilianorum declamationes.* . . . London, 1641.

R. W. *The English Orator: or Rhetorical Descants upon Some Valuable Themes Both Historical and Philosophical.* In two parts. London, 1680.

Radau, Michael. *Orator extemporaneous seu artis oratoriae breviarum bipartitum.* London, 1657.

Rainolde, Richard. *A Booke Called the Foundacion of Rhetorike, Because All Other Partes of Rhetorike Are Grounded Thereupon, Every Parte Sette Forthe in an Oracion upon Questions.* . . . Made by Richard Rainolde. London, 1563.

Rainolds, John. *An Excellent Oration of That Famously Learned John Rainolds, D.D.* . . . Very useful for all such as affect the studies of logick and philosophie, and admire profane learning. Translated out of Latin into English by J[ohn] L[eycester] Schoolmaster, London, 1638. [Said to be the *Oratio post festum S. Michaelis 1573*, which appeared in *V. CL. D. Joannis Rainoldi, olim graece linguae praelectoris in collegio Corporis Christi apud Oxoniensis, orationes duodecim*. . . . London, 1619.]

Ramus, Peter. *The Logike of the Moste Excellent Philosopher P. Ramus Martyr*. Newly translated, and in diuers places corrected after the mynde of the author, per M. R. Makylmenaeum Scotum. London, 1574.

────── *P. Rami dialecticae libri duo*. A. Talaei praelectionibus illustrati. London, 1560.

Rapin, René. *A Comparison between the Eloquence of Demosthenes and Cicero*. Translated out of the French [of René Rapin]. Oxford, 1672.

────── *Reflections upon the Use of the Eloquence of These Times*. Translated out of the French [of René Rapin]. Oxford, 1672.

Richardson, Alexander. *The Logician's School-Master*. . . . *Whereunto Are Added His Prelections on Ramus His Grammar; Talaeus His Rhetoric*. . . . London, 1657.

Robinson, Hugh. *I. Preces. II. Grammaticalia quaedam. III. Rhetorica* [Anon.] Oxford, 1616.

Robinson, Robert. *The Art of Pronuntiation*. London, 1617.

Rutherford, J. *Commentariorum de arte disserendi*. London, 1577.

Sanderson, Robert. *Logicae artis compendium*. 2nd ed. Oxford, 1618.

Seton, John. *Dialectica*. London, 1545. [Interesting treatment of the "rhetorical syllogism."]

Sherry, Richard. *A Treatise of Schemes and Tropes . . . Gathered Out of the Best Grammarians and Oratours*. . . . London, 1550.

────── *A Treatise of the Figures of Grammer and Rhetorike Profitable for Al That Be Studious of Eloquence*. . . . London, 1555.

Siluayn, Alexander [A. van den Busche]. *The Orator: Handling a Hundred Severall Discourses, in Forme of Declamationes*. . . . Tr. by Lazarus Pyott [Anthony Munday]. London, 1596.

Smith, John. *The Mysterie of Rhetorique Unvail'd Wherein above 130 of the Tropes and Figures are Severally Divided from the Greek into English together with Lively Definitions and Variety of Latine, English Scriptural Examples*. London, 1657.

Spencer, Thomas. *The Art of Logick, Delivered in the Precepts of Aristotle and Ramus*. London, 1628. ("Logic is an Art of discoursing well.")

Stephens, Thomas. *Troposchematologia: maximam partem ex indice rhetorica Farnabii deprompta: additis insuper anglicanis exemplis.* London, 1648.

Stockwood, John. *The Treatise of the Figures at the End of the Rules of Construction in the Latin Grammar* [Lyly's]. Construed . . . by John Stockwood. London, 1686.

Sturmius, Johann. *A Ritch Storehouse or Treasurie Called Nobilitas literata.* Tr. by T. Browne. London, 1570. [Said to treat of rhythm and composition, etc.]

Susenbrotus, Joannes. *Epitome troporum ac schematum et grammaticorum et rhetoricorum.* London, 1562.

Talaeus, Audomarus. *M. Tullii Ciceronis de Orator . . . dialogi tres, Audomari Talaei explicationibus illustrati.* . . . London, 1553.

———— *Rhetorica.* London, 1577.

———— *A. Talaei rhetorica.* Edinburgh, 1621.

Temple, William. *P. Rami dialecticae libri duo.* Scholiis G. Tempelli Cantabrigiensis illustrati. . . . Cambridge, 1584.

Tesmarus, John. *Exercitationum rhetoricam libri viii.* London, 1621.

Thorne, William. *Ducente deo.* London, 1592.

Tommae, Petrus. *The Art of Memory.* London, 1548.

Trelcatius, Lucas. *Scholastica et methodica locorum communium institutio.* London, 1604.

Vaughan, William. *The Golden-Groue, Moralized in Three Bookes: A Worke Very Necessary for All Such as Would Know How to Gouerne Themselues, Their Houses, or Their Countrey.* London, 1600 [Contains a section on rhetoric.]

Vicars, Thomas. Χειραγωγια. *Manuductio ad artem rhetoricam.* London, 1619.

Vives, J. L. *De tradendis disciplinis.* [London?], 1531.

Vossius, Gerandus. *Rhetorices contractae, sive partitionum oratoriarum libri.* . . . *Edito altera.* . . . Oxford, 1631.

———— *Elementa rhetorica, oratoriis ejusdem partitionibus accommodata.* . . . London, 1663.

Walker, Obadiah. *Some Instructions concerning the Art of Oratory.* London, 1659.

Walker, William. *Troposchematologiae. Rhetoricae libri duo.* London, 1672. [Included are two books: *De argumentorum inventione, libri duo;* and *De inventione rhetorica.*]

Willis, John. *Mnemonica, sive reminiscendi ars.* London, 1617.

Wilson, Thomas. *The Arte of Rhetorique, for the Use of All Suche as are Studious of Eloquence.* . . . London, 1553.

———— *The Rule of Reason, Conteining the Arte of Logique.* London, 1551.

Wotton, Samuel [tr.?]. *The Art of Logick, Gathered Out of Aristotle, and Set in Due Forme, according to His Instructions.* By Peter Ramus. . . . Published by A. Wotton. London, 1626.

B. WORKS ON RHETORIC PRINTED ON THE CONTINENT

Agricola, Rodolphus. *Rodolphi Agricolae Phrisij dialectica* [with head-title "De inuentione dialectica"]. Louvain, 1515.

Aicker, Otto. *Iter oratorium.* Salzburg, 1675.

Alcuin (Albinus Flacus). *De arte rhetorica dialogus.* In *Antiqui rhetores latini.* . . . Paris, 1599.

Alexander (Numenius) Sophista. *De figuris sensuset dictionis.* In Manutius, *Rhetores in hoc volumine habentur.* . . . Venice, 1508-09.

———— *De figuris sententiarum ac elocutionum,* N. de Comitibus interprete. Venice, 1556.

———— *De figuris sententiae atque elocutionis libri II . . . de schematibus oratoriis scholia.* . . . Upsala, 1690.

Allacci, Leone. *De erroribus magnorum virorum in dicendo dissertatio rhetorica.* Rome, 1635.

Almarini, Gasparis. *Artes rhetoricae viridarium ex Aristotle, Cicerone, Quintiliano, & aliis rhetoribus.* Venice, 1609.

Alstedius, J. H. *Orator, sex libris informatus.* . . . Herborn, 1612.

———— *Rhetorica, quatuor libris proponens universam ornate dicendi modum.* . . . Herborn, 1616.

Alvarez Caldera, Juan. *Rhetorica—Isagoge.* Madrid, 1618.

Anonymous. *La rhétorique de l'honnéte homme, ou la manière de bien écrire des lettres, de faire toutes sortes des discours, & de les prononcer agreablement.* . . . Paris, 1699.

Arnauld, Antoine. *Réflexions sur l'eloquence des prédicateurs.* . . . Paris, 1695.

———— *La rhétorique françoise qui enseigne la manière de bien discourir de chacque chose.* Par L. D. P. Paris, 1657. [This has been attributed to Cardinal du Perron.]

———— *L'arte oratoria, secondo i modo della lingua volgare, divisa in III. libri, ne' quali si ragiona tutto quello che all' artificio appartiene, cos del poeta, come dell' oratore, con l' autorita dei nostri scrittori.* Venice, 1646.

———— *Operum graecorum, latinorum, et italorum rhetorum tomus primus (-octavus. De labore et virtute prolegomena rhetorum graecorum . . . opiubus praeposita, Italice inscripta.* Avvisi precedenti). 8 vols. Venice, 1644.

―――― *Philippo Ramerum rhetoricae artis systema ex praeceptis Rami.* Steinfurt, 1606.

―――― *Precetti necessarj sopra cose di grammatica, retorrica, topica, loica, poetica, e istoria.* Venice, 1567.

―――― *Rhetorica en lengua castellana en la qual se pone muy en breve lo necessario para saber bien hablar y escriver y conoscer qui en habla y escrive bien. n. p.* 1541.

―――― *Rhetorica ad Herennium.* In *Rhetorica Tullii.* M. T. Ciceronis . . . rhetorices libri quattuor ad C. Herennium . . . ac ejusdem M. T. Ciceronis de inventione libri duo. . . . [Lyonss, 1510?]

―――― *Tableau de l'orateur françoise.* Lyon, 1624.

Antiqui rhetores latini. Rutilius Lupus, Aquila Romanus, J. Ruffianus, de figuris sententiarum et elocutionis. C. Fortunatiani . . . artis rhetoricae scholiae libri iii. M. Victorini expositio in libros rhetor. Cicer. S. Victoris institutiones oratoriae. Emporius Rhetor de ethopoeia ac locco communi. Ejusdem demonstrative ac deliberative materiae praecepta. A. Augustini principia rhetorices. I. Severiani syntomata. Ruffinus de compositione et metris oratorum. Priscianus Caesariensis de praeexercitamentis rhetoricae. A. Cassiodorus de arte rhetorica. Beda de tropis sacrae scripturae. Isidorus de arte rhetorica. Anonymus de locis rhetoricis. Albini Aleuini de arte rhetorica dialogus. Omnia ex codd. manusc. emendatoria vel auctiora ex bibliotheca F. Pithoei. Paris, 1599.

Aphthonius of Antioch. *Progymnasmata commentarii innominati autoris.* . . . 2 vols. Venice, 1508-09. See Manutius, *Rhetores in hoc volumine habentur.* . . .]

Apsinis. *De arte rhetorica.* In Manutius, *Rhetores in hoc volumine habentur.* . . . Venice, 1508-09.

―――― *De memoria liber singularis.* . . . Paris, 1618.

Aquilla, Romanus. *Liber retoricus de nominibus figurarum et exemplis; seu de figuris sententiarum et elocutionis.* Venice, 1513.

Arias Montano, Benito. *Rethoricorum libri iiii.* . . . *Cum annotationibus A. Moralij Episcopi Meschaucanensis.* Antwerp, 1569.

Aristotle. Ἀριστοτέλους Ἅπαντα. *Aristotelis opera omnia.* Per D. Eras. Roterodamum. . . . 2 vols. Basle, 1531.

―――― *Aristotelis opera . . . omnia, latinitate . . . donata.* . . . Item supra censuram I. L. Vivis de libris Aristotelis & P. Melanchthonis commentationem.* . . . 3 vols. Basle, 1542.

―――― *Aristotelis rhetoricorum ad Theodecten libri tres. Ejusdem rhetorica ad Alexandrum. . . . Ejusdem ars poetica.* In Manutius, *Rhetores in hoc volumine habentur.* . . . Venice, 1508-09.

——— *Aristotelis topica inventio in octo secta libros. A magno A. Nipho interpretata atque exposita.* Paris, 1540.

——— *Declaratio compendiosa per viam divisionis Alpharabii super libris rhetoricorum Aristotelis.* . . . *Explicit rhetorica Aristotelis cum . . . Egidii de Roma comentariis.* . . . Venice, 1515.

——— *Expositiones magni A. Niphi in libros de sophisticis elenchis Aristotelis. Cum textu recognito & ab ipso auctore interpretatio.* Paris, 1540.

Aromatii, G. degli (ed.). *Degli autori del ben parlare per secolari, e religiosi opere diverse, Intorno, 1. Alla favella nobile d'Italia. 2. Al barbarismo, e solecismo, tropi, figuri, ed altre virtù e vitii del parlare. 3. Agli stili, ed eloquenza. 4. Alla retorica. 5. All'eloquenza ecclesiastica.* 5 pt. 19 tom. Venice, 1643.

Auge (Augentius), Daniel. *Two Dialogues Concerning Poetical Invention: The True Knowledge of the Art of Oratory, and of the fiction of the Fable.* Paris, 1560.

Augustine, Saint Aurelius. *Quattuor divi Augustini libri, de doctrina christiana.* . . . Leipsic, 1515.

——— *Principia rhetorices.* In *Antiqui rhetores latini.* . . . Paris, 1599.

Averroes. *Paraphrasis in Aristoteles rhetoricam.* . . . Venice, 1560.

Bader, Matthaeus. *Rhetoricarum institutionum libri ii, ex D. Philippi [Melanchtonis] rhetorices et C. Crussii commentariis collecti. Additus est libellus de copia verborum et rerum Erasmi.* . . . *In fine quoque Aphthonii rhetores.* . . . Frankfort, 1593.

Balthazar, Andre. *Quaestiones rhetoricae breves admodum et expeditae in gratiam eorum qui disputationibus rhetoricus oblectantur . . . authore Andrea Balthazar.* . . . Editio tertia. Paris, 1554.

Barbaro, Daniello. *Della eloquenza, dialogo di Monsignor Daniello Barbaro.* . . . Mandato in luce da Girolamo Ruscelli. Venice, 1557. *Also see Barbaro, Ermalao.*

Barbaro, Ermalao. Ἀριστοτέλους Τεχνης ῥητορικης βιβια τρια. *Aristotelis de arte dicendi libri tres.* Ad fidem uetustiss. codicum . . . à Petro Victorio correcti & emendati. Iidē latinitate per Hermolaū Barbarū. Paris, 1549.

——— *Rhetoricorum Aristotelis libri tres.* Interprete Hermolao Barbaro . . . commentaria in eosdem Danielis Barbari. Venice, 1544.

——— *Martini Borrhai . . . in tres Aristotelis de arte dicendi libros commentaria.* Hermolai Barbari, eorundem versio, cum graeco textu capitibus suis distincto. . . . Basle, 1551.

Barlandus, Hadrianus. *Institutionem artis oratoriae.* Louvain, n.d.

Barry, Rene. *La rhètorique françoise, où l'on trouve de nouveaux exemples sur les passions et sur les figures; où l'on traitte à fonds de la matière des genres oratoires.* . . . Paris, 1653.

Bartholin, Caspar. *Rhetorica.* Copenhagen, 1603.

Bede, the Venerable. *De schematibus et tropis sacrarum literarum liber Bedae Presbyteri.* Basle, 1527.

Benedictus, Benedictus de. *De arte rhetorica libri 3.* Venice, n. d.

Bernardo, G. B. *Thesaurus rhetoricae ex antiquis & recentibus oratorum monumetis congestus.* Venice, 1500.

Bersmanus, Gregorius. *De dignitate atque praestantia poetices, id est antiquissimae philosophiae, oratio.* . . . Leipsic, 1575.

———— *Erotemata rhetorica.* Leipsic, 1602.

———— *Orationes duo, vna, de cura loquendi.* . . . Leipsic, 1576.

Beumlerus, Marcus. *Elocutionis rhetoricae, libri duo.* Zurich, 1598.

Bilstein, Joannis. *Rhetorica: ex Philip. Melanchtone, Audomaro Talaeo, & Claudio. Minoe selecta, atque exemplis philosophicis & theologicis illustrata.* . . . Herborn, 1591.

Blebelius, Thomas. *Rhetoricae artis progymnasmata . . . ad puerilem institutionem.* . . . Leipsic, 1584.

Boissimon, de. *Les Beautez de l'ancienne éloquence opposées aux affections de la moderne.* Paris, 1698.

Bonaccursius, Cenobius. *Institutio oratoris, sive de arte rhetorica, ab omnibus qui recte de illa scripserunt, artificiosa collect.* Venice, 1603.

Boulai, Caesar Egasse de. *Speculum eloquentiae.* Paris, 1658.

Brandolinus, Aurelius. *De ratione scribendi libri tres.* . . . Basle, 1549.

Bretteville, Abbé E. de. *L'éloquence de la chaire N du barreau selon les princeps les plus solides de la rhétorique sacrée N profane.* Paris, 1689.

Brocardus, Jacobus. *Partitiones oratoriae, quibus rhetorica omnia Aristotelis praecepta breviter et dilucide explicantur.* . . . Venice, 1558.

Bumann, Carl. *Rhetoricorum commentariorum libri duo . . . conscripta opera et studio M. Caroli Bumanni.* . . . Frankfort, 1602. [1st ed. 1601?]

Camariota, Matthaeus. *Synopsis rhetoricae . . .* a Davide Hoeschelio edita [Greek]. Augsburg, 1595.

Camerarius, Joachim. *Elementa rhetorica.* Basle, 1551.

———— *Notatio figurarum orationis et mutatae simplicis elocutionis in Apostolicis scriptis.* . . . Leipsic, 1572.

———— *Notatio figurarum sermonis in libris quatuor Euangliorum, et indicata verborum significatio, et orationis sententia.* . . . Leipsic, 1572.

Camillo Delminio, Giulio. *Due trattati, l'uno delle materie, che possono venire sotto lo stile dell' eloquente, e l' altro dell' imitazione (contra il Ciceroniano, dialogo di Erasmo, già suo amico, ma non in questo).* Venice, 1544.

———— *La topica, ouvero della elocutione.* In *Degli autore del ben parlare.* . . . Venice, 1643.

———— *Topica della figurati locuzioni.* Venice, 1560.

Campanella, Thomas. *Philosophia rationalis partes quinque, videlicet: grammatica, dialectica, rhetorica, poetica, historiographica.* . . . Paris, 1638.

Campanile, Filiberto. *Lè idee, ovvero forme dell' eloqunza, di Filiberto Campanile, secondo la dottrina di Ermogene, e di altri retori antichi.* Naples, 1606.

Campian, Edmund. *Orationis, epistolae, tractatus de imitatione rhetorica. A. R.* Turnero . . . collecta. Et nunc primum è MS edita. . . . Ingolstadt, 1602.

Capella, M. M. F. *De nuptijs Philogiae et Mercurij, libri duo, de grammatica, de dialecticae. de rhetorica.* . . . *libri septem.* Venice, 1499.

Cappel, Jacques. *Rhetorica, multis exemplis tam ex scriptura, quam aliunde petitis illustrata.* Sedan, 1623.

Caesarius, Joannes. *Rhetorica . . . in septem libros sive tractatus digesta.* . . . Paris, 1538.

Caselius, J. C. *Ρ'ητωρ, sive magistro dicendi.* Helmstadt, 1596.

Casmann, Otto. *Rhetoricae tropologiae praecepta.* . . . Frankfort, 1600.

Cassander, Georgius. *Tabulae breves in praeceptiones rhetoricas.* Antwerp, 1548.

Cassiodorus, M. A. *De arte rhetorica.* In *Antiqui rhetores latini.* Venice, 1599.

Castro, Francisco de. *De arte rethorica.* Cordoba, 1611.

Catena, G. G. *Discorso di Girolamo Catena sopra la traduzione delle scienze, e di altre facultà.* Venice, 1581.

Caulerius, Simon. *Rhetoricorum libri quinque.* Paris, 1600. [2nd ed.]

Caussin, Nicolas. *De eloquentia sacra et humana libri xvi.* Paris, 1630. [3rd ed.]

Cavalcanti, Bartolomeo. *La rettorica . . . divisa vii. libri, dove so contiene tutto quello, che appartiene all' arte oratoria.* Venice, 1559. [2nd ed.]

Celsus, A. C. *De arte dicendi libellus, primum in lucem editus, curante Sixto à Popma.* Cologne, 1569.

Cerda, Melchor de la. *Campi eloquentiae.* 2 vols. Lyons, 1614.

17

Champier, Benedict C. Symphorien. *Libri vii. De dialecteca, rhetorica, geometria.* . . . Basle, 1537.

Chytraeus, David. *Libri rhetorices, continens praecepta de elocutione et de figuris grammaticis et rhetoricis.* Rostoch, 1574.

Chytraeus, Nathan. '*Ποηκαπαοη, seu de affectibus movendis Aristotelis ex ii. rhetoricorum doctrina explicata.* Wurzburg, 1586.

Cicero, M. T. *Opera Ciceronis, rhetorica, oratoria, et forensia.* 4 vols. Paris, 1531.

———— *De inventione.* In *Rhetorica Tullii. M. T. Ciceronis . . . rhetorices libri quattuor ad C. Herennium . . . ac ejusdem M. T. Ciceronis de inventione libri duo.* . . . [Lyons, 1510?]

———— *De oratore librittres, a P. Melanchthone scholiis ac notulis quibusdam illustrati.* Paris, 1534.

———— *De partitiones oratoriae.* In *Ciceronis partitiones commentaria G. Vallae.* Paris, 1533.

———— *Orator.* In *Rhetoricorum ad C. Herennium lib. iiii. De inventione. De oratore. De clarius orationibus qui dicitur Brutus. Orator ad Brutum.* . . . Paris, 1544.

———— *Topica.* In *Topica Ciceronis A. M. S. Boetii commentarius.* Paris, 1528.

Comes, Natalis. *Natalis de Comitibus . . . de terminis rhetoricis libri quinque . . . : praetera inventionis oratoriae tabellae, per Anatolium Frontium.* . . . Basle, 1560.

Costa, Juan. *De utraque inventione oratoria et dialectica.* Pamplona, 1570.

Costacciaro, L. C. a. *De dispositione oratoria disputationes XXX.* . . . Venice, 1590.

———— *De elocutione oratoria, libri iiii.* Venice, 1592.

———— *De oratoria ac dialectica inventione, vel de locis communibus libri quinque.* Venice, 1589.

———— *De questionibus oratoriis libri duo.* . . . Venice, 1593.

Courcelles, Pierre de. *La rhétorique.* Paris, 1557.

Crebs, A. B. *Praxis rhetorica, et delineatio partis secundae praxeos rhetoricae ecclesiasticae de formandis concionibus.* Danzig, 1611.

Cresollius, Ludovic. *Theatrum veterum rhetorum, oratorum, et declamatorum . . . libri v.* Paris, 1620.

———— *Vacationes autumnales; sive, de perfecta oratoris actione et pronunciatione, libri iii.* Paris, 1620.

Crusius, Martinus. *Philippi Melancthonis elementorum rhetorices libri duo, Martini Crusii quaestionibus et scholiis explicati in Academica Tybingensi.* . . . Basle, 1570.

Cyllenius, R. A. *Tabulae rhetoricae, seu Aristotelicarum partitionum, libri tres.* Venice, 1571.

Dannhauer, J. C. *Epitome rhetorica,* Strassburg, 1651. [2nd ed.]

Dante, Alighieri. *Dante de la vulgare eloquenzia.* (Tradatto in lingua Italiana [by G. C. Trissino]). Venice, 1529.

———— *De vulgari eloquentia libri duo.* Venice, 1529.

Dati, Agnostino. *In elegantiarum A. Dathi codice contenta. Et primo I. J. Badij Ascensij de epistolis compendiolum. . . . IIII. A. Dathi elegantiae cum duplici commentario. . . .* Paris, 1501.

———— *Isagogicus libellus ad eloquentie praecepta recussus.* Marburg, 1608.

Demetrius, Phalereus. *De elocutione.* Florence, 1542. [See Gemistus, Georgius.]

———— *De elocutione, ac Dionsii Halicarnassensi opuscula quaedam. . . .* Basle, 1557.

———— *De interpretatione.* In Manutius, *Rhetores in hoc volumine habentur. . . .* Venice, 1508.

Dieu, Lewis de. *Sacra rhetorica.* Utrecht, 1695.

Dionysius of Halicarnassus. *Ars rhetorica.* In Manutius, *Rhetoris in hoc volumine habentur. . . .* Venice, 1508.

———— Διονυσιου Του ῾Αλικαρνασσεως ῾Ρωμαης ᾿Αρχαιολογιας βιβλιαδεκα *Dionysii Halicarnassei antiquitatum Romanarum libri X. . . . De compositione. . . .* [*Ed by R. Estienne*]. Greek. 2 pt. Paris, 1546-47.

Dresser, Matthew. *Rhetorica inventionis et dispositionis, illustrata & locupletata. . . .* Edita denuò correcta. . . . Basle, 1573.

Ducci, Lorenzo. *De elocutione libri duo.* n. p., 1600.

Du Flos, Jean. *Rhetoricarum praeceptionum tabulae.* Paris, 1554.

Du Pont, Gratien. *Art et science rhétorique métriffiée.* Paris, 1539.

Dupré, Jacques. *Portrait de l'eloquence.* Paris, 1620.

Durant, J. H. *Les Elemens de l'éloquence.* Paris, 1603.

Du Vair, Guillaume. *De l'éloquence, françoise et des raisons pourquoi elle est demeurie si bassé.* Paris, 1595.

Emporius (Rhetor). *De ethopoeia ac loco communi liber. Demonstrativae ac deliberativae materiae praecepta.* In *Antiqui rhetores latini. . . .* Paris, 1599.

Erasmus, Desiderius. *De duplici copia rerum ac verborum commentarii duo. De ratione studii, et instituendi pueros commentarii totidem. . . .* Paris [1510?]

———— *De formis oratoriarum argumentationum libellus.* Paris, 1537.

———— *De recta latini graecique sermonis pronuntiatione D. Erasmus dialogus. Ejusdem dialogus cui titulus Ciceronianus, sive de optimo genere dicendi.* . . . Paris, 1528.

―――― *Ecclesiastae sive de ratione concionandi libri quatuor.* Basle, 1535.

Erythraeus, Valentinus. *De elocutione, libri iii.* Strassburg, 1567.

Espinosa de Santayana, Rodrigo de. *Arte de retorica, en . . . tres libros: el primero enseña el arte generalmente, el segundo, particularmente el arte de hystoriador, el tercero escrivir epistolos y dialogos.* . . . Madrid, 1578.

Faber, J. R. *Enchiridion artis oratoriae.* Geneva, 1626.

Faber, P. S. *Le grant et vray art de pleine rhetorique.* Rouen, 1521.

Fortunatianus, Chirius. *Artis rhetoricae scholiae, libri iii.* In Trapezuntius, *Continentur hoc volumine.* . . . Venice, 1523.

―――― *Rhetorica a P. Nannio.* Louvain, 1526.

Fouquelin, Antoine. *La rhétorique françoise.* Paris, 1555. [Contains a reprint of Talaeus's *Institutiones oratoriae.*]

Fox Morzillo, Sebastian. *De imitatione, sive de informandi styli ratione libri duo.* Antwerp, 1554.

Francius, Peter. *Oratio de perfecto et consummato oratore.* Amsterdam, 1689.

Frisius, Paul. *La comparison de la rhétorique de Melanchthon, tant avec la logique de Ramus, qu' avec la rhétorique de notre auteur* [Talacus?]. Frankfort, 1600.

Frontinus, Anatolius. *Tabulae oratoriae inventionis.* Basle, 1560.

Furius, Frederick (Coeriolanus). *A Treatise on Rhetoric.* Basle, 1556. [In Latin?]

Garsias, Alphonsus. *De ratione dicendi libri duo, quibus accessere singulorum generum orationes.* Alcala de Henares, 1548.

Gaudin [le P. Jean?]. *Rhétorique françoise, autrement l'art de bien dire, traité par une methode nouvelle.* . . . Paris, 1645.

Gemistus, Georgius. *De gestis graecorum post pugnam ad Mantineam. . . . Ad haec Dionysii Halicarnassei praecepta, de oratione panegyrica, de oratione nuptiali, de eptholamiis. Demetri Phaleri praecepta, de membris et incisis, de periodis, de componendis epistolis, de characteribus dicendi.* . . . Basle, 1540.

Goosens, Gerardus. *Compendium rhetorices ex praelectionibus Petri Guersii.* Antwerp, 1567.

Górski, Jakób. *De figuris, tam grammaticis, tam rhetorcis, libri v.* Cracow, 1550.

―――― *De generibus dicendi.* Cracow, 1549.

―――― *De periodis atque numeris oratoris, libri duo.* Cracow, 1558.

Granada, F. Luis de. *Rhetoricae ecclesiasticae, seu de ratione con-ciononodi, libri sex.* [Cologne?], 1576.

Grosse, J. G. *De formandis orationibus.* Basle, 1613

Gueret, Gabriel. *Entretiens sur l'éloquence de la chaire et du barreau.* Paris, 1666.

Guntherus, Petrus. *De arte rhetorica, libri duo.* Strassburg, 1521.

———— *De arte rhetorica, libri ii, cum scholiis Valentinus Erythraeus.* Strassburg, 1568.

Hammerick, Johann. *Questionum rhetoricarum libri duo. . . . Accesserunt Cicerone orationes duae.* Jena, 1602.

Hauteville, Nicolas de. *L'art de bien discourir, ou la méthode aysée pour inventer, former, établir et multiplier un solide discours dans la chaire et dans le barreau. . . .* Paris, 1666.

Henisch, Georg. *Praeceptionum rhetoricarum libri v, et exercitationum libri ii. . . .* Strassburg, 1593.

———— *Praeceptiones rhetorica. Tabulis comprehense. Adiuncta est methodus docendi et discendi. Rhetoricam per praxin in uno exemplo. Item aliquot declinationes.* Strassburg, 1613.

Hermogenes of Tarsus. *Ars rhetorica absolutissma.* Paris, 1530.

———— *Ars rhetorica. In Manutius, Rhetores in hoc volumine habentur. . . .* Venice, 1508-09.

———— *De formis orationum et de inventione.* 2 vols. Paris, 1531, 1536.

———— *De methodo gravitatis, sive virtutis commode dicendi.* Paris, 1531.

———— *Progymnasmata. In Manutius, Rhetores in hoc volumine habentur. . . .* Venice, 1508-09.

Horace (Quintus Horatius Flaccus). *Epodom liber, ejusdem de arte poetica, item epistolarum libri duo.* Strassburg, 1515.

———— *Horatius de arte poetica.* [Deventer], 1500.

Hyperius, Andreas. *Dialecticae liber unus. Ejusdem rhetoricae liber unus.* Editio 2. . . . Zurich, n. d.

Ingolstetter, Johann. *Isagoge in rhetoricam Aristotelis, hoc est, praecepta eloquentiae methodica, ex Aristotelis excerpta.* Leipsic, n. d.

Isidore, Saint. *De arte rhetorica liber. In Antiqui rhetores latini.* Venice, 1599.

Jacob, Paul. *La clavicule, ou la science de Raymond Lulle, avec toutes les figures de rhétorique, par le sieur Paul Jacob.* Paris, 1646.

Jesu-Maria, J. A. *Rhetorica ecclesiastica, et ars concionandi.* Cologne, 1610.

Junius, Melchior. *Methodus eloquentiae comparandae, scholis rhetoricis tradita a Melchior Junio.* . . . Editio postrema. Antwerp, 1609. [1st ed. 1591?]

Keckermann, Bartholomaeus. *Rhetoricae ecclesiasticae, siue artis formandi et habendi conciones sacras, libri duo.* . . . Hanover, 1600.

———— *Systema rhetoricae.* Danzig, 1606.

Kelhaimannus, G. A. *Partitiones in M. T. Ciceronis de rhetorica libros quatuor ad C. Herennium.* Basle, 1549.

Kirchner, L. J. *Medulla praeceptionum rhetoricarum.* Coburg, 1594.

Lamy, Bernard. *La rhétorique, ou l'art de parler.* Paris, 1675.

Le Faucheur, Michel. *De l'action de l'orateur, ou de la prononciation et du geste.* Paris, 1657.

Le Grand, Jean-Francois. *Discours oratoires et dissertationes critiques.* Paris, 1657.

Le Gras, Le Sieur. *La rhétorique françoise, ou lès précepts de l'ancienne et vrai éloquence, accomodés a l' usage des conversations et de la société civile, du barreau et de la chaire.* Paris, 1671.

Le Gris, Claude. *Discours de la langua, et le thrésor de bien dire.* Rouen, 1604.

Leonini à Grenevoude, Albert. *Rhetorica, siue de arte dicendi libri duo.* Speier, 1588.

Longinus, Dionysius. *Liber de grandi sive sublimi orationis genere, nunc primum a Fr. Robortello in lucen editus.* . . . Basle, 1554.

Lulle, Antonio. *De oratione libri vii, quibus non modò Hermogenes ipse totus, verùm etiam quisquid ferè à reliquis Graecis ac Latinis de arte dicendi traditum est, suis locis aptissmè explicatur.* Basle, 1558.

———— *Progymnasmata rhetorica.* Basle, 1550.

Lulle, Raymond. *Ars magna.* . . . Barcelona, 1501.

———— *Artificum, sive ars brevis D. Raymundi Lullii ad absolvendam omnium artium encyclopediam.* [J. Villeta edidit.] Barcelona, 1565.

———— *Opusculum raymundinum de auditu kabbalistico sive ad omnes scientias introductorium.* Venice, 1533.

———— *Rhetoricorum Raimundi Lullii nova evulgatio, qua perspicuo faciliaque traduntur de omnibus tum scientiae, tum eloquentiae, generalia principia.* Paris, 1638. [Chiefly extracts from *Ars brevis* and *Ars magna.*]

Lupus, Rutilius. *De figuris sententiarum et elocutionis, libri duo.* Venice, 1513.

Macropedius, George. *Methodus de conscribendis epistolis, et epitome praeceptionum de paranda copia verborum et rerum, item ix. speciebus argumentationum rhetoricarum.* Paris, 1580.

Major (Meier), Georg. *Quaestiones rhetoricae ex libris M. Ciceronis, Quintiliani, et P. Melanch.* . . . Middleburg, 1535.

Manutius, A. P. (ed.?). *Rhetores in hoc volumine habentur hi. Apthonii Sophistae progymnasmata. Hermogenis ars rhetorica. Aristotelis rhetoricorum ad Theodecten libri tres. Ejusdem rhetorica ad. Alexandrum. Ejusdem ars poetica. Sopatri Rhetoris quaestiones de comp* [on] *endis declamationibus in causis praecipuae judicialibus. Cyri Sophistae differentiae statum. Dionysii Alicarnesei ars rhetorica. Demetri Phaleri de interpretatione. Alexandri Sophistae de figuris sensus & dictionis. Adnotationes innominati de figuris rhetoricis. Menandri Rhetoris divisio causarum in genere demonstrativo. Aristeidus de civili oratione. Ejusdem de simplici oratione. Apsini de arte rhetorica praecepta.* [This is volume 2, in *Apthonii progymnasmata commentarii innominati autoris. Syriani. Sopatri. Marcellini commentarii in Hermogenis rhetorica.* Greek. 2 vols. Venice, 1508-09]

Masen, Le P. Jacob. *Ars nova argutiarum eruditae et honestae recreationis, in duas partes divisa. Prima est epigrammatum, altera inscriptorum argutarum.* . . . Editio 2. Cologne, 1660.

———— *Exercitationes oratoriae, quae generum diversorum progymnasmata et orationes, vario stylo et disserendi ratione, complectitur libris duobus.* . . . Cologne, 1660.

———— *Palaestra eloquentiae ligatae novam . . . tam concipipiendi quam scribendi quovis stylo poetico methodum complectitur.* . . . 3 vols. Cologne, 1661-64.

———— *Palaestra oratoria . . . in progymnasmata eloquentiae atque exercitationes rhetorum proprias . . . distributa cum resolutione et artificio tullianarum orationum adjuncto.* . . . Cologne, 1659.

———— *Palaestra styli romani, quae artem et praesidia latine ornatèque quovis styli genere scribendi complectitur cum brevi graecarum et romanarum antiquitatum compendio, et praeceptis ad dialogos, epistolas et historias scribendas legendasque necessariis.* . . . Cologne, 1669.

Matienzo, Sebastian de. *Rhetorica.* Pamplona, 1618.

Melanchthon, Philip. *Contenta in hocci libello: Eloquentiae encomium, authore P. Melanchthone.* . . . Cologne, 1525.

———— *De arte dicendi declamatio.* Paris, 1527. (*See also* Schade. *De ratione studii.* . . . Basle, 1541.)

———— *De rhetorica libri tres.* Basle, Wittenburg, 1519.

———— *Elementorum rhetorices libri duo.* Haganau, 1532.

———— *Institutiones rhetoricae Philippi Melanchthonis.* Cologne, 1521.

250   BIBLIOGRAPHY

Merclin, M. J. *Quaestionum rhetoricarum libri duo.* Basle, 1559.

Moschopulus, Emanuel. *De ratione examinandae orationis libellus.* . . . [Greek.] Paris, 1545.

Mothe-le-Vayer, Francois de. *La rhétorique du Prince.* Paris, 1651.

Nebrija, Antonio de. *Artis rhetoricae compendiosa coaptatio.* Alcala, 1515.

Neideccerus, Laurentius. *Rhetoricarum oratoriarum institutionum liber 3, tan ad tum, in iuris ciuilas palestram, quam ad eloquentiae decus ab interitu vindicandum emissi.* Ivrea, 1600.

Neldelius, M. J. *Schediasmata μη' αὐτοσηχζδαλογ prodromi solidiotis atque illustrioris futurae, de universae rhetoricae natura ac constitutione disputationis.* Erfurt, 1687.

Nores, Jason de. *Breve trattato dell' oratore alla studiosa e valorosa gioventù d' nobli . . . con un discorso intorno alla distinzione, definizione, e divisione della retorica.* . . . Padua, 1574.

———— *Della rettorica di Giason de Nores libri iii, ne' quali oltra i precetti dell' arte si contengono venti orazioni tradotte da' più famosie illustri filosofi e oratori.* Venice, 1584.

Nunnensius, P. J. *Rhetoricae institutiones.* Barcelona, 1556.

Oliverus, Arnoldus. *De arte concionandi.* n. p., 1611.

Olivier, Petrus. *Dissertationes academicae; de oratoria, historia, et poetica.* Paris, 1672.

Pallavicino, Sforza. *Trattato dello stile e del dialogo . . . in questa terza diuolgazione emendato ed accresciuto.* Rome, 1662.

Palmireno, J. L. *Campi eloquentiae, in quibus L. Palmireni ratio declamandi, orationes, praefationes, epistolae, declamationes, et epigrammata continentur.* . . . Valencia, 1574.

———— *Rhetoricae. Pars secunda in duos libros distributa.* Valencia, 1565.

———— *Rhetoricae. Prima pars.* Valencia, 1567.

———— *Rhetoricae prolegomena.* . . . 3 pt. Valencia, 1567.

———— *Rhetoricae.* Tertia et ultima pars. Valencia, 1565.

Panigarola, Francesco. *Il predicatore, overo Demetrio Falereo dell' elocutione. Con le paraphrasi, e commenti, e discorsi ecclesiastici.* . . . n. p., 1609.

———— *Rhetorica ecclesiastica: sive, de modo componendae concionis libellus. Nunc primum in lucem editus.* Cologne, 1605.

Patrizi, Francesco. *Della retorica dieci dialoghi . . . nelli quali si favella dell' arte oratoria.* . . . Venice, 1562.

Pelletier, Le P. Gérard. *Palatium reginae eloquentiae, sive exercitationes oratoriae.* Paris, 1641.

Perez, Juan. *Progymnasmata artis rhetoricae, Joannis Petreii Toletani una cum annotationibus in Senecae declamationes, controversiae et deliberativae.* Alcala, 1539.

Perpina, P. J. *Aliquot epistolae, ubi, praeter caetera, de artis rhetoricae locis communibus, ac de juventute graecis latinisque literis erudienta agitur....* [Ed. P. J. Lucas.] Paris, 1683.

———— *De rethorica discenda.* Cologne, 1561.

Pico della Mirandolo, G. F. *Jo.-Francisci Pici ad Petrum Bembum de imitatione libellus.* Venice, 1530.

Pomey, F. A. *Novus candidatus rhetoricae, altero se candidior, comptiorque, non Aphthonii solum progymnasmata ornatius concinnata, sed Tullianae etiam rhetoricae praecepta clarius explicare repraesentans. ... Accessit ... dissertatio de panegyrico.* Lyons, 1682.

Quintilian, M. F. *Institutiones oratoriae.* Paris, 1510.

———— *Quintiliani institutionum oratoriarum libri duodecim quam emendatissimi sine vllis commentariis.* Venice, 1513.

Raberius, Anton. *Tabulae rhetoricae.* Basle, n. d.

Ramus, Peter. *Dialecticae libri duo, A. Talaei praelectionibus illustrati.* Paris, 1560.

———— *Scholae in liberales artes. ... Grammaticae libri xx, rhetoricae libri xx, dialecticae libri xx. ... Pro philosophica ... disciplina proemium reformandae Parisiensis Academicae. De sua professione oratio....* Basle, 1578.

Rapicius, Jovita. *De numero oratorio libri quinque. ...* Venice, 1554.

———— *Sermo de praestantia earum artium, quae ad recte loquendi, subtiliter disputandi, et bene dicendi ... rationem pertinant.* Venice, 1544.

Rapin, René. *Réflexions sur l'usage de l'éloquence de ce temps en géneral.* Paris, Oxford, 1672.

Regius, Emerici. *Isagoges rhetoricae libri duo, quorum prior de inuentione & dispositione, posterior vero de elocutione agit.* Hieron, 1612.

Regius, Hieronymus. *Linguae latinae commentarii tres; de emendata elocutione, de figurate sermone, de amplificanda oratione. ...* Venice, 1568.

Resenius, P. J. *Parva rhetorica.* n. p., 1619.

Reuschius, Joannes. See Ruffianus.

Reusner, Nicolas. *Elementorum artis rhetoricae.* Strassburg, 1578.

Rhenius, Johannes. *Compendium rhetoricae tribus libris adornatum de inuentione, dispositione, & elocutione.* Leipsic, 1621.

———— *Sylloge rhetorica, brevem et perspicuam continens σμγοψιγ omnium praeceptionum necessariarum.* . . . Leipsic, 1621.

Ricci, Bartholomeo. *De imitatione libri tres.* Venice, 1541.

Riccoboni, Antonio. *Commentarius, in quo explicatur rhetoricorum Ciceronis librorum doctrina.* Venice, 1560.

———— *Commentarius in universam doctrinam oratoriam Ciceronis.* . . . *Simulque libri rhetoricae Aristotelis perstringuntur. Addito compendio totius rhetoricae ex Aristotele et Cicerone junioribus ediscendo.* Frankfurt, 1596.

———— *De usu "Artis rhetoricae" Aristotelis commentarii viginti quinque* . . . *quibus accessit ejusdem Antonii Roccoboni a Jo. Mario Matio Brixiano dissensio de quibusdam locis Quintilaini probantibus rhetorica ad Herennium esse Cornificii.* Frankfurt, 1595.

Richer, Edmond. *De arte et causis rhetoricae, ac method eam ad usum vitae civilis revocandae liber unus.* Paris, 1629.

Robortello, Francesco. *De artificio dicendi* . . . *liber. Eiusdem tabulae oratoriae in Or. Cic. qua gratias agit Senatur post reditum.* . . . 3 pt. Bonaniae, 1567.

Roderici de Arriaga, R. F. *De oratore libri quatuor.* Cologne, 1637.

Roman, Nicolas. *De arte rhetorica libri 4.* Ingolstadt, 1581.

Ruffianus, Julius. *De figuris lexeos et dianoias libell'. Adjecto J. Reuschii de tropis orationis et dictionis opusculo.* Leipsic, 1521.

Rust, Johann. *Rhetoricae libri duo.* Bern, 1612.

Saint Paul, R. P. Charles de. *Tableau de l'éloquence Françoise, où l'on voit la manière de bien écrire.* Paris, 1632. [In the edition of 1657 is included *Traité de la rhétorique,* attributed to Cardinal du Perron.]

Salinas, Miguel. *Rhetorica en lengua Castellana.* Alcala, 1540.

Sanchez de las Brozas, Francisco. *De arte dicendi.* Salamanca, 1585.

———— *De partibus orationis et de constructione,* n. p., n. d.

———— *Organum dialecticum seu rhetoricum.* Salamanca, 1582.

Sansovino, Francesco. *Dell' arte oratoria libri iii, nella quale si contiene il modo, che si dee osservare nello scrivere ornatamente e con eloquenza così nelle prose, come ne' versi volgari.* Venice, 1569.

———— *In materia dell' arte (oratoria) libri iii, ne' quali se contiene l'ordine dell cose, che si recercano all' oratore.* Venice, 1561.

Santiago, Juan. *De arte rhetorica.* Seville, 1595.

Schade, Petrus. *De ratione studii, deque vita juventutis instituenda, opuscula diversorum autorum perquam erudita.* . . . Basle, 1541.

———— *Tabulae de schematibus et tropis Petri Mosellani. In rhetorica tabulae P. Melanchthonis. In Erasmi* . . . *libellum duplici copia.* Antwerp, 1529.

Scheffer, Joannes. *De stylo ad consuetudinem veterum liber singularis.* Upsala, 1653.

———— *Gymnasium styli sive do vario scribendi exercitio ad exemplum veterum.* Upsala, 1657.

Schollius, Joannes. *Praxis rhetorica, siue scholae & exercitationes eloquentiae.* Lubeck, 1612.

Segni, Bernardo (tr.). *Rettorica / et poetica / d'Aristotile /.* Tradotte de Gre / co in lingua vulga / re Fiorentian da Bernardo Segni. . . . Venice, 1551.

Seneca, M. A. *Ioannes Frobenius verae philosophiae studiosis S. D. En tibi lector optime, L. Annaei Senecae . . . lucubrationes omnes additis etiam nonnullis, Erasmi Roterdami.* . . . (*Declamationum libri decem.—Suasoriarum et controversiarum libri sex* [of Marcus A. Seneca]. . . . Basle, 1515.

Severianus, Julius. *Praecepta artis rhetoricae summatim de multis, ac syntomata.* . . . Basle, 1556.

Siberus, A. T. *Institutio rhetorica, epistolica elocutoria, una cum elogio in Ciceronem.* Wittenburg, 1608.

Sities y Vidal, Juan. *Apparatus ad publicam rhetoricae ac poesis academiam.* n. p., 1663.

Soarez, P. Cipriano. *De arte rhetorica, libri III ex Aristotele, Cicerone, et Quinctiliano depromptu.* Antwerp, 1575.

———— *Tabulae rhetoricae.* Venice, 1589.

Soudier, Jean de (Sieur de Richesource). *L'art de bien dire, ou les topiques françoise.* Paris, 1662.

———— *Méthode des orateurs, ou l'art de lire les auteurs, de les examiner, et de faire des lieux communs.* Paris, 1668.

Spangenberg, Johann. *Artificiosae memoriae libellus.* . . . (*Organon eloquentiae, hoc est de studio . . . commonfactiones . . . ex optimus authoribus collectae.*) Wittenburg, 1570. [1st ed. Paris, 1544?]

Stampel, Georg. *Tabulae rhetoricae praecepta artis dicendi, breuiter & plene collecta.* Frankfurt, 1607.

Streaebus, J. L. *De electione & oratoria collocatione verborum libri duo.* [Paris, 1539.]

———— *De figuris.* In *Operum graecorum, latinorum.* . . . Venice, 1644.

Sturmius, Johann. *De imitatione oratoria libri iii. cum scholis ejusdem authoris, antea nunquam in lucem editi.* [Ed. by V. Erythraeus.] Strassburg, 1574.

———— *De universa ratione elocutionis rhetoricae, libri iiii.* Nunc primum lucem editi opera et studio C. Thretii Poloni. Strassburg, 1576.

———— *In partitio-/nes oratorias Ciceronis. Dialogi qua-/tuor, ab ipso authore emen-/ dati, & aucti. / Nunc vero captibus distincte, et castigatiores editi, addi-/ tis singulorum capitum οικονομια, seu dispositione. / Adiumximus praetera, propter studiosos eloquen-/ tiae, eusdem authoris libros duos, de amissa / dicendi ratione, & quomodo ea / recuperanda sit. Strassburg, 1539. [Date of dedication.]

―――― *Institutiones literatae, sive de discendi atque docendi ratione.* Strassburg, 1591.

Sulpicius Victor. *Institutiones oratoriae.* In *Degli autori del ben parlare.* . . . Venice, 1643.

Susenbrotus, Joannes. *Epitome troporum ac schematum et grammaticorum & rhetorum.* . . . Figuri, [1540?].

Sylvius, Franciscus. *Progymnasmatum in artem oratoriam F. Sylvii . . . centuriae tres.* [Paris], 1520.

Talaeus, Audomarus. *Institutiones oratoriae.* 2nd ed. Paris, 1548. [1st ed. 1544?]

Theodoricus, D. C. *Epitome praeceptorum rhetoricae.* Erfurt, 1617.

―――― *Institutiones rhetoricae ex Aristotele, Quintiliano, Cicerone & aliorum praeceptis method conscriptae.* Jena, 1624.

Theonis, Aelius. Θεωγος σοφιστον προγυμγασματα. *Theonis rhetoris de modo declamandi libellus.* Rome, 1520.

Tholdius, Christain. *Rhetorica praeceptis, theorematis, ac cannonibus methodici dispositis conscripta, exemplis sacris & profanis, oratoriis et poeticis illustrata.* Frankfurt, 1623.

Timpler, Clemens. *Rhetoricae systema methodicum, per praecepta et questiones. Adiectus est de methodo eloquentiae libellus.* Hanover, 1613.

Tomitano, Bernardino. *Quattro libri della linqua Thoscana . . . ove si prova, la philosofia esser necessaria al perfetto oratore, & poeta, con due libi nuovamente aggionti, dei precetti richiesti à lo scrivere e parlare con eloquenzia* [Ed. by I. Olmo]. Padua, 1570.

―――― *Ragionamenti della lingua Toscana. . . . I precetti della rhetorica secondo l'artificio d'Aristotle e Cicerone nel fine del secondo libro nuovamente aggionti.* Venice, 1546.

Torres, Alfonso. *Progymnasmata rethoricae.* Alcala, 1569.

―――― *Tabula in rethoricam.* Alcala, 1569.

Toscanella, Orazio. *Applicamento de i precetti della inventione, dispositione, et elocutione, che propriamente serve allo scrittore di epistole latine, et volgari, ritratto in tavole, da Oratio Toscanella.* . . . Venice, 1575.

Trapezuntius, George, *Opus absolutissimum rhetoricorum . . . cum additionibus herrariensis* [i.e. of F. de Herrara]. n. p., 1511.

―――― *Continentur hoc volumine: Georgii Trapezuntii rhetoricorum libri v. Consulti C. Fortunatiani libri iii. Aquilae Romani de figuris sententiarum & elocutionis liber. P. Rutilii lupi earundem figurarum e Georgio Trapezuntio interprete libri iii. Ejusdem* [*or rather of Anaximenes of Lampsacus*] *rhetorices ad Alexandrum a F. Philelpho in latinum versae liber. Paraphrasis rhetoricae Hermogenis ex Hilarionis monachi Veronensis traductione. Priscianus de rhetoricae praeexercitamentis ex Hermogene. Aphthonii declamatoris rhetorica progymnasmata J. M. Catanaeo tralatore.* Venice, 1523.

Treutler, Hieronimo. *Annotata philosophica, in rhetorica, logica, ethica & physica praecepta.* Marburg, 1595.

Valerius, Cornelius. *In universam bene dicendi rationem tabulae, summam artis rhetoricae complectens.* Antwerp, 1567.

———— *Rhetorica . . . universam bene dicendi rationem . . . complectens . . . nunc ad majorem puerorum commoditatem per interrogationes et responsiones . . . digesta . . . per L. Schenckelium.* Antwerp, 1596.

Valiero, Agostinio. *De rhetorica ecclesiastica, sive modo concionandi.* Venice, 1574.

———— *Libri tres, de rhetorica ecclesiastica. Synopsis ejusdem rhetoricae . . . contexta. Adjunctis tribus praelectionibus, ab eodem habitus, quibus omnis hujus rhetoricae explicandae ratio traditur. . . .* Paris, 1575.

Vavasseur, Francois. *De ludicra dictione liber.* Paris, 1658.

Vechner, Daniel. *Amplificationum rhetoricarum pars prior rationem orationis dilatandae iusta method demonstrans.* Breslau, 1614.

Vietor, Theodore. *Examen rhetoricum.* Hanover, 1597.

Villavicentius, Laurentius. *De formendis sacris concionibus, sive de interpretatione scripturarum populari, libri tres,* 1570.

Vives, J. L. *De ratione dicendi, libri tres.* Louvain, 1533.

Vossius, G. J. *Commentariorum rhetoricorum, sive oratoriaium institutionum, libri vi.* Lyons, [1606?]. [3rd ed., Frankfurt, 1616.]

———— *De logices et rhetoricae natura et constitutione, libri ii.* Hagenau, 1658.

———— *Elementa rhetorica.* Middleburg, 1640.

Westhovius, Willichius. *Introductio ad rhetoricam Melanchthonis. . . .* Leipsic, 1607.

III. General Works Consulted

A. books

Abbott, E. A. *Bacon and Essex: A Sketch of Bacon's Life.* London, 1877.

———— *Francis Bacon: An Account of his Life and Works.* London, 1885.

Abercromby, David. *On Conversation*. London, 1683.

Aiken, Lucy. *Memoirs of the Court of King James the First*. 2 vols. London, 1822.

Allen, P. S. *The Age of Erasmus*. Oxford, 1814.

The Ancient Laws of the Fifteenth Century for King's College, Cambridge, and for the Public School of Eton College. Collected by James Heywood and Thomas Wright. London, 1850.

Aristotle. "Analytica posteriora." Translated by G. R. G. Mure. *The Works of Aristotle*. Ed. by W. D. Ross. Vol. 1. Oxford, 1928.

———— "Analytica priora." Tr. by A. J. Jenkinson. *Works*. Ed. by W. D. Ross. Vol. I. Oxford, 1928.

———— *The Nichomachean Ethics of Aristotle*. Tr. by J. E. C. Welldon. London, 1902.

———— "Rhetorica." Tr. by W. Rhys Roberts. *Works*, Ed. by W. D. Ross. Vol. XI. Oxford, 1928.

———— "Topica and de sophisticis elenchis." Tr. by W. A. Pickard-Cambridge. *Works*. Ed. by W. D. Ross. Vol. I. Oxford, 1938.

The Rhetoric of Aristotle, with a commentary by the late Edward Meredith Cope. Ed. by J. E. Sandys. 3 vols. Cambridge, 1877. *See also* Cooper, Lane.

Atkins, J. W. H. *Literary Criticism in antiquity: a sketch of its development*. Cambridge, 1934.

Austen-Leigh, Augustus. *King's College*. London, 1899.

Bacon, Francis. *Francis Bacon: The Advancement of Learning*. Ed. by W. A. Wright. Oxford, 1891.

———— *Essays Or Counsels, Civil and Moral, and Wisdom of the Ancients*. With Biographical notice by A. Spiers, Preface by B. Montagu, and Notes by Different Writers. Boston, 1868.

———— *Essays*. With Introduction, Notes and Index by E. A. Abbott. 2 vols. London, 1886.

———— *Essays, and Colours of Good and Evil*. With Notes and Glossarial Index by W. A. Wright. London, 1885.

———— *Letters of Sir Francis Bacon . . . Written during the Reign of King James the First. Now Collected and Augmented with Several Letters and Memories*. . . . Ed. by Robert Stephens. London, 1702.

———— *Novum organum*. Ed. by Thomas Fowler. Oxford, 1878.

———— *Physical and Metaphysical Works*. Ed. by J. Dewey. London, 1889.

———— *The Promus of Formularies and Elegancies*. Illustrated . . . by Passages from Shakespeare by Mrs. Henry Pott. Preface by E. A. Abbott. London, 1883.

—————— *The Promus of Formularies and Elegancies.* Collected with the Original MS by F. B. Bickley and Revised by F. A. Herbert. In Lawrence, Sir Edwin D. *Bacon Is Shakespeare.* 1910.

Bain, Alexander. *English Composition and Rhetoric.* New York, 1868.

—————— *Logic: Deductive and Inductive,* New York, 1874.

Baker, Thomas. *History of the College of St. John the Evangelist, Cambridge.* Cambridge, 1869.

Baldwin, C. S. *Ancient Rhetoric and Poetic.* New York, 1924.

—————— *Medieval Rhetoric and Poetic.* New York, 1928.

Bartlett, A. C. *Larger Rhetorical Patterns in Anglo-Saxon Poetry.* New York, 1935.

Baxter, Richard. *Reliquiae Baxterianae.* Ed. by M. Sylvester. London, 1696.

Birch, Thomas. *The Court and Times of James the First.* 2 vols. London, 1849.

—————— *The Life of the Most Reverend Dr. John Tillotson.* London, 1753.

—————— *Memoirs of the Reign of Queen Elizabeth from the Year 1581 till Her Death.* . . . 2 vols. London, 1754.

Blair, Hugh. *Lectures on Rhetoric and Belles Lettres.* London, 1783.

Blount, T. P. *De Re Poetica.* London, 1694.

Bornecque, Henri. *Les déclamations et les déclamateurs d'après Sénèque le Père.* Lille, 1902.

Bozell, R. B. *English Preachers of the Seventeenth Century on the Art of Preaching* (Cornell University Doctoral Dissertation). Ithaca, New York, 1939.

Brown, Basil. *Law Sports at Gray's Inn* (1594) . . . *together with Reprint of Gesta Grayorum.* New York, 1921.

Bryant, D. C. *Papers in Rhetoric.* Ed. by D. C. Bryant. Saint Louis, 1940.

Buckle, H. T. *History of Civilization in England.* 3 vols. London, 1925-1931.

Burgh, James. *The Art of Speaking.* Philadelphia, 1775.

Campbell, George. *The Philosophy of Rhetoric.* London, 1776.

Castiglione, Baldassare. *The Book of the Courtier.* Tr. by Thomas Hoby. London, 1561.

Cato variegatus or Catoes Morall Distichs. Translated and Paraphrased with Variations of Expressing, in English Verse by Sir Richard Baker. London, 1636.

Chaignet, A. E. *La Rhétorique et son histoire.* Paris, 1888.

Chamberlain, John. *Letters Written by John Chamberlain during the*

Reign of Queen Elizabeth. Ed. by Sarah Williams, Camden Society Publications, 1861.

Channing, E. T. *Lectures Read to the Seniors in Harvard College on Rhetoric and Oratory.* Boston, 1856.

Chrysostom, Saint. *Six Books on the Priesthood.* Augsburg, 1599. (In Nicene and Post-Nicene fathers. Ed. by Philip Schaff. Buffalo, 1887.)

Church, R. W. *Bacon.* New York, 1884.

Clark, D. L. *Rhetoric and Poetry in the Renaissance.* New York, 1922.

Cole, P. R. *A History of Educational Thought.* London, 1931.

Cooper, Lane. *Aristotle on the Art of Poetry: An Amplified Version.* New York, 1913.

Cornwallis, Lady Jane. *The Private Correspondence of Lady Jane Cornwallis: 1613-1644.* London, 1842.

Cotton, Sir Robert. *Cotton posthuma.* Ed. by J. Howell. London, 1651.

Craik, G. L. *Bacon, His Writing and His Philosophy.* 2 vols. London, 1846.

Crane, W. G. *Wit and Rhetoric in the Renaissance.* New York, 1937.

Cubberley, E. P. *Readings in the History of Education.* New York, 1920.

Cust, Lionel, *History of Eton College.* London, 1899.

Denniston, J. D. *Greek Literary Criticism.* New York, 1924.

D'Ewes, Simonds. *Autobiography and Correspondence.* Ed. by J. O. Halliwell. London, 1845.

Dill, Samuel. *Roman Society in the Last Century of the Western Empire.* London, 1905.

Dionysius of Halicarnassus. *On Literary Composition.* Ed. by W. Rhys Roberts. London, 1910.

Dixon, W. H. *Personal History of Lord Bacon, from Unpublished Papers.* Boston, 1861.

Dorchester, Dudley Carleton. *Letters from and to Sir Dudley Carleton . . . from January 1616 to December 1620.* London, 1757.

Draud, Georg. *Bibliotheca classica.* . . . Frankfurt, 1625.

Drummond of Hawthornden. *Notes of Ben Jonson's Conversations with William Drummond of Hawthornden.* London, 1619.

Duff, J. W. *A Literary History of Rome in the Silver Age, from Tiberius to Hadrian.* London, 1930.

Early Statutes of Christ's College, Cambridge. Ed. and tr. by H. Rackham. Cambridge. 1927.

Elyot, Thomas. *The Book Called the Gouvenour.* London, 1531.

Erasmus, Desiderius. *The Apophegmes of Erasmus.* Tr. by Nicholas Udall. London, 1542. Ed. by Robert Roberts. Boston, 1877.

―――― *Colloquies.* Tr. by N. Bailey. London, 1725.

―――― *De Ratione studii.* Strassburg, 1511.

―――― *The Epistles of Erasmus.* Ed. and tr. by F. M. Nichols. 3 vols. London, 1901-1918.

―――― *Proberbs, Chiefly Taken from the Adagia of Erasmus, with Explanations.* . . . Tr. by Robert Bland. 2 vols. London, 1814.

Evelyn, John. *Diary and Correspondence of John Evelyn.* Ed. by William Bray. 4 vols. London, 1859-1862.

Fletcher, Anthonie. *Certain Very Proper and Most Profitable Similies.* London, 1595.

Fowler, John. *Bacon.* New York, 1881.

Genung, J. F. *Practical Elements of Rhetoric.* Boston, 1887.

Gibert, B. *Jugements des savants sur les auteurs qui ont traité de la Rhetorique.* 3 vols. Paris, 1713.

Glanville, Joseph. *An Essay concerning Preaching.* . . . London, 1678.

―――― *A Seasonable Defense of Preaching: And the Plain Way of It.* London, 1678.

Goiyet, C. P. *Bibliothèque francoise, ou histoire de la litterature francoise,* 18 vols. Paris, 1741-1756. (Part II, vols. I-II, is entitled "Des Livres qui traitent de la Rhétorique, ou de l'Art de l'Eloquence.")

Gosse, Edmund. *Life and Letters of John Donne.* London, 1899.

Graves, F. P. *A History of Education during the Middle Ages and the Transition to Modern Times.* New York, 1923.

―――― *Peter Ramus and the Educational Reformation of the Sixteenth Century.* New York, 1912.

Grierson, H. J. C. *The First Half of the Seventeenth Century.* London, 1906.

Haarhoff, Theodore. *Schools of Gaul: A Study of Pagan and Christian Education in the Last Century of the Western Empire.* Oxford, 1920.

Hallam, Henry. *View of the State of Europe during the Middle Ages.* New York, 1880.

Hamilton, Sir William. *Discussions on Philosophy and Literature.* London, 1853.

―――― *Lectures on Metaphysics and Logic.* 2 vols. Boston, 1860.

Harrison, W. H. *Desiderius Erasmus concerning the Aim and Method of Education.* Cambridge, 1904.

Herbert, Edward of Cherbury. *The Autobiography of Edward, Lord Herbert of Cherbury.* Ed. by Sidney Lee. New York, 1908.

13

260   BIBLIOGRAPHY

Herbert, George. *The English Works of George Herbert*. 3 vols. New York, 1905.

Herrick, M. T. *The Poetics of Aristotle in England*. Cornell Studies in English, XVII. New Haven, 1930.

Hobbes, Thomas. *Leviathan, or The Matter, Form and Power of a Common-wealth, Ecclesiastical and Civil*. London, 1651.

Hooker, Richard. *Of the Laws of Ecclesiastical Polity*. London, 1592-1662.

Howell, James. *Instructions for Forreine Travell*. London, 1642.

Hultzén, L. S. *Aristotle's Rhetoric in England to 1660*. Cornell University Doctoral Dissertation. Ithaca, New York, 1932.

Hume, David. *Essays and Treatises on Several Subjects*. 2 vols. London, 1767.

Hutchinson, Lucy. *Memoirs of the Life of Colonel Hutchinson*. London, 1908.

Hyperius, Andreas. *The Practice of Preaching, otherwise Called The Pathway to the Pulpit*. . . . Ed. by John Ludham. London, 1577.

Innes, A. D. *England under the Tudors*. London, 1905.

James the First. *Correspondence of King James VI of Scotland with Sir R. Cecil and Others*. Ed. by John Bruce. London, 1861.

Jones, R. F. *Ancients and Moderns: A Study of the Background of the Battle of the Books*. Washington University Studies. New Series, No. 6. Saint Louis, 1936.

Kay, M. M. *The History of Rivington and Blackrood Grammar Schools*. Manchester, 1931.

Keckerman, B. *Gymnasium logicum in iii libres,* Hanover, 1605.

Kelso, Ruth. *The Doctrine of the English Gentleman in the Sixteenth Century*. University of Illinois Studies in Language and Literature, XIV, No. 1-2. Urbana, 1929.

Knight, Samuel. *The Life of Dr. John Colet*. Oxford, 1823.

Krapp, G. P. *The Rise of English Literary Prose*. New York, 1915.

La Ramée, Pierre. *Dialecticae libri duo*. London, 1576.

Laurie, S. S. *The Rise and Early Constitution of Universities, with a Survey of Medieval Education*. New York, 1887.

Lawson, John. *Lectures concerning Oratory*. London, 1752.

Leach, A. F. *English Schools at the Reformation, 1546-8*. Westminster, 1896.

Lee, Sidney. *Shakespeare's England: An Account of the Life and Manners of his Age*. Ed. by Sidney Lee, Oxford, 1917.

The Legacy of the Middle Ages. Ed. by C. G. Crump and E. F. Jacob, Oxford, 1926.

Livius, Titus. *The Roman Historie: Also the Breuiaries of L. Florus.* Tr. by P. Holland. London, 1600.

Locke, John. *An Essay concerning the Understanding, Knowledge, Opinion, and Assent.* London, 1671.

Lupton, J. H. *A Life of John Colet . . . with an Appendix of Some of his English Writings.* London, 1887.

Lyly, John. *Euphues.* London, 1868.

Mallett, C. E. *A History of the University of Oxford.* 3 vols. New York, 1924.

Manly, J. M. *Chaucer and the Rhetoricians.* London, 1926.

Mantuanus, Baptista. *The Eclogues of Baptista Mantuanus.* Tr. by George Turberville. London, 1567.

Mayor, J. E. B. *Early Statutes of the College of St. John the Evangelist in the University of Cambridge.* Cambridge, 1859.

Mill, J. S. *Dissertations and Discussions: Political, Philosophical, and Historical.* 3 vols. Boston, 1864.

―――― *A System of Logic.* 2 vols. London, 1851.

Milton, John. *The Prose Works of John Milton.* Ed. by J. A. St. John. 5 vols. Bohn Standard Library. London, 1848.

Mitchell, W. F. *English Pulpit Oratory from Andrewes to Tillotson.* London, 1932.

Montagu, Basil. *The Life of Francis Bacon.* London, 1833.

Montaigne, Michel de. *The Essays, or Morall, Politike Discourses: Done in English by J. Florio.* London, 1603.

More, Thomas. *The Life of Sir Thomas More, Knight.* London, 1726.

Mulcaster, Richard. *The First Part of the Elementarie which Entreateth of Right Writing of our English Tung. . . .* London, 1582.

―――― *Positions wherein those Circumstances be Explained Necessarie for the Training up of Children.* London, 1581.

Mullinger, J. B. *The University of Cambridge from the Earliest Times to the Royal Injunctions of 1535.* Cambridge, 1873.

―――― *The University of Cambridge from the Royal Injunctions of 1535 to the Accession of Charles I.* Cambridge, 1884.

Napier, M. *Lord Bacon and Sir Walter Raleigh.* Cambridge, 1853.

Nashe, Thomas. *The Anatomie of Absurditie.* London, 1589.

Neale, J. M. *Mediaeval Preachers and Mediaeval Preaching.* Tr. and ed. by J. M. Neale. London, 1856.

Nichol, John. *Francis Bacon: His Life and Philosophy.* 2 vols. Edinburgh, 1888-1889.

Orderne, James. *Directions concerning the Matter and Stile of Sermons.* London, 1671.

Osborne, Dorothy. *The Letters from Dorothy Osborne to Sir William Temple.* New York, 1914.

Owst, G. R. *Literature and Pulpit in Mediaeval England.* Cambridge, 1933.

Pater, Walter, *The Renaissance.* London, 1877.

Paule, George. *The Life of John Whitgift, Archbishop of Canterbury.* London, 1699.

Perkins, William. *The Arte of Prophecying or A Treatise concerning the Sacred and Only True Manner and Methode of Preaching.* London, 1892.

Petty, William. *The Advice of W. P. to Mr. Samuel Hartlib, for the Advancement of Some Particular Parts of Learning.* London, 1648. (Harlean Miscellany, VI.)

Plato. *The Dialogues of Plato.* Tr. by B. Jowett. 2 vols. New York, 1937.

Plimpton, G. A. *The Education of Shakespeare.* New York, 1933.

Plinius Secundus, Caius. *A Summarie of the Antiquities, and Wonders of the Worlde, out of the Sixtene First Books of Plinie.* Tr. by J. A. London, 1566.

Plutarch. *The Education or Bringinge up of Children.* Tr. by Syre T. Eliot. London, 1535.

———— *The Lives of the Noble Grecians and Romans.* Tr. out of the French by T. North. London, 1579.

———— *The Philosophie, Commonlie Called the Morals.* Tr. by Philemon Holland. London, 1603.

Pollard, A. F. *Thomas Cranmer and the English Reformation.* New York, 1904.

———— *Wolsey.* New York, 1929.

Prideaux, Matthias. *Sacred Eloquence, or the Art of Rhetoric, as It Is Laid Down in the Scripture.* London, 1659.

Priestley, Joseph. *Lectures on Oratory and Criticism.* London, 1777.

Puget de la Sieur, Jean. *The Secretary in Fashion: Or, a Compendious and Refined Way of Expression in All Manner of Letters. . . .* Tr. by John Massinger. London, 1640.

Quarles, Francis. *Emblemes.* London, 1639.

———— *Enchyridion containing Institutions Divine and Morall.* London, 1640.

Rackham, Harris. *Early Statutes of Christ's College, Cambridge.* Cambridge, 1927.

Rainolds, John. *Oratio in laudem artis poeticae.* Introduction and commentary by William Ringler. Tr. by Walter Allen, Jr. Princeton, 1940.

Rashdall, Hastings. *The Universities of Europe in the Middle Ages.* 2 vols. Oxford, 1895.

Rawley, William. *A Translation of the Thirty-two Latin Poems in Honor of Francis Bacon, Published by Rawley in 1626.* Boston, 1904.

Remusat, C. F. M. *Bacon, sa vie, son temps, sa philosophie et son influence jusquà nos jours.* Paris, 1877.

Richard, J. W. *Philip Melanchthon, the Protestant Preceptor of Germany.* New York, 1898.

Richardson, Alexander. *The Logicians Schoolmaster.* London, 1629.

Richardson, C. F. *English Preachers and Preaching, 1640-1670.* New York. 1928.

Roper, Thomas. *The Life of Sir Thomas More.* London, 1817.

Sandford, W. P. *English Theories of Public Address, 1530-1828.* Columbus, Ohio, 1931.

Sandys, J. E. *History of Classical Scholarship.* 3 vols. Cambridge, 1921.

Scott, M. A. *The Essays of Francis Bacon.* New York, 1908.

Seebohm, Frederic. *The Oxford Reformers, John Colet, Erasmus, and Thomas More.* London, 1869.

Selden, John. *Table-Talk,* Ed. by E. Arber. English Reprints. Birmingham, 1868.

Sellery, G. C., and A. C. Krey. *Mediaeval Foundations of Western Civilization.* New York, 1929.

Seneca, L. A. (the Elder). *The Suasoriae of Seneca the Elder.* Tr. by W. A. Edward. Cambridge, 1928.

Sheridan, Thomas. *A Course of Lectures on Elocution together with Two Dissertations on Language.* . . . London, 1763.

Sidney, Philip. *An Apologie for Poetrie.* London, 1595.

Smith, G. G. (ed.). Elizabethan Critical Essays. 2 vols. London, 1904.

Smith, Preserved. *The Age of Erasmus.* New York, 1920.

South, Robert. *Sacred Eloquence: Or the Art of Rhetoric as It is Layed Down in the Scriptures.* London, 1659.

Spedding, James. *The Collection of Books Used by James Spedding as His Working Library in Preparing his Edition of the Works of Sir Francis Bacon.* London, 1916.

────── *Evenings with Reviewer, or Macaulay and Bacon.* 2 vols. London, 1881.

264   BIBLIOGRAPHY

Spencer, Thomas. *The Art of Logick, Delivered in the Precepts of Aristotle and Ramus.* London, 1628.

Spingarn, J. E. (ed.). *Critical Essays of the Seventeenth Century.* Oxford, 1908.

Sprat, Thomas. *The History of the Royal Society of London for the Improving of Natural Knowledge.* London, 1722.

Statutes of the Colleges of Oxford . . . Printed by Desire of Her Majesty's Commissioners for Inquiring into the State of the University of Oxford. 3 vols. Oxford, 1853.

The Statutes for Corpus Cristi College, All Souls College, and Magdalen Ward. London, 1843.

Statutes of the University of Oxford, Codified in the Year 1636 under the Authority of Archbishop Laud. Ed. by J. Griffiths. Oxford, 1888.

Steeves, G. W. *Francis Bacon; A Sketch of His Life, Works, and Literary Friends.* . . . London, 1910.

Stockwood, John. *Disputationcularum grammaticalium libellus.* London, 1589.

Strype, John. *Memorials of Thomas Cranmer.* London, 1694.

Symonds, J. A. *Renaissance in Italy: Revival of Learning.* London, 1877.

Tacitus, P. C. *The Annales of Corn. Tacitus.* Tr. by R. Greneway. London, 1598.

Taylor, H. O. *Thought and Expression in the Sixteenth Century.* 2 vols. New York, 1930.

Tenison, E. M. *Elizabethan England.* 6 vols. Glasgow, 1932-1937.

Trevelyan, G. M. *England Under the Stuarts.* London, 1925.

—————— *History of England.* New York, 1929.

Virgilius, M. P. *The Bucolikes, Drawne Into English by A. Fleming.* London, 1575.

—————— *The Bucoliks, Georgiks, Tr. by A.* F[leming]. London, 1589.

—————— *The Whole XII Bookes of the Aeneidos.* Tr. by T. Phaer and T. Twyne. London, 1573.

Waddington, Charles. *Ramus: sa vie ses écrits et ses opinions.* Paris, 1855.

Walker, John. *Elements of Elocution, in Which the Principles of Reading and Speaking are Investigated . . . to Which is Added a Complete System of the Passions.* . . . London, 1759.

Ward, John. *A System of Oratory.* . . . 2 vols. London, 1759.

Watson, Foster. *The English Grammar Schools to 1660: Their Curriculum and Practice.* Cambridge, 1908.

────── *Tudor Schoolboy Life, Being a Translation of Latinae Exercitatio (1539) of Vives.* London, 1908.

────── *Vives: On Education. A Translation of the De Tradendis Disciplinis (1531) of Juan Luis Vives.* Cambridge, 1913.

Webbe, William. *A Discourse of English Poetrie.* . . . London, 1586.

Weever, John. *Epigrammes, in the Oldest Cut, and Newest Fashion.* London, 1599.

Weld, C. R. *A History of the Royal Society.* . . . 2 vols. London, 1848.

West, A. F. *Alcuin and the Rise of the Christian Schools.* New York, 1892.

Whately, Richard. *Elements of Rhetoric.* London, 1828.

Wheatley, H. B. *The Early History of the Royal Society.* Hertford, 1905.

Whitaker, V. K. *Bacon and the Renaissance Encyclopedists.* (Stanford University Doctoral Dissertation.) Polo Alto, 1933.

Wilkins, John. *Ecclesiastes, or, A Discourse concerning the Gift of Preaching.* . . . London, 1647.

Williams, Charles. *Bacon.* London, 1933.

Wilson, Mona. *Sir Philip Sidney.* New York, 1932.

Wolff, Emil. *Francis Bacon und seine Quellen.* Berlin, 1910.

Wood, Anthony à. *Athenae Oxioniensis.* 2 vols. London, 1721.

Woodward, W. H. *Erasmus concerning the Aim and Method of Education.* Cambridge, 1904.

────── *Studies in Education during the Age of the Renaissance, 1400-1600.* Cambridge, 1906.

────── *Vittorino da Feltre and Other Humanist Educators.* Cambridge, 1897.

Wotton, Sir Henry. *Reliquiae Wottonianae, or a Collection of Lives, Letters, Poems, with Characters of Sundry Personages and other Incomparable Pieces of Language and Art.* . . . London, 1651.

Wright, L. B. *Middle-Class Culture in Elizabethan England.* Chapel Hill, North Carolina, 1935.

Wright, Thomas. *Queen Elizabeth and Her Times, a Series of Original Letters, Selected from the Unedited Private Correspondence* . . . *of the Distinguished Persons of the Period.* 2 vols. London, 1838.

B. ARTICLES

Barnes, H. E. "The Historical Background and Setting of the Philosophy of Francis Bacon," *Scientific Monthly,* XVIII (May, 1924), 475-495.

Bensley, Edward. "Dr. Andrews and Bacon's Apophthegms," *Notes and Queries*, CXLVI (February 2, 1942), 85-86.

Boissier, M. "Lés écoles de déclamation à Rome." *Revue des deux Mondes*, II (1902), 480-508.

Bundy, M. W. "Bacon's True Opinion of Poetry," *Studies in Philology*, XXVII (1930), 244-264.

――― " 'Invention' and 'Imagination' in the Renaissance," *Journal of English and Germanic Philology*, XXIX (1930), 535-545.

Caplan, Harry. "Classical Rhetoric and the Medieval Theory of Preaching," *Classical Philology*, XXVIII (1933), 73-96.

――― "The Four Senses of Scriptural Interpretation and the Medieval Theory of Preaching," *Speculum*, IV (1929), 282-290.

――― "A Late Medieval Tractate on Preaching," *Studies in Rhetoric and Public Speaking in Honor of James A. Winans*, New York, 1924.

――― "Rhetorical Invention in Some Medieval Tractates on Preaching," *Speculum*, II (1927), 284-295.

Crane, R. S. "The Relation of Bacon's Essays to His Program for the Advancement of Learning," *Schelling Anniversary Papers*, New York, 1923.

Croll, M. W. "Attic Prose in the Seventeenth Century," *Studies in Philology*, XVIII (1921), 79-128.

――― "Attic Prose: Lipsius, Montaigne, Bacon," *Schelling Anniversary Papers*, New York, 1923.

――― "Muret and the History of Attic Prose," *Publications of the Modern Language Association*, XXXIX (1924), 254-309.

Emperor, John. "The Rhetorical Importance of Lucan's Pharsalia," *Quarterly Journal of Speech*, XVI (1930), 463-471.

Hale, E. E., Jr. "Ideas of Rhetoric in the Sixteenth Century," *Publications of the Modern Language Association*, XVII (1903), 424-444.

Harrison, B. S. "Medieval Rhetoric in the Book of the Duchesse," *Publications of the Modern Language Association*, XLIX (1934), 428-442.

Hendrickson, G. L. "Origin and Meaning of the Characters of Style," *American Journal of Philology*, XXVI (1905), 248-290.

――― "The Peripatetic Mean of Style and the Three Stylistic Characters," *American Journal of Philology*, XXV (1904), 125-146.

Herrick, M. T. "The Early History of Aristotle's Rhetoric in England." *Philological Quarterly*, V (1926), 242-257.

Howell, W. S. "Nathaniel Carpenter's Place in the Controversy between Dialectic and Rhetoric," *Speech Monographs*, I (1934), 20-41.

Hudson, H. H. "Jewel's Oration against Rhetoric: A Translation," *Quarterly Journal of Speech,* XIV (1928), 374-392.

Hultzén, L. S. "Charles Butler on Memory," *Speech Monographs,* VI (1939), 43-65.

Hunt, Everett. "Plato and Aristotle on Rhetoric and Rhetoricians," *Studies in Rhetoric and Public Speaking in Honor of James A. Winans,* New York, 1924.

Jones, R. F. "The Attack on Pulpit Eloquence in the Restoration," *Journal of English and Germanic Philology,* XXX (1931), 188-217.

———— "Science and Prose Style in the 3rd Quarter of the 17th Century," *Publications of the Modern Language Association,* XLV (1930), 977-1009.

———— "Science and Language in England of the Mid-Seventeenth Century," *Journal of English and Germanic Philology,* XXXI (1932), 315-331.

Paetow, L. J. "The Arts Course at Medieval Universities with Special Reference to Grammar and Rhetoric," *The Universitiy Studies,* University of Illinois, III (1910), 497-624.

Ringler, William. "The Immediate Source of Euphuism," *Publications of the Modern Language Association,* LIII (1938), 678-686.

Sandford, W. P. "English Rhetoric Reverts to Classicism," 1600-1650, *Quarterly Journal of Speech,* XV (1929), 503-525.

———— "On English Rhetorics," *Quarterly Journal of Speech,* XV (1929), 250-251.

Schoell, F. L. "G. Chapman's 'Commonplace Book'," *Modern Philology,* XVII (1919), 199-218.

Smith, Bromley. "Some Rhetorical Figures Historically Considered," *Quarterly Journal of Speech,* XX (1924), 16-29.

Thonssen, Lester. "A Functional Interpretation of Aristotle's Rhetoric," *Quarterly Journal of Speech,* XVI (1930), 297-310.

———— "Thomas Hobbes's Philosophy of Speech," *Quarterly Journal of Speech,* XVIII (1932), 200-206.

Van Hook, LaRue. "Greek Rhetorical Terminology in Puttenham's *The Art of English Poesie," TAPA,* XLV (1914), 111-128.

Wagner, R. H. "The Text and Editions of Wilson's Arte of Rhetorique," *Modern Language Notes,* XLIV (1929), 421-428.

———— "Wilson and His Sources," *Quarterly Journal of Speech,* XV (1929), 525-537.

Wallace, K. R. "Bacon's Conception of Rhetoric," *Speech Monographs,* III (1936), 21-48.

———— "Early English Rhetoricians on the Structure of Rhetorical

Prose," *Papers in Rhetoric*. Ed. by D. C. Bryant. Saint Louis, 1940.

—————— "Rhetorical Exercises in Tudor Education," *Quarterly Journal of Speech*, XXII (1936), 28-51.

—————— "Bacon's Contribution to the Theory of Rhetoric," *Humanistic Studies in Honor of James Calvin Metcalf*, University of Virginia Studies, I (1941), Charlottesville, 1941.

Wright, L. B. "Translations for the Elizabethan Middle Class," *The Library*, XIII (1932), 312-331.

Zeitlin, Jacob. "The Development of Bacon's Essays—with Special Reference to the Question of Montaigne's Influence upon Them," *Journal of English and Germanic Philology*, XXVII (1928), 496-519.

INDEX

Aaron, 49

Abbott, E. A., 70, 71

Advancement of Learning, The, its point of view, 3; style of, 153. *See also De augmentis scientiarum*

Accent, 15. *See also* Grammar

Acroamatic method. *See* Disposition, methods of

Affections, 32; their orientation, 33; meaning of, 107. *See also* Moral Philosophy

Alcibiades, 74

Alexander, 64

Alphabets, 8

Analogy, the, as a proper commonplace, 75; Bacon's use of in *The Wisdom of the Ancients,* 75-76. *See also* Invention

Analytic method. *See* Disposition

Andrewes, Launcelot, 95

Anglican clergy, authority weakened by unwise controversy, 130-131

Antitheta, 56; nature of, 68; construction of, 69; as provoking analytical thought, 70; general utility of, 169; originality of, 205-207; Bacon followed by Whately, 224. *See also* Invention, Common-places

Aphorisms on the Composition of the Primary History, and *topica,* 62

Aphoristic method. *See* Disposition

Aphthonius, mentioned, 169, 186; *Progymnasmata,* 198

Apophthegmes, New and Old, and their bearing on rhetoric, 2, 74

Apothegms, 56; function and use, 74; originality of, 205-207. *See also* Invention, Common-places

Aristotelian categories, as general *topica,* 57

Aristotle, mentioned, 32, 41, 67, 112n, 123, 166, 169, 176, 193, 205, 206, 224; *Rhetoric,* 3, 41; *Nicomachean Ethics,* 41; Bacon's knowledge of the *Rhetoric,* 170, 170n; *re* Bacon's view of rhetoric, 171-179; Sidney's translation of the *Rhetoric,* 194; inspired Bacon's *Colours,* 206; *De sophisticis elenchis* and Bacon's *colours,* 206

Arrangement of discourse. *See* Disposition

Ascham, Roger, mentioned, 52, 184, 202, 203n; love of words, 200, 209

Assertions with proofs, method of. *See* Disposition, methods of

Asteley, John, 203n

Attic style, 152. *See also* style

Audience, classes of, 23-24; perfect adaptation to, 42; adaptation of reason to, 108-110; large groups and argument, 120; and praise, 120-121; and wit and humor, 121-122; knowledge of, 122-123. *See also* Pathos, Ethos

Austin, Gilbert, 225

Bacon, Anthony, 78

Bacon, Francis, ability as a speaker, 4; fondness for analogy, 75-76; use of conversation, 79-80; use of praise, 120n; use of the acromatic method, 136; and the Ramean "Methode" of arrangement in the *Advancement,* 140; use of other methods of disposition, 141-142; concern for his own style, 148; style of speeches, 148; variety of style, 152-154; delivery, 163; preparation for delivery, 165; rhetorical heritage, 169-170

Blount, Thomas, mentioned, 222, 225; *Academy of Eloquence* indebted to Bacon, 220

Brinsley, John, 169n, 184; *Ludus literarius,* 199-200

Bundy, M. W., 38

Burghley, Lord William Cecil, 165

Butler, Charles, mentioned, 212, 215; *Oratoriae libri duo,* 187; his *Rhetoricae libri duo,* 188, 194

Caesar, Julius, 165, 169; *Analogy,* 10

Cambridge University, Bacon at, 169; lectures on rhetoric at, 201-202

Campbell, George, *Philosophy of Rhetoric* indebted to Bacon, 222-223, 224